Sixty Years a Hunter

SIXTY YEARS A HUNTER

BY BILL QUIMBY

SKETCHES BY THE AUTHOR

Safari Press

The trademark Safari Press ® is registered with the U.S. Patent and Trademark Office and in other countries.

Quimby, Bill

First edition

Safari Press

2010 Long Beach, California

ISBN 978-1-57157-340-7

Library of Congress Catalog Card Number: 2008937817

10 9 8 7 6 5 4 3 2 1

Printed in China

Readers wishing to receive the Safari Press catalog, featuring many fine books on big-game hunting, wingshooting, and sporting firearms, should write to Safari Press Inc., P.O. Box 3095, Long Beach, CA 90803, USA. Tel: (714) 894-9080 or visit our Web site at www.safaripress.com.

Dedication
This is for Stephanie, Natalie, and Logan

TABLE OF CONTENTS

Foreword

It seems to me that I have known Bill Quimby my entire working life. Technically, that isn't exactly true. Bill is a bit older than I am (never mind how much), and we came from altogether different paths. We were first brought together nearly thirty years ago, when he began taking the reins of *Safari* magazine, the official publication of a then fledgling, nonprofit organization. He came to that job as a seasoned newspaperman, a real journalist, with decades of "OJT" (on-the-job training) in perhaps the most difficult schools of journalistic endeavor. I was still the new kid on the block, a former marine and occasional freelance writer who had somehow found himself as the editor of *Petersen's Hunting* magazine.

I had been doing some writing for *Safari* for Bill's predecessor, Sally Antrobus (also a real journalist), so Bill inherited me as part of his stable of writers. Truthfully, there was such a gap in knowledge and experience between us that the only thing we had in common was a passion for hunting. I can't say it was a fortuitous thing for Bill, but for darned sure it was for me. As he grew into his new job at *Safari*, and as I stumbled along and felt my way at my magazine, he proved to be a role model I could follow, a real editor who knew exactly what he wanted from his writers and who had a clear vision of what his magazine should be.

Over the years, we hunted together infrequently—for the first time when he, *Field & Stream*'s Dave Petzal, and I formed a team for the famous Lander One Shot Antelope Hunt. Petzal and Quimby were old hands, and they each took their pronghorns with one shot. I'm sure neither doubted that this would be the outcome. I had doubts! When it was my turn to make a stalk, I had no idea how my teammates were faring, but I didn't want to let them down. In the many years since, I have made a lot of pressure shots (and missed a few), but I don't recall ever again being that nervous or feeling that much weight riding on the final press of a trigger. I made the shot, and my teammates, who were both friends and mentors, made theirs. In that year, 1982, two teams took their three pronghorns with three shots—an unusual occurrence. Our team won on elapsed time, which is blind luck, so Petzal, Quimby, and I danced with the Shoshone warriors that night.

Over the years, we shared campfires at various events and had long conversations when we chanced to meet, and our correspondence was full of ideas about hunting, writing, and editing. I learned much from Bill Quimby in all three areas. Though we hunted together very little, my primary takeaway in that arena was Quimby's steadfast balance and love for the sport. We worked together on the initial founding of Safari Club International's *Record Book of Trophy Animals*, which has become a standard reference for hunters. While Quimby put his heart and soul into the project and must be given tremendous credit for the product it became, in his personal hunting he never succumbed to "record-book fever." He hunted because he loved it. As you will see in this book, the primary trophies he took home are not measured in inches, but in the quality and breadth of the experiences he gathered.

As an editor he was tough and direct, but he always provided clear guidance that he expected to be followed. He didn't blindly accept all the stuff I sent him, nor did he sit on it with no comment. I always knew where he was coming from, and if he rejected a piece, I always knew why. This was a mark I strove for in my own editorial tasks, and Bill Quimby is one of the guys I learned it from. Recently, I commented to him that he was "one of the best editors I ever worked for." He seemed genuinely touched, which surprised me. After all, Bill and I probably have something else in common: We consider ourselves writers first and hunters and editors somewhere farther down the line. After all, as another mentor of mine, the great outdoor writer John Wootters, once told me, "Them's as can, writes; them's as can't, edits."

Truthfully, as anyone who has tried both can attest, writing original material is a vastly different skill from the meticulous massaging (editing) of another person's writing, and it is also different from the planning, handholding, cajoling, and disciplining of undisciplined writers that is so necessary when editing a periodical. Relatively few in our business are equally adept as hunters, writers, and editors. Bill Quimby is one; our friend Dave Petzal is another. It is possible that I am a third, but this foreword isn't about me, or about Petzal, so that is said only in the context that I have done enough hunting, editing of other writers' words, and writing of my own to have some familiarity with the processes involved.

As a hunter, Bill Quimby's experience is global and in some areas, especially in his native southwest, extremely deep. You will read about his experiences in this book. I especially remember when he drew his desert sheep tag. This was in 1993. Factor in thirty-nine years of unsuccessful applications, and you understand that Bill Quimby was no longer a young man. Add an arm badly broken at the beginning of the hunt and a shot taken resting over the new cast that encased his left arm. This is the essence of Bill Quimby the hunter, on a hunt that concluded a lifelong desire to be among the very few who have taken all ten of Arizona's big-game species.

Bill Quimby's work at *Safari* and the other Safari Club International publications speaks for itself, but there is much more. After his retirement from the magazine, he set about "assisting" certain high-profile hunters in the writing of their memoirs. This was done as a business, it's true, but thanks to Bill Quimby, we are all the beneficiaries of the legacies of hunting greats such as Prince Abdorreza Pahlavi, C. J. McElroy, Watson Yoshimoto, Arnold Alward, David Hanlin, and Hubert Thummler. One necessary comment: As a writer or as an editor, I know of nothing more difficult than trying to get inside the mind of another person who is not a writer. This takes a different and very special skill. I tried it once, once only, when I helped my old friend, mentor, and African legend Geoff Broom write his autobiography. It was the most difficult writing task I have ever undertaken, and this is not a skill that I possess! I estimate I could have written three or four of my own books in the time it took me to help Geoff write his, and it left me in awe of the body of work in this genre that Bill Quimby has delivered in the last decade.

As a writer, Bill Quimby was a successful newspaper columnist for most of his career. As you will see, he wrote under a pseudonym for many of his years at SCI, but, under any name, his many fans, including me, could always recognize his no-nonsense style. And, of course, when so many of us write for glory, it is the mark of a true professional to produce work that is constant and consistent, whether the byline is an unknown nom de plume or that of the crown prince of Iran. Now, in this book we have the real Bill Quimby telling his own story in his own way—after so many years of serving other editors, the executive director and board of SCI, and the great hunters whom he has assisted in writing their memoirs. As you will find, it's a fine story of a great life of hunting and editing and writing. I hope my old friend Bill is granted much more time to continue all three passions. And I do hope that our paths will often cross on the mountain. As you read on, you will come to know, as I have, that Bill Quimby is a man from whom we can all learn.

Craig Boddington
Douala, Cameroon
March 20, 2008

Acknowledgments

Everything I have accomplished is due to two remarkable women: Helen Dixon Quimby, my mother who encouraged a boy to dream of something better, and Jean Potts Quimby, my partner and lover who took that gullible, gangling boy and shaped him into what I am more than a half century later.

Many other people have earned my gratitude for their friendship, favors given, or contributions to the memories that resulted in this book, however.

Among these (in alphabetical order) are: Arnold Alward; Paul and Maureen Bamber; Boris Baird; Jim Bedlion; Bill Berlat; Jack Brody; Pat Bollman; Holt Bodinson; Craig Boddington; Bud Bristow; Robert Douglas Campbell; Fiona Claire Capstick and Adelino Serras-Pires; Paul Casey; Gene Clayburn; Sandy Cox; Don Deluca; L. V. "Whitey" DeVries; John Doyle; U. C. "Charlie" Drayer; Rick Furniss; Stephanie, Robbie, Natalie and Logan Greene; David Hanlin; Bill Gustin; Larry Heathington; Eric Hubbell; Tudor Howard-Davies; Larry Hughes; Alex Jacome; Burt D. Klineburger; Halena and Jerome Knap; Jim and Seymour Levy; C. J. McElroy; Lynton McKenzie; Grant Maclean; Harold Mares; Rob Martin; José Martinez de Hoz; Bill, Ben, Billy, David and Daniel Mattausch; Ricardo Medem; Wilbur Minderman; Eddie Norgard; George Parker; Ernest "Bud" and Anna Potts; S. E. "Fanie" and Joyce Pretorius; George Proctor; Dick Remaly; Don Saelens; Roland "Fritz" Selby; Jack Schwabland; Trevor Shaw; Eric Sparks; Ted Sweetnam, Bill Tate; Don Taylor; Hubert Thummler; Hank Thompson; Henri and Riana van Aswegen; Pierre van der Walt; Tom Waddell; Glenn Wadsworth; Anthony "Ant" Williams; Ludo Wurfbain and his competent staff; and Peter Zidec.

I thank all of you.

Introduction

This is a book about my experiences as an outdoor writer, editor, publisher, author, and hunter. I could not have written it without letting readers know what shaped me, and it is for this reason that I have allowed you to see my father as he was. An analyst might say I became obsessed about hunting to prove I was better at something than my parent. I can't deny that this may have been true when I was younger, but it doesn't explain why I still have such a strong desire to pursue wild animals, even though my skills and experiences long ago surpassed his.

My motives for hunting are much deeper than merely wanting to prove something to someone, especially myself. It is simplistic to say I hunt because I must, but it is true. If domesticated animals such as dogs and cats can be excused for possessing uncontrollable instincts they no longer need, why can't we humans? Hunting is a noble tradition that predates the lesser men who scratched in the dirt for their food.

Although this is a book about hunting, I'll also give the reader a glimpse of what it was like to visit South Africa as apartheid was ending. I grew up in the United States when government-sanctioned racism was called "segregation," and I found the similarities in our countries at similar stages of our history to be great. I'll also provide a few insights into Safari Club International, the world's largest and most influential international hunting organization, and its founder, C. J. McElroy, gained during my long association with that club.

I apologize for having no photos of myself with some of my better trophies, especially the mule deer, Coues white-tailed deer, and wild turkeys I took in Arizona during sixty years of hunting them. The few photos I had showing me with those animals were destroyed when firefighters pumped nearly a thousand gallons of water into a bedroom in my home, where the photos were stored in a closet. Although I shot a deer in Arizona nearly every year for more than a half-century (and four or more deer every year during the fifteen years I hunted in the Texas Hill Country), I had few photographs taken of myself with them.

The reason had a lot to do with my job. As an outdoor writer for a newspaper, I needed to take photographs to illustrate my columns and articles, and the *Tucson Citizen* alone required three photos a week. That meant nearly five thousand of my photos were published over the three decades my work appeared in that newspaper and in Associated Press and Gannett News Service newspapers across the country. I must have photographed many hundreds of fishermen and hunters with their trophies during all those years at the newspaper; however, of all the things I did, I despised having to take pictures. And I seldom photographed my own trophies, the people I hunted with, or the places I hunted. It was too much like work.[1]

I have always considered myself an editor and author who specialized in big-game hunting. Although I've sold firearms articles to gun magazines, done some competitive rifle shooting and amateur gunsmithing, loaded nearly every round of ammunition ever fired from my shotguns and rifles, and owned more rifles and shotguns than anyone needs, and although I am foolish enough to believe I know more about ballistics and firearms history than the average hunter, I am not a gunwriter. That genre is best left to the guys who write as if they go hunting only because they need targets to test the goodies that manufacturers loan or give them. I grant that just as there are hammers, saws, and shovels for specific purposes, there are calibers and mechanisms that are best for certain types of hunting, but this is well covered in other books and numerous magazines, and you should not look for bits of wisdom about firearms and ammunition choices here. What I will say I'll say now: It is where a hunter puts his bullet— and not that bullet's brand, type, caliber, or velocity—that is the most important factor in killing an animal humanely.

---

[1] I found it interesting that my camera equipment grew smaller and less complicated as the years passed. Near the end of my time with the *Citizen,* I was using a simple 35mm "point-and-shoot" camera that fit in my pocket. It was especially handy for the trite "grip-and-grin" shots (people smiling and shaking hands) that sources expect a reporter to snap of them but that are seldom published in larger newspapers.

Also, although I've taken big-game animals that qualify for record books, I will seldom mention the size of my trophies in this book. It bothers me that some hunters judge their hunting success strictly by the horns, antlers, or skulls they bring home. After serving as de facto editor of the *SCI Record Book of Trophy Animals* for five years and as editor-in-name for another eleven years, I am not obsessed with records. I have never taken a measuring tape on a hunt, and I never will.

I also will not bore you with a chronological account of every hunt I made over the past sixty years. There simply were too many.

EVERYTHING MUST START SOMEPLACE

CHAPTER 1

One of my earliest memories is of my father skinning a mule deer. Watching the hide being peeled off that buck was the most fascinating thing I had seen during my short life. Under all that hair and skin was a layer of fat and blue membrane, and under that lay muscle and red meat. More than sixty years later, I remember that the skinned carcass was cold when I touched it. I was only five years old,[1] but I can remember other things that happened between the day my father brought home that deer and the day he shipped off to the Philippines just over a month later.

We were on a family outing in the San Diego Mountains in California, three hours west of our home in Yuma, Arizona, and I remember my three-and-a-half-year-old brother and me playing in the first snow either of us had seen. Our family's Sunday holiday was ruined when we heard on our car radio that Japanese airplanes were bombing a place called Pearl Harbor. I remember how shocked my parents were, but I was too young to know what President Franklin Delano Roosevelt meant when he announced over the radio in our living room that 7 December 1941 was a day that would live forever

---

[1]Among the boys and girls attending my fifth birthday party, nine weeks before the attack on Pearl Harbor, were Jean and June Potts, twin sisters who lived next door to our home. They are the same age as I am, and their father also worked for the Southern Pacific Railroad. Their father was a conductor; mine was a machinist. Jean still remembers that party. She had broken her arm six weeks earlier, and the sling was removed the morning of the party. Her still-weak bones snapped again during a wheelbarrow-race game we children played. She and I were married fifteen years later. At the time of this writing, we have celebrated our fifty-second year together.

in infamy. I had no concept of what a war was or why thousands of men lined up across America to join the U.S. Armed Services the next day.

My father was one of those men, but he was thirty-two years old, and the navy, army, and marines didn't want him. The war was only a day old, and recruiters could only follow the prewar rules, which said he was too old to serve. Joining the Seabees was the only choice open to him in the first days following the attack. That branch of the navy wanted recruits who could build things. The navy didn't care that my father was married and had two young sons. He left for boot camp in California within the week and spent the duration of the war in the Philippines and New Guinea. I didn't see him again until after the war.

My father's return in 1945 was a rude shock for me. He was a stranger who suddenly stepped off a train and reappeared in my young life. I resented it. Other men came back from the war to families who didn't know them. But other men, I'm sure, strove to restore relationships with their sons and daughters. To make matters worse, my father moved us from Yuma to Sparks, Nevada, a month after he returned, taking me away from everything I had known. It didn't help that I was diagnosed simultaneously with pneumonia and scarlet fever after we arrived, followed by mumps and whooping cough (also together), or that our doctor in Reno was a quack. His prescription for my illnesses was to sit outside in direct sunlight and slurp big spoonfuls of cod-liver oil, a thick, awful-tasting and foul-smelling, sticky brown syrup that no sane person would take willingly.

In addition to being sickly, I was a redhead covered with freckles and was as skinny as a straw. I knew none of my classmates and was too timid to make friends. This made me a target for some of my grammar school's worst bullies. I tried taking a different route home every day to escape them, but this worked only briefly. When they eventually caught me, they held me down and ripped off my pants and threw them up a tree. They then proceeded to chase me home. My father showed no sympathy. When I came home crying and pantless, he said that I should have "fought like a man." I was nine years old.

I had not yet seen him drunk, but he already was well on his way to becoming a world-class miser. Twice a month he would present my mother some small amount for groceries for our family of four, carefully counting out each dollar and coin on the kitchen table. First, though, she had to show receipts to account for every penny she had spent at the grocery store the previous two weeks.

It didn't matter that I was in poor health most of the time we were in Nevada; if I could walk, I was expected to help remodel the run-down house my father had bought for us. After school and on weekends, I painted, carried things, laid floor tile, and pounded nails. After-school activities were out. I had to work. I had no playmates other than my brother, and we were never close, even then. I cannot describe how elated I was when another doctor recommended we return to Arizona, where my health was expected to improve in the desert's drier weather.

We had been back in Yuma only a short time when I heard the *Daily Sun* was hiring boys to deliver papers. Jerry and I rode our bikes the mile and a half to the newspaper's office downtown. Jones Osborne, the editor and publisher, took one look at us and pronounced us too young for a paper route. The *Sun* had never had anyone hawk papers on the streets downtown, he said, but we could be the first if our parents approved. The papers sold for five cents each, and he would sell them to us for half that amount. If we could sell two dozen copies each, we'd each earn sixty cents a day! I did the math in my head and figured I'd earn $3.60 for the six days the paper was published. This was big money for a boy when new cars sold for $850 and a union man in the building trades earned less than $5,000 a year. Jerry and I rode our bikes home as fast as we could pedal. We not only needed permission, but we also needed seed money for our enterprise.

Upon hearing about our proposed venture, my father made a show of opening his coin purse and magnanimously handing each of us a dime.

"I want you to pay this back," he said, scowling.

I was crushed. I could buy just four newspapers with my dime, and then I would have to sell them and buy eight more, and sell those and buy twelve more to reach my goal of earning sixty cents that first day. The worst was yet to come, however. When I returned the dime to my father, he announced that now that I was working, I could use my earnings to pay for my room and board and buy the things I needed, such as clothes and school supplies. (Because Jerry was younger and didn't sell as many papers, my father waited a while before charging him.)

My brother and I eventually established routes we traveled daily to sell our papers to our regular customers. Young as we were, we soon knew the inside of every bar and hotel in downtown Yuma. I witnessed several knife fights—one of them fatal—and an attempted rape. A pervert propositioned Jerry. The experiences we had while selling newspapers in Yuma's sleaziest spots in the second half of the 1940s have stayed in my memory for a lifetime. I told myself someday I would make a little boy's week by buying every one of his newspapers. The problem is that I never saw a little boy selling newspapers after I was old enough to keep my pledge. Most of the newspaper peddlers I've seen since then were adults who looked as if they had held "will work for food" signs on the same corners an hour earlier.

Three of the things I bought over the next two years of selling newspapers were a bicycle (a pinstriped black Western Flyer with chrome wheels, fat tires and fenders, and a battery-powered horn built into the frame) from Yuma's Western Auto store; a used Remington bolt-action .22 rimfire repeater; and a 16-gauge Winchester single-shot shotgun, also secondhand. I still have that little shotgun, but I sold the .22 to help pay for my first semester of college. I wish I'd kept the bike, after seeing one identical to mine at an antique fair recently.

Jerry and I were given a BB gun (one for the two of us) when he was six and I was almost eight, and we soon were good shots with it. We could stand a dozen feet from a line of scurrying ants and pick them off one by one, or toss up a vanilla wafer and smash it to smithereens like a skeet target. It was my .22 that opened up a new world for me, however. I could place it across the handlebars of my bike and ride a mile or two into the desert for solo expeditions after jack rabbits, badgers, ground squirrels, rattlesnakes, and any other big game that presented itself. Today, a boy on a bike carrying a firearm wouldn't get far before someone called a cop. Heaven help that boy if he says he only intends to plink a few critters. Animal activists have spent a lot of money trying to convince the public that boys who hunt small things grow up to be serial killers. This ignores the fact that Adolf Hitler and a couple of his henchmen opposed hunting and believed all animals (except certain humans) had rights.

I've forgotten all the types of creatures and how many fell to my .22, but I remember shooting a great horned owl (they were not protected in the 1940s) and then mounting it, using skills I learned from a Great Northwestern School of Taxidermy correspondence course. I also remember everything about shooting my first bird on the wing with my shotgun. I'd been on one or two dove hunts by then, but the only dove I'd brought home was one I'd shot off a fence wire. On this great day of my first successful venture into the fine art of wingshooting, my father allowed me to tag along when he and a friend hunted ducks in Yuma's Gila Valley.

We soon found several ducks swimming in a drainage canal, and I stayed behind while the two of them stalked the ducks. I heard them shoot, and then a lone bird flew toward me. I threw up my shotgun, yanked the trigger, and watched the bird tumble into the canal. I was thrilled and would have liked to pose for a photo with that bird and hear my father say, "Nice shot." Instead, he took one look at the dark-feathered lump wedged in the tules where the current had taken it, then turned his back and walked away.

"It's a coot. A damned ol' mud hen," he said.

Six months before my twelfth birthday, my father said someone was selling a Savage Model 99 rifle chambered for .303 Savage and he thought I should buy it. Few hunters today have heard of this obsolete cartridge, but it was popular in its day. My father claimed it "hit harder" than his long-barreled .30-30 Winchester, though I now know the ballistics of the two cartridges are virtually identical. I think I paid $35 for the Savage and two boxes of 180-grain Winchester Silver Tip ammunition. It was a lot of money for me, but by then I had a paper route, which meant I probably was earning as much as ten dollars a week.

I was taller than most boys my age, but that rifle's recoil and its crescent-shaped buttplate punished me terribly whenever I fired it, and I had to get used to its heavy trigger pull. I spent the next few months anticipating my first deer hunt. My father neither encouraged nor discouraged me. It was understood that his sons would hunt deer with him when they were twelve years old, the legal age for hunting big game in Arizona then. "We need the meat" was as close as he got to saying he wanted to take us.

I visited my father's distant relatives in Arkansas and Washington State when I was too young to remember much. Other than that, I knew nothing about and had no other contact with my father's side of the family. My mother said my father moved to Arizona from Arkansas and took a job in the copper mine in Bisbee while still in his teens. He was working for the railroad in Tucson when she married him in 1934. My mother's parents arrived in Tucson by way of Los Angeles in the 1920s. Her father owned a radiator and body repair shop but moved to Alamogordo, New Mexico, to work as a foreman of the machine shops at the White Sands Proving Grounds during World War II. I apparently have good genes, at least on my mother's side. My grandfather lived to be 94; my grandmother, 96. My mother outlived three more husbands after divorcing my father. She was a beautiful, talented woman who entertained children with tricks of magic and ventriloquism on television and stage and traveled to every U.S. state as the national president of the American Legion Auxiliary. She died of cancer at age 91 in January 2005.

My father was an alcoholic by the time I was a sophomore in high school. At first he bought rum in brown ceramic jugs in San Luis del Rio Colorado, across the border in Mexico, seventeen miles south of Yuma. It wasn't long before he was buying colorless, inexpensive grain alcohol in clear gallon bottles and mixing it with grapefruit or grape juice to save even more money. As far as I know, he always drank alone and at home, probably because he didn't want to pay what it cost to drink in a bar. He worked the 3 to 11 P.M. shift and often was drunk within an hour after getting home. I never knew what to expect as a teenager when I walked through our back door after staying out late. He frequently abused me verbally, and on one occasion he hit me with the buckle end of his navy belt after I "talked back" to him.

Another example of his attitude toward money came after I was in an auto accident during my junior year of high school. I was riding with a friend, who lost control of his 1939 Ford, skidded along the curb on the left, overcorrected, and crashed into a pickup truck parked on the right side of the street. When my father visited me in the hospital, he said he had paid the bill so I could be released, but I would have to repay him, which I eventually I did. Many years later, I realized he also would have collected my medical expenses from his railroad worker's medical insurance policy.

My mother stayed with him until my youngest brother, Tom, graduated from high school. When my father learned she was seeing a lawyer, he hid their assets from the court. Even before the decree was final, he bragged to friends that he had withdrawn all of the cash from several bank accounts, instructing his brother in San Francisco to hold it while the divorce proceedings were under way. The joke was on him. When his brother died suddenly, the widow said she knew nothing about the money.

I am convinced my father treated me differently because I not only was the eldest son but was also the only one who rebelled at his demands. My brothers sided with him during the divorce. I supported our mother. This, and his belief that I owed him money, resulted in his writing me out of his will. When an aneurism killed him in the mid-1980s, his estate consisted of six houses, several bank accounts, stocks, and miscellaneous real estate in Arizona and Iowa. In his will he specifically denied me anything except stocks worth about $2,500 and his .30-30 rifle. The only reason I got the securities was that, unknown to me, he had bought them in my name to avoid paying tax on the dividends, which he somehow was able to cash without my signing the checks.

After the dime that financed my first day of selling newspapers, the only money I received from my father were one hundred silver dollars when Jean and I were married in 1956, and another $600 that

I borrowed in six installments to help pay for tuition and books at the University of Arizona. As he counted out the money and had me sign a note, he would always say the loan would be "paid in full upon graduation," meaning it would not have to be repaid if I graduated. Then he would promptly forget what he'd said. Though I repaid the loans by graduating, he kept asking me to return the money for the rest of his life. When I reminded him the debt was paid, he would agree at first, but a few months later I would receive a dunning letter that he obviously had written while drunk.

Jean and I cared for her grandmother, who lived with us, and I worked at a variety of jobs while going to school. Our daughter Stephanie was born in 1958, and I graduated with a degree in marketing and a minor in commercial design a year later. I spent several years working in the advertising departments of local department stores before becoming the creative director of an advertising and public relations firm.

It wasn't long before I grew tired of the job. My time was billed to clients in quarter-hour segments, and I had to account for every segment of the day. The final straw came when we prepared a campaign for the opening of a developer's model homes. We'd produced a logo, billboards, newspaper ads, brochures, entry signs, and price sheets, using a name I've forgotten for the project. Three weeks before the development's grand opening, the client's wife changed the name. The agency had to scramble and pressure its suppliers, but we somehow made the necessary changes in time for the opening. It made me realize I wasn't happy doing what my education had trained me to do.

Next, I launched a small hunting and fishing newspaper. In high school I'd taken journalism classes and worked on our school's newspaper and yearbook. I also had taken a couple of university journalism courses as electives under some excellent teachers, one of them the retired editor of the *New York Times*. My *Arizona Outdoor News* was doomed from the start because I was the world's worst advertising salesman. Jean and I kept the paper going for three years, hoping it would be our salvation to make it the official organ of the Arizona Wildlife Federation, which I thought would give the paper the circulation and credibility we needed to sell more advertising. Unfortunately, when I was awarded the AWF contract, I learned the federation had fewer than one thousand members and not the six thousand I was promised. We published another three or four issues before we mailed refunds to our subscribers and shut it down.

I learned the intricacies of printing, publishing, advertising sales, and distribution the hard way, but the greatest lesson I learned was that it didn't matter how good the content of a publication might be. Advertising is the key to its success. It was an expensive learning experience, but it would serve me well later.

A month or so after we closed *Arizona Outdoor News,* printers at the company that published Tucson's two separately owned newspapers quit to protest the installation of technology that soon would replace most of them. I knew the company's production manager well, and when he asked if I wanted a job, I took it. Because of my background in the local graphic arts industry, he put me in charge of "ad alley," which meant I supervised three twenty-person crews who worked shifts around the clock, building ads and sending proofs to clients.

My crews and I were among the first in the newspaper industry to set type photocomposition machines and build pages with pieces of paper and hot wax. Being responsible for sixty people under the deadlines of a daily newspaper was stressful, doubly so because we were inventing systems and learning skills and technology as we went.

Although those of us in the back shop had little contact with the people working on the editorial side of the two newspapers, I had made friends with Bill Davidson, the *Tucson Citizen*'s outdoor editor. When he left to become a regional representative for the National Rifle Association, he recommended that the *Citizen* hire me to produce its outdoor columns. I soon was writing twice-weekly columns and freelancing magazine articles while supervising ad alley. When I left ad alley and took a job as the advertising manager of a local department store, I continued to write the *Tucson Citizen*'s outdoor columns.

A dilemma arose when the *Citizen* wanted me to become a full-time employee a couple of years later. I wanted the job, but the store was paying me more than the newspaper would. I decided to work from

4 A.M. to 11 A.M. at the paper and launch a small business that produced color catalogs for local department stores. I worked with store executives and buyers, hired models and photographers, contracted printers, and produced catalogs for Christmas, white sales, and clearances. I might still be doing this if national retail chains hadn't started buying up local stores or forcing them out of business. Chains produced their advertising materials at regional headquarters a long way from Tucson.

I freelanced for a while, producing brochures and artwork for other local businesses and selling an occasional magazine article, but the work was sporadic. Meanwhile, my position at the *Citizen* expanded to include serving as a member of the editorial board and helping shape the paper's editorial positions. As far as I know, I was the only outdoor editor ever to serve on a Gannett newspaper's editorial board.

In 1983, in addition to my work on the newspaper, I began what would be a long association with Safari Club International, about which you'll learn in the last chapter. My position as the club's director of publications brought me friends and enabled me to build contacts all over the globe. It also gave me the desire and the means to hunt around the world.

Mule Deer: My First Big-Game Animal

Chapter 2

There is nothing like the smell and sound of pine burning and crackling in an old-fashioned, red-hot, potbellied iron stove, especially when you are twelve years old and in a wood shanty that has been wallpapered with newspapers to keep the wind from blowing through its widest cracks. The corner with the stove was uncomfortably hot, while the other corners were cold enough to hang meat in. The place belonged to someone my father had befriended, a man named Theodore Gallardo. Theo was a veteran who had found this spot on Lynx Creek near Prescott after the Spanish-American War. In those days people could "patent" government land if they found valuable minerals on it. They only had to "improve" (mine) their claim and live on it for a specified number of years to get full ownership of the land. Theo dug a tunnel with a pick and shovel and claimed he was getting gold from it. I doubt that the gold he found (if any) amounted to much, however.

His "guest house" was my first hunting camp. I still remember struggling to get under the heavy, hand-sewn quilts that covered the iron bed my father and I shared the night before my first deer hunt began in October 1948. I still can see myself going outside to relieve myself while wearing only socks and my first pair of long underwear. It was so cold I wanted to run back inside, but I gritted my teeth and did what I needed to do—on the firewood stacked outside the door. The smell of the ponderosa pines and the sight of a dusting of snow in the moonlight made everything seem magical. The smell of urine-soaked wood burning in a crowded shack was something else, I soon learned.

My first deer hunt did not last long. We were out before daylight, after a breakfast of bacon, eggs, and coffee (my first taste of it) that my father cooked in a tin skillet and a blue-enameled pot on top of the little stove. Everything about this hunt was memorable. I still can see the stars above us as we ventured out of our shelter in the dark and started climbing the hill behind Gallardo's house. I was wearing an old pair of leather-soled street shoes, not boots, and I constantly slipped on rocks and loose dirt. Over my long underwear I wore a heavy shirt and a thin, olive-colored military jacket I'd bought at one of the hundreds of army surplus stores that opened after World War II. In my pocket was my first hunting license and deer tag, which had cost a total of four dollars—three dollars for the license, one dollar for the tag. (I kept the license for a long time under the buttplate of my rifle. I lost it several years later, when I installed a stock with a flatter plate.)

Many years after this hunt, the U.S. Forest Service and the Arizona Game and Fish Department built a dam across Lynx Creek, and the lake that flooded Gallardo's place began attracting hundreds of visitors from Phoenix and Prescott on weekends. In 1948, though, Lynx Creek was as remote and unknown as anyplace in Arizona. There were pine trees in the canyons and along the creek, but the slopes were covered with manzanita, an awful brush whose name means "little apple" in Spanish. The stuff grows reddish purple branches that intertwine and make it impossible for a human to walk through it. Deer eat its leaves and twigs, and they also use its dense growth for cover. Other than that, it has no other reason for existing that I can see.

We had climbed only one or two ridges when a mule-deer buck ran out of a patch of manzanita, and my father shot at it and missed. I started shooting, too. My father stopped to reload just as the deer was about to go out of sight across the canyon. I fired my last shot, saw the deer drop, and immediately heard the "splat" of my bullet hitting the deer. There was no doubt I had killed that buck, but all my father would say later was that "we" had gotten it.

In the late 1940s the only reasonable way to reach Prescott and points north by car from Phoenix, Yuma, or even Tucson was via a two-lane road that twisted up Yarnell Hill and on to Prescott. That part of the road was the only stretch of pavement between Yuma and the Grand Canyon, except for the streets in Prescott and Flagstaff. Every other inch of the trip was on gravel and dirt. Near the base of Yarnell Hill was a gasoline station and café at a junction called Aguila, or "eagle" in Spanish, although I doubt that any self-respecting eagle was ever seen there. A sign pointed toward a place called "Bagdad" somewhere down a dirt road. Despite the misspelling, it brought visions of *The Arabian Nights* to my young mind.

The opening of Arizona's annual deer-hunting season was a major event in the late 1940s. There was a continuous line of hunters' vehicles going up Yarnell Hill on the night before the season opened, and a long line of vehicles going down two or three days later. An itinerant photographer had set up shop in Aguila to photograph successful hunters with their deer, and I convinced my father to stop at the man's stand. I don't remember how much he charged to photograph me with my buck, but I do remember that I paid for it. You can imagine my disappointment when the photo arrived in the mail a couple of weeks later and I opened the envelope to find that glare on the camera lens had obliterated most of my image. The photographer staged the photo with the deer in the trunk of my father's car while I held its antlers, and my father sitting on the bumper. All that could be seen of me in that photo were my waist and legs.

✳ ✳ ✳

Four months later, in February 1949, my father, one of his friends, and I hunted javelinas in the foothills of the Tortolita Mountains north of Tucson. We had separated when I walked into a herd that was bedded in a thicket of ocotillo, a nasty plant with tall, thorn-covered stalks, and shot the animal that was closest to me. When I walked up to it, though, there was another javelina standing next to the one I'd killed. When it trotted off, making "woofing" noises as it went, I reached down to drag my kill away from a pile of prickly pear, and that's when the

13

javelina that had just run off turned around, ran back, and grabbed my pant leg with its tusks. It doesn't take much imagination to know how terrified I was at age twelve and a half. I've since heard about javelina and European wild boar using their tusks to "slash" dogs and humans. This animal bit through my jeans and briefly shook its head, fortunately without touching my leg, before it got its teeth untangled and ran off for good. My father and his friend would not believe my story until they saw my pants.

There were lots of far-fetched stories going around in the 1940s and 1950s, even the 1960s, about javelina herds attacking cowboys and forcing hunters to spend hours in trees to escape snapping teeth. After that javelina grabbed and shook my pant leg, I believed every such story, even those I should have known were too off-the-wall to have happened. I now know my experience was a rare event. Of the seventeen reported attacks on humans by javelinas in southern Arizona's Pima County in 2005, fifteen incidents involved owners who were attempting to protect their dogs.

* * *

I had a rude surprise on my second trip to Gallardo's place on Lynx Creek. I was convinced I was a seasoned hunter when my father and I drove there in October 1949. After all, I already had killed a deer, a javelina, a great horned owl, some jack rabbits and cottontails, a couple of doves, a coot, several rattlesnakes, and a whole bunch of lizards. I again went to sleep in Gallardo's shack, anticipating our next day's hunt. It was long after sunrise the next morning when my father shook me awake.

"Give me your tag. I got your deer," he said.

"No!" I fired back, without hesitating.

I had paid for my license and deer tag, and I expected to shoot my own buck. My refusing his demand was something he never forgot. He angrily tagged his deer and loaded up our gear. We drove back to Yuma in silence. It was the only year between 1948 and 2000, when I couldn't draw a tag in the state's annual hunting lottery, that I didn't hunt a deer in Arizona.

From then on, although my father took me with him on his deer-hunting trips every year until I left for college at age seventeen, we left camp in different directions. I killed only two deer in those five years, but I found them, shot them, and field-dressed them myself, with no help from anyone.

Jerry was old enough for his first deer hunt in 1950. While he accompanied our father, I went out by myself and missed the only deer I saw. They killed two deer, and Jerry tagged one of them. I never knew if he shot it himself. I do know I was married and living in Tucson nine years later when my youngest brother called and asked if he could hunt with me. Tom had gone out twice with our father and hadn't been allowed to kill his own deer. I took him into the Santa Rita Mountains thirty miles south of Tucson, where he shot a three-by-three Coues white-tailed deer.[1] I think I was happier with his buck than he was. As far as I know, it was the only big-game animal he ever shot.

✳ ✳ ✳

As a newspaper outdoor writer in the 1970s, I interviewed many of southern Arizona's most successful deer hunters, and among them were Tom and Mary Knagge. They consistently brought home trophy mule deer from the fabled Arizona Strip, that isolated area between the Colorado River and our state's borders with Utah and Nevada, and Mary's bucks often were larger than Tom's. Interviewing her for a feature article and seeing their antlers lined up on a wall in their garage got me interested in hunting a "Strip deer," too.

There was no direct way to reach the place where Mary and Tom suggested we hunt. Alex Jacome, Larry Wheeler, and I drove to Boulder Dam, crossed the river and entered Nevada, and had dinner

---

[1]Whenever I mention the number of tines on deer antlers, I follow the western tradition of ignoring eyeguards. A four-by-four buck in the West, for example, is a ten-pointer in the East. With elk, however, we count every tine more than three or four inches long. Many of us count only the better side on elk and deer. For example, we call a buck with two eyeguards and four tines on one side and three tines on the other a "four-pointer."

in Las Vegas. From there we continued on to St. George, Utah, where we drove back into Arizona and took a slippery, muddy dirt road about ninety miles south to a place called Pigeon Canyon, not far from the northern shore of Lake Mead. Our route took us past a site called Wolf Hole, which author Edward Abbey claimed as his address. All I saw there were corrals and a windmill.

We'd driven all night to get there, but we couldn't wait to start hunting. We set up my tent trailer, unpacked my truck, and gathered some firewood. Then the three of us started up one side of the canyon on foot. We soon were separated. After climbing a while, I looked back and decided the opposite slope looked as if it would be a better spot for deer. I should have let my friends know what I was about to do, but I didn't. Instead, I turned around, walked down to camp, crossed the road, and began climbing again. I'd gone about a mile when I spotted several deer up against a row of sandstone cliffs, and one of them was a good buck.

To reach them I'd have to cross a slope covered with loose shale. I was halfway across it when the entire side of the mountain seemed to give way, taking me over a small ledge, and I landed on my back! It took a minute or two before I could breathe without pain. I've done some dumb things, but this would rank near the top of the list. If I'd been injured and unable to walk, no one would have known where I was. A search party would have looked for me on the other side of the canyon.

Larry Wheeler and I didn't shoot a deer on that trip, but Alex did. It was a typical Strip deer, a big buck with heavy, wide antlers, and I was happy for Alex.

Our trip home was something we'd like to forget. The road north to Wolf Hole now was a boggy mess, thanks to hunters who had been stuck before us and had to dig out their vehicles. Thinking we'd have fewer problems by waiting until the mud froze, we left for St. George at midnight. We'd been driving only about an hour when we came upon a quarter-mile stretch of churned-up, wet mud. I stopped, shifted into low-range four-wheel drive, and started across, and my truck suddenly was buried up to its doors. It took us at least three hours to dig it out and get back to frozen ground.

We were covered with brown mud and exhausted when we finally reached the pavement at St. George at sunrise. Larry was cleaner than we were, so we parked around the corner from a motel and sent him to get us a room. The shower stall must have had an inch of mud on its floor after we three had taken our showers. We didn't use the beds. After changing into clean clothes, we continued on to Las Vegas for breakfast, and then drove nonstop to Tucson without sleeping. We were younger then.

✳ ✳ ✳

During the 1980s I went through a period when I did most of my hunting with muzzleloading rifles I built with locks, triggers, trigger guards, buttplates, and barrels ordered separately from a Dixie Gun Works catalog and with slabs of walnut and maple donated by friends in Texas and Ohio. In Arizona I used these black-powder rifles mostly for javelinas, but I did shoot a desert mule deer south of Tucson with one of them. All my other muzzleloaders had full stocks, but this one had a .45-caliber barrel with a half stock (short for a muzzleloader). I based its design loosely on the rifles the Hawken brothers of St. Louis had built for the buffalo hunters, Indian fighters, and farmers heading west in the mid-1800s. Hawken rifles were heavy, sturdy things, but I purposely scaled mine down to make it lightweight.

A .45-caliber round ball, which my barrel shot more accurately than Minié balls or cast bullets, was not the best choice for a big mule deer, but I had just completed my miniature Hawken and really wanted to try it when I drew a tag for a muzzleloader-only hunt near Sierra Vista. This small city near the Mexican border, about eighty miles southeast of Tucson, was close enough that Alex Jacome and his son Kiko and I could sleep at our homes and drive there and back each day to hunt.

Where we'd chosen to hunt was a line of steep, grassy hills on Coronado National Forest land, overlooking a privately owned wildlife sanctuary. From the road, it seemed more like pronghorn antelope country, and in fact we sometimes saw them there. The canyons, though, had Gambel oak and other vegetation that provided plenty of cover for mule deer. The perfect place to glass for deer would have been from below on the refuge, but it was closed to hunting. Instead, we stayed a few yards below each ridge and walked around the heads of the canyons where the deer were bedded. We jumped a few deer that way, but we kept pushing them ahead of us, and all were out of the limited range of our muzzleloaders.

Our friends Holt and Ilsa Bodinson parked their vehicle next to mine when we struck out to hunt at first light the second morning. They went in one direction, and Alex, Kiko, and I went in another. Holt shot his buck right away, and he and his wife returned to Tucson with it. Alex, Kiko, and I hunted until dark, still without getting close enough to a deer in that open country.

When all of us returned before sunup, we parked our two vehicles on the same high ridge. Holt and Ilsa went off to look for a buck for her, while Alex, Kiko, and I hunted the same places we'd covered for two days. When we returned at noon, Alex and Kiko walked over to the edge of the canyon below the truck to see what was there. I had just dragged an ice chest out to my truck's tailgate to make sandwiches for lunch when Alex suddenly fired his rifle. He was frantically trying to reload when I grabbed my rifle and ran to him.

"Shoot him! Shoot him!" he said.

"Where is he?"

I expected to see a deer running down or across the canyon below us.

"Right there!" Alex said, pointing almost straight down.

I couldn't believe it. A mule deer buck was in the canyon, looking up at us. I quickly checked to see if a percussion cap was on the lock's nipple, cocked the hammer, set the hair trigger, and shot as soon as the rifle's buttplate hit my shoulder. The angle was so steep that the little round ball broke the buck's spine, slamming the deer to the ground. It was a two-year-old buck, with only three tines per side and no eyeguards, but I'd killed it with a rifle I'd built from an assortment of parts and a slab of wood, and I was proud of it.

This story isn't over, though. That evening, when Holt and Ilsa returned to their truck, we learned that they had seen several bucks, but Ilsa was not able to get a shot. We stood around our trucks talking for a while, and then they got into their vehicle and drove off. We still could see their taillights when Alex, Kiko, and I climbed into my truck and discovered its battery was dead! The three of us had no choice but to walk to a gravel road about a mile away and get someone to help get us moving again. Fortunately for us, the driver of the first vehicle we flagged down had jumper cables and was nice enough to drive two miles out of his way to help us. Since then, we've never driven away from a remote parking spot before making certain every vehicle in our group was started.

✳ ✳ ✳

A quagmire south of Wolf Hole and a dead battery were not the only problems I had with vehicles while hunting with Alex. He and I were looking for mule deer on the Babocomari Ranch, a huge Spanish land-grant property ninety miles southeast of Tucson, when a little-used Jeep track took us to a creek we hadn't crossed on previous hunts. There were tire tracks running into the water on the trail forty yards away on the other bank, and from where we were we could see they'd been made since the rain, which had raised the usually calm stream and left it running fast and muddy.

To make certain we could cross, though, I took a stick and waded halfway across the creek. I found the water to be only about a foot deep. My pickup truck had big tires and four-wheel drive, so I shifted into low range and started across. I'd driven only a few feet past where I'd walked when we suddenly dropped into a ditch the stream had dug along the far bank! My truck's front end was submerged at a steep angle, and water was spurting into the cab through the doors and floor. While I picked up everything that floated out from under the seat and piled it on the dash, my friend didn't say a word. Taking his rifle, binocular, and jacket, he calmly crawled through the window onto the bed of the truck, then leaped from rock to rock and onto dry land without getting his boots wet.

I soon was sitting in water up to my waist. Instead of bothering to crawl through the window, I opened the door and waded to the bank. Alex looked as if he could have been a model for a Cabela's hunting catalog. I was as soaked as a rat.

After we walked the two miles to the ranch headquarters, one of the cowboys drove us back to the site and pulled my truck out of the hole with a chain. At least fifty or sixty gallons of water flowed out of the cab when I opened the doors. If this had been a cartoon instead of real life, there would have been fish flopping on the ground around my truck. Amazingly, we were able to get the engine running, after waiting an hour or so for things to dry out. The clutch had to be replaced; the engine oil and the grease in the transmission, transfer case, and differentials needed changing; and every grease fitting required flushing and filling after I drove the truck home. I also had to remove the seat cushions and set them out in the sun while the clutch was being repaired. Otherwise, the truck was none the worse for its bath.

The cowboy who had rescued us had answered my question before I could ask it.

"You know, this is the second truck I've dragged out of that creek since the rain. The other fellows tried to cross it from the other side," he said.

* * *

I've lost count of the mule deer I've taken in Arizona since my first buck in 1948. Early on, they came from places above the Mogollon Rim, but in recent years all of my mule-deer hunts have been closer to Tucson. My best desert buck came from the Santa Rita Experimental Range, about midway between Tucson and the Mexican border.

In those days, two of the best places to swap hunting information were John Doyle's taxidermy shop and John Myrmo's blacksmith shop. Anyone who hung around these places eventually would meet every serious hunter, trapper, and houndsman in southern Arizona. I made a point of stopping by each of them at least once a month for hunting and fishing news to use in my newspaper columns. It was on one of those visits to his shop that Myrmo told me about a big mule-deer buck he had seen where I'd drawn my hunting permit that year. I reciprocated by telling him about a special Coues white-tailed buck Alex Jacome and I had watched in February while hunting javelinas in another mountain range along the border.

On the opening morning of our hunt a few weeks later, Alex, Eric Sparks, and I parked where Myrmo had suggested and headed toward where he'd been seeing the deer. The rolling terrain was covered with thorny brush. It was not a place to use binoculars to look for deer, so we soon were moving about a quarter-mile apart, heading north, crossing each shallow arroyo, hoping to push deer out of their beds in front of us. We had gone about a mile when a forked-horn buck jumped up, stopped and looked at me, and then ran over the ridge and out of sight. The only thing that kept me from shooting that little deer was hearing rocks rolling below me. A small four-by-four buck appeared first. I had my rifle up when a third buck showed itself. I had no doubt which deer I wanted when I saw its much larger body and wider, taller antlers.

There was only enough time for two quick offhand shots before it disappeared over the ridge about two hundred yards away, and I wasn't certain that either of them had hit that deer. I was grateful that the ground was damp, making the tracks where the three deer had run out of the canyon easy to see. There was no blood, but after I had followed the tracks for a while, my deer suddenly stood up in the hip-high grass—and then collapsed, almost at my feet! It was the largest mule deer I've ever killed, with the best antlers.

All the while I was gutting it, I worried about how I would get that big deer back to my truck. Before I had finished, Sparks showed up. I forget who first saw the lone utility pole on the ridge a few hundred yards above us, but where man plants poles, he usually makes a road, so we climbed to it and found an ancient two-track trail that led back to where I'd parked my truck. I marked the spot above the deer by piling a few rocks on the trail, and we started back for the truck.

We were in sight of it when Alex, who was approaching us from another ridge, spooked several deer toward us. When I saw they were running straight for my truck, I yelled for Sparks to wait until they passed it before he shot the buck that was running with the little herd, and that's what he did. His deer went down no more than thirty steps from my truck's front bumper. I had only to turn the truck around and drop the tailgate to load it.

The antlers on Eric's deer had eyeguards and three long points on each side. They could have passed for those of a white-tailed deer. That buck also had a smaller body and more hair on its tail than most mature mule deer have. I've been told that hybridization of mule deer and white-tailed deer seldom occurs in wild populations—even when both species are found together, as they were during that hunt—but if any deer I've seen in Arizona was a hybrid, it would have been Eric's.

We were able to drive to the old pole, then go down the ridge to my buck and load it whole. I never knew what that deer weighed, but this was one of the few times I didn't cut up my own venison, and I couldn't believe how many packages I came home with when I picked up the meat from the butcher shop. Typically, the largest desert mule deer taken south of Tucson will weigh one hundred and fifty to one hundred and seventy pounds. That buck weighed much more than that.

As for Myrmo and "our" whitetail, he found it near where Alex and I had seen it, and his son killed it. Its antlers were among the largest taken in Arizona that year.

Eric Sparks also was along when I shot my last mule deer. He is an attorney, and we were hunting on farms north of Willcox as guests of one of his clients. It was a long way from anywhere that resembled mule-deer habitat to me, but deer were attracted to the farm's apple orchids and chili and maize fields.

Eric's buck was feeding in a field of red chili peppers when we found it, which taught both of us that we should forget everything we'd heard about mule deer being less wary than other deer. Eric and the farmer walked around the field and entered it with the wind in their faces, while I covered what we thought would be the buck's exit route. Rolling watering machines across the field allowed us to know exactly where we'd last seen the deer, and the farmer's son and I used hand signals to direct Eric and the farmer to the spot. We couldn't believe it when we watched them walk back and forth in waist-high chili plants without spooking the deer. Through my binocular I could see Eric raise his hands and hunch his shoulders, as if to say, "I don't know where it could have gone." Seconds later, I saw him quickly raise his rifle, point it at what I thought was the ground almost in front of his feet, and shoot.

"That buck wouldn't get up, even when I walked up to it," Eric said, after he and the farmer dragged it out of the field to the road.

My deer came much easier. There were at least a dozen bucks in a field of maize with stalks so tall we couldn't see the deer when they fed with their heads down. But after a while, one head would pop up, and then another. They were all young bucks, and I shot the one that was closest to me.

Amazingly, the other deer didn't run out of the field. They merely moved to the other side of it.

THE ONLY CREATURE
I'M SMARTER
THAN

CHAPTER 3

In Arizona, Texas, and New Mexico (the only U.S. states where they occur), as well as in northern Mexico, the collared peccary is called a javelina. You may have read that the name is derived from javelin because of the animal's thin, spearlike tusks, but javelina actually is an Americanization of *jabalí*, the Spanish word for wild boar. In that language, when *ina* or *ino* is added to a noun, it means the speaker is talking about something small or young. The first Spaniards who encountered peccary in the New World apparently called them *jabalína*, or little wild boar. To the untrained ear of someone who speaks no Spanish, a *b* sounds like a *v*.

Many of the same authors also will call them "pigs," and, believe it or not, I've also read reports that claim these little animals are hoofed rodents. I can understand why someone might believe javelina are swine—they look like and behave like pigs—but how anyone could believe javelina are related to rats, rabbits, and squirrels is puzzling to me. Peccary are New World animals and are not related to Old World swine or any member of the Rodentia family. They are entirely covered with coarse hair (it is very long along their backbones), and they have only one dewclaw on each rear leg. Their tails are nearly nonexistent, and they have an odoriferous musk gland resembling a small breast (complete with a nipple) on their backs.

After elk, javelina are my favorite North American animal to hunt. One reason is that I usually can find a herd of javelinas no matter which direction from Tucson I might want to hunt, and when I find a herd, it usually is not hard to get close to it. I've sat and watched javelinas for up to an hour and enjoyed every minute. On a cold day, they'll pile up on top of each other for warmth in a sunny spot or den up in a cave. On warm days, they seek shady places where breezes cool them. Javelinas in Arizona breed throughout the year, so there are always a couple of piglets to entertain me.

Individual herds apparently use the same bedding and feeding areas generation after generation because I still can find javelinas on the same hillsides where I found them a half-century ago. Their senses of hearing and smell are excellent, but they are as nearsighted as Mr. Magoo. A hunter who knows this can get close enough to hit them with a rock, if he moves slowly and quietly and can throw accurately. This makes them perfect prey for short-range hunting tools, which is why Arizona has a special HAM (handgun, archery, or muzzleloader) javelina-hunting season every year.

On my second javelina hunt, my mother's brother, my father, and I hunted along the San Pedro River near a place called Cascabel (Spanish for rattler) in February 1950. It is aptly named because there are lots of snakes there, but it was a winter day and we saw none. I didn't want my father to shoot my javelina, so I went one way and he went another. We had been separated for about an hour when I became lost for the only time in my life. I was thirteen now, but I was crying, not knowing which way to go in a grove of cholla "jumping cactus" taller than my head. I couldn't see fifty yards in front of me when I suddenly came upon five or six javelinas using their crusty snouts to dig up cholla roots. I shot one of the animals with my .303 Savage and began dragging it by its rear feet. I didn't stop crying until I eventually stumbled upon the road that ran along the riverbank and found my father's old panel truck.

My father's response on seeing me with my javelina was to chastise me for not gutting it. If nothing else, I should have removed its musk gland, he said.[1]

---

[1]He always tried to shoot two or three javelinas, and he took home only the largest sow whenever he found a herd because he believed sows were better to eat. I now know that boars and sows taste no different, and that it's best to remove the gland when skinning the animal in a clean environment.

"The meat will taste like it smells," he said.

There was no way I would tell him that I was lost when I shot that animal.

This was the second of maybe fifty collared peccaries I have taken with centerfire rifles, bows, and muzzleloading rifles over the past sixty years in Arizona. I love hunting these little piglike animals, and I especially enjoy watching them.

* * *

On one hunt I'll never forget, I didn't kill a javelina. My friends Whitey DeVries and Boris Baird and I had driven to the Mustang Mountains, about eighty miles southeast of Tucson, on opening morning of the 1990 javelina season. We reached those rugged low hills at daybreak.

I knew where a herd usually could be found, but, as we often do, I parked my truck before we reached the mountain, and we set up our spotting scopes to glass every likely looking canyon before moving another half-mile or so and checking out another canyon. We were parked just off a two-track trail that led to a rugged knob called Biscuit Peak, where "my" herd lived, when two hunters in a red Jeep roared past us. They apparently knew about the same herd and were racing to beat us to it. We waved at them as they drove past, but they didn't respond.

The three of us were inspecting another long canyon a half-hour later when we heard three or four shots fired behind Biscuit Peak, which could only mean the other two hunters had found the herd. We had a good place to glass from, so we stayed where we were for another hour, using our binoculars and spotting scopes constantly to search for javelinas. We saw several white-tailed deer and a very good mule-deer buck but no "pigs." We were ready to move to another vantage point when the Jeep returned. There was only one man in it, and he was almost hysterical. He was afraid his partner was in trouble. The two of them had found the javelinas, and this man had killed one.

"He ran over the hill after them," the man said, meaning his partner. "When he didn't come back, I went looking for him, but I couldn't find him. He has a bad heart, and I'm afraid something happened. Will you help me look for him?"

I moved the spotting scope so I could see the head of the canyon, where he said his partner had gone. Boris did the same with his scope, and almost simultaneously we found a suspicious-looking white spot in our scopes. It was more than a mile away, but the more we watched it, the more we were convinced we were looking at someone stretched out on a rock. Whatever it was, it wasn't moving, and we needed to get a closer look.

Boris got to the man first and yelled down to us that the guy was dead. The man apparently had taken off his shirt and jacket after climbing the peak, and the white spot we'd seen from so far away was his undershirt. As best we could figure, he'd sat down on a rock with his rifle in his lap and died. His partner was horrified and kept saying, over and over, "What am I going to tell his wife?"

We had left home in my truck, so the three of them stayed with the corpse while I worked my way down to the vehicle and drove a few miles to the little town of Elgin, population maybe seventy-five or eighty persons. It had only one public telephone, and it was mounted on the outside wall of a real estate office that was closed for the weekend. When I called 911, I was connected with the Santa Cruz County sheriff's office in Nogales and told that Biscuit Peak was in another county and out of its jurisdiction. I then asked the operator to connect me with the Cochise County sheriff's office in Sierra Vista, the closest town of any size in that county.

"We can't do anything for at least an hour," a woman said.

She told me the only deputy on duty in the Biscuit Peak area was at a fatal car crash thirty miles away.

Then I remembered that Fort Huachuca, a U.S. Army post, was nearby.

"Can't you get a helicopter out of the fort to come get the guy?" I asked.

"Nobody can move the body until the deputy inspects the scene," she said. "Stay where you are so you can guide him to it."

There was no way I was going to wait at a telephone booth in Elgin until a deputy showed up while my friends were on a hillside with a dead man, wondering what had happened to me. I gave the woman directions to where we could be found and headed back to the peak.

Instead of parking on the Jeep trail, I shifted into four-wheel drive and drove off-road up the mountain to get as close as I could to where my friends were waiting above me. I was surprised to see that the ground in a fifty-foot circle around them was blackened. My friends had built a fire to keep warm, and it had gotten away from them before they could stomp it out. It had burned almost to the corpse's feet!

The four of us sat with a dead man on Biscuit Peak, high above the Sonoita Valley, not talking as we watched the sun drop behind the Santa Rita Mountains. If a coyote had yodeled, the sound would have set the small hairs on my neck on end. Around 11 P.M. we finally saw the headlights of a vehicle following my tracks up the mountain. When the deputy drove up to my truck, we called down to him in the dark to let him know where we were. He climbed up to us, carrying a small flashlight and an aluminum stretcher that resembled a flattened lawn chair laced with plastic webbing. After interviewing us, he took several flash-lit photos of the deceased and the area around the corpse.

"I need you to help me get him down," he said. "Any of you have health problems?"

I was being treated for a heart condition and told him so.

"I don't want anybody to die getting him out. You can't believe how many people do that," he said.

He then proceeded to lecture me about climbing mountains in my "condition." I didn't try to explain that I could walk up and down mountains all day if I set my own pace.

We started off the peak in the dark with the deputy holding his flashlight, the four of them carrying the stretcher on which the dead man was strapped. I was at the rear, carrying the dead man's backpack and two rifles—Whitey's and the dead man's—and stumbling a lot because I was the last in line and the deputy's flashlight was of no use to me. I couldn't see my feet in the dark.

Graythorn is one of the most common types of brush in javelina country, and the side of that peak was covered with it. A similar type of thorny bush in Africa is called wait-a-bit. Believe me, our graythorn is worse than its African counterpart. Its terrible thorns are slanted backward, and to get through it you have to force yourself through, ripping clothes and flesh whenever you're snagged, which is constantly and nearly everywhere. My friends and the deputy began our trip off the mountain by trying to protect the corpse, but they soon were using the stretcher to part the brush.

When we reached the deputy's pickup truck, they slid the stretcher into the bed of the truck. There was no tailgate, and I asked if the stretcher needed to be tied down. The deputy said something about this wasn't the first time he'd brought a dead man out. I didn't say anything after that.

Whitey, Boris, and I followed the deputy's truck off the mountain in my truck. I drove at least fifty yards behind the deputy. I didn't want to run over the body if the stretcher slipped out while we were driving across country. Whenever the deputy crossed a gully, the stretcher would slam into the cab end of the box as he went downhill and then slide almost out of the truck as he climbed out of the gully. He somehow reached the road without losing the corpse. It was nearly 2 A.M. before we got home.

✳ ✳ ✳

The hunt I'm about to describe began with a call from a woman I thought would have been the last person to ask me to help someone kill an animal. She was well known for her association with the Arizona–Sonora Desert Museum, which, at the time, was a bastion of antihunting sentiment. Nonetheless, there she was, asking me to help Mexico's ambassador to the United States hunt a javelina that weekend.

This was an important person, with full diplomatic immunity as the top representative of a foreign nation. Although he didn't need a license—or even a hunting season—I didn't know where I might stand under the law if I aided him, so I called the Arizona Game and Fish Department. I was surprised to learn that the agency also wanted to help the ambassador.

When I called the woman back, we made an appointment for me to pick up the ambassador at her ranch on the east side of Tucson at a very early hour two days later. I then arranged to meet my friends Alex Jacome and Grant Maclean on the way out of town. Grant was certain he could find a herd of javelinas he had seen recently.

I met the ambassador, a friendly man named José Juan de Olloqui, over a breakfast cooked and served by the pillar of Tucson society. Then we hooked up with Alex, Grant, and wildlife manager Gerry Perry and drove an hour or so to a small range of hills southeast of town. I was curious why an ambassador from Mexico would want to hunt in Arizona, when javelinas are found from one end of his country to the other.

"The problem is, I don't get to do much hunting when I'm there," he said. "Everyone wants to hold a party for me. If we do go out, we just drive around."

I was shocked when he said he intended to shoot his javelina with a .375 H&H Magnum. Sopping wet, a really big boar might weigh fifty to sixty pounds on the hoof. His rifle was better suited for Alaskan brown bear, Cape buffalo, and elephant, but I didn't say anything.

The herd Maclean knew about wasn't where he had last seen it, and after about an hour of glassing places, we thought it might have gone. At that point, the ambassador announced he needed to make a telephone call. This was before cellular phones, and the closest phone I knew about was in Elgin, a half-hour away. The call couldn't wait, Olloqui said, so I drove him to the phone while our three companions continued to look for the herd. They found it soon after we returned, we made a short stalk, and the ambassador had his javelina.

I was gutting the animal when the ambassador asked me how I felt. I felt fine, I said.

"That's good," he said. "My last guide died on me. I don't want it to happen again."

Olloqui then told about someone who had dropped dead of a heart attack a week earlier while gutting a mule-deer buck the ambassador had killed in New Mexico. There were just the two of them, so he got the keys out of the dead man's pocket, hiked back to the truck, and drove off to find help. The problem was, he'd traveled to the hunting area in the dark and had no idea where he was or which of the dozens of dirt roads he needed to take to reach pavement.

"I must have wasted an hour just getting to the highway," he said. "And when I got to town, I had no idea where I'd been. I drove around with the sheriff, and just before it was too dark to see, we finally found where I'd left the man."

A formal reception for the ambassador already was under way when I returned him to the woman's ranch that evening, and Olloqui and his host asked me to stay for it. Before I could politely decline, the ambassador left me alone with some of our city's best-known animal activists while he went off to change clothes. I was thankful nobody wanted to debate the morality of hunting. In fact, everyone seemed pleased that the ambassador had collected the animal he wanted. Olloqui, wearing a black suit and tie that made him look like the important diplomat he was, returned, and I was then able to make a quick exit.

He called my home a few weeks later to invite Alex, Grant, and me to be his guests at the Mexican embassy the next time we were in Washington, D.C.

*　*　*

The first of perhaps six or seven javelinas I have taken with black powder was one I shot with a flintlock .54-caliber muzzleloader I'd built using parts from Dixie Gun Works of Tennessee. Someone had told me about a herd he had seen regularly on the southern end of the Santa Rita Mountains, not far from the little town of Patagonia and the Mexican border. I went there by myself, parked my truck at the town dump where he'd said I should park, and spent the first hour of daylight searching from the truck with my binocular. I was ready to move to another spot when I suddenly saw several dark objects moving into the head of a steep canyon at least three-quarters of a mile above me. There were javelinas exactly where he'd said they would be.

It took me at least an hour to climb to the spot, select one of the largest javelinas in the little herd, take aim with the muzzleloader's open sights, and shoot it. It was a damp morning, and the cloud of white smoke from my barrel immediately obscured my view. It seemed to take a minute before I could see that I'd killed the animal, but it probably was much less than that. This is not just a story about shooting a javelina with a muzzleloader, though.

After gutting the animal, I tied a rear leg to its snout and slung it from my shoulder. The mountain was covered with a horrible plant that Mexicans call *lechuguilla*. We gringos know it as "Spanish bayonet" or "shin-dagger" because it is nearly impossible to walk through it without its sharp points stabbing our ankles. The only way I've found to navigate a field of the stuff is to carefully put my heel down first and try to purposely flatten the plant before it jabs me. Sometimes it works, sometimes it doesn't. To try to escape the fields of shin daggers growing on the hillsides and ridges, I stayed in the bottom of the canyons as I walked back to my truck carrying the javelina.

I was halfway there when I heard something that sounded like someone crying. At first I thought it might be an animal, but the closer I got to the sound, the more I was convinced that it was human, even though there was nobody in sight. It wasn't until I was walking past a dead tree that I spotted the young woman. She was crouched inside the hollowed-out cavity in the huge tree's trunk, and she was absolutely terrified of me.

It took a while before I could convince her that I wouldn't harm her. She had become lost, I soon learned, after she and her boyfriend started climbing the opposite side of the peak on which I'd killed my javelina. She grew tired and lost interest in hunting about halfway up the mountain and decided to return to their truck alone. Instead of retracing their path to the peak, she followed the easiest route down the canyon to where I'd found her. Because the canyon she had chosen ran at an angle from the ridge where they had parked, it meant their truck was a long way off. She followed me off the mountain, and I drove her to where her friend was waiting. She never told me why she'd taken refuge inside a tree. Who knows what she would have done if I hadn't come along!

*   *   *

I have never been accused of being an expert bow hunter, but I have done some hunting with a bow. After I graduated from the University of Arizona, I bought a Ben Pearson Javelina recurve bow and lost a lot of Herter's Famous Port Orford Cedar arrows and single-blade, stamped-metal broadheads while trying to kill one of the big-antlered mule-deer bucks still found across the foothills of the Tucson Mountains west of Tucson. This was before homes popped up all over the place in the mid-1970s, and long before the National Park Service annexed nearly all of the public land on that mountain. I even managed to stick an arrow into a doe in the last few minutes before dark one evening. When I returned the next morning, I followed a scant blood trail and found coyotes had left only its head—minus its nose and ears—and a whole lot of hair scattered over a quarter-acre.

Alex Jacome, Grant Maclean, and I also spent a couple of seasons flinging arrows at elk southeast of Flagstaff, until I wounded and lost a young bull. The two experiences made me realize I didn't have what it took to be an ethical bow hunter of large game. This was before someone decided to put sights on bows, which meant we all shot "instinctively"—we pulled back the string and guessed where our arrow would go. To gain the skill needed to consistently hit a target more than a few yards away, I needed to practice several times every week for months, and this was something I wasn't willing to do.

You don't have to be a skilled archer to hunt javelinas with a bow and arrow if you limit yourself to short-distance shooting, however. They're usually found in herds of five to a dozen, and at least one of them will be rolling rocks, rooting, or pushing brush around, so they usually don't pay much attention to minor noises around them. Combine this with their nearsightedness, and that should be proof enough that javelinas are made for bowhunting.

My only bow-killed javelina that was farther away than the length of my pickup truck—my self-imposed limit for bowhunting—was one that taxidermist John Doyle and I called to us with our voices. John and a couple of his friends pioneered the use of optics to hunt big game in southern Arizona, and John had found a small herd of javelinas feeding about a mile above us in the Tumacacori Mountains south of Tucson. Someone had told me that javelinas could be called to bow range by making woofing noises, so when we were within seventy-five yards of the herd, I whispered to John that we should try it.

The animals immediately stopped feeding and milled around when we imitated the sound javelinas make when alarmed. A minute or two later, one of them started toward us. The long hair on its back was erect, and it was snapping its teeth. When it was about thirty yards away, I held over the animal and released my heavy wooden arrow. It flew in an arc, dropped, and broke that javelina's hip, anchoring it where it was.

"You hit him!" John said.

"Wasn't I supposed to?" I whispered, acting as if it were something I could do every time.

I was as surprised as he was when my arrow hit that javelina, but I would never admit it to him.

We both were shocked when the other javelinas piled on their wounded companion and bit it repeatedly and noisily. They stopped only when John and I started woofing again. When another javelina left the herd and approached us, John waited until it was only a couple of yards away and sent an arrow through it before it ran off. While he went after his animal, I walked over to mine and found it dead. My arrow apparently had cut its femoral artery.

I tried "woofing up" javelinas several times after that with no success. I was alone each time, though. It may take two "woofers" to make the technique work.

I had much better luck bringing javelinas to me using a mouth-blown varmint call, but it took a while to refine the technique. Grant Maclean and I tried it for the first time after we found a herd of javelinas about three hundred yards away on a hillside covered with shin daggers. When Grant brought out his varmint call and started calling, the herd bolted and began running away. When he continued calling, the herd stopped, turned, and moved toward us in a line, stopping only when Grant stopped calling. I missed the first animal as it passed by me, but the second dropped instantly when my arrow caught it under its chin and sliced through its heart.

The secret to calling javelinas, we decided, was to keep calling, even when they ran off or stopped. Their first reaction to the squeaks and squawks of a varmint call was to run away, but they usually returned to investigate what had frightened them. As long as we called, they moved toward us, almost always with their long hair erect and their teeth snapping.

✳ ✳ ✳

The best way to hunt javelinas in southern Arizona is to sit on a hillside in an area where you know there is a herd, and then spend at least an hour in that spot with your eyes glued to a binocular. I can't tell you how many times I did that and was ready to give up and go look for another place to glass when I suddenly spotted movement on a far-off hillside. Minutes later, I would be looking at four or more javelinas that had been there all the while I was searching for them.

I remember such a time in the early 1970s on the northern slope of the Tumacacori Mountains south of Tucson. I had been watching a cone-shaped peak nearly a mile away when I thought I saw a barrel cactus move. There were dozens of these short, thorn-covered cacti scattered all over the hill. When I saw the movement, I thought I had seen a javelina, but as I concentrated on it I could see that I hadn't. It definitely was a barrel cactus that had fallen over sometime earlier. I was ready to move to another hill when I saw the cactus roll a couple of feet. Those things can't move by themselves, I told myself, as I got up to check it out.

I approached and was about fifty yards from the cactus when I saw it move again. This time, when I checked it with my binocular, I could see the rear legs of a javelina, which had hollowed out the cactus and was inside it, eating its wet pulp. It would have been an easy shot from where I stood, but I decided to see how close I could get to the animal. It was so preoccupied with what it was doing that I was able to sneak within a few steps of it and yell, "Hey, pig!" before it realized I was there. It backed out of the cactus in panic and bounced down the hillside on its short legs before stopping about a hundred yards away. I was there to hunt a javelina, so I shot it.

✳ ✳ ✳

In my opinion, javelinas are inedible unless slathered with lots of barbecue sauce and slow-roasted overnight in a covered pit filled with at least a foot of hot mesquite coals. It's a lot of work to prepare them that way, and I was having trouble finding people to give them to. I had stopped applying for hunting permits until Whitey DeVries wanted to hunt them again about five or six years before this writing. He and I filled our tags the first morning on the western slope of the Tumacacori Mountains. After that, I decided I wouldn't hunt them again.

It's a funny thing, but working on this chapter got me interested in javelinas again, and I applied for and drew another tag. It didn't worry me that I could only hunt the last two days of the season, and the only javelina I saw was the one my friend Bill Mattausch shot when he went one way and I went another. I did see two Coues white-tailed bucks and a coyote, and I had a great time with good friends. What else could a hunter want?

Arizona Whitetails Are Special

Chapter 4

One of the first things I did when I left Yuma in August 1954 to attend the University of Arizona was to call Jean Potts, who was living in Tucson at the time. I'd dated her a couple of times, even though we attended high school in separate cities. I even rode the train to Tucson on my father's pass to escort her to her senior prom.[1] We were married eighteen months after I moved to Tucson. We lived with Jean's grandmother at her family's home on East Fort Lowell Road while we attended the university.

Jean's parents had given her and her sister a Jeepster convertible while they were in high school, but I knew better than to take it hunting, so I left home on foot at 4 A.M. on the third Friday of October 1956, the opening of Arizona's annual deer-hunting season, with my .303 Savage and a steel U.S. Army canteen filled with water. Tucson was much smaller than it is now, and Campbell Avenue was one of the few roads that cut into the foothills north of River Road. Dogs barked at me as I walked in the dark past the last of the houses, but I apparently awoke no one. This was quite a hike I undertook, perhaps seven or eight miles just to reach the Santa Catalina Mountains, where I'd been told I could find Coues white-tailed deer. Although I walked through what then was prime mule-deer country, I saw nothing other than several large coveys of Gambel's quail and cottontail rabbits.

---

[1]My birth certificate says I was born "at home in Pima County, three miles east of Tucson" in 1936. The little house is still standing, but the city limits are now at least fifteen miles east of there. We moved to Yuma when I was three years old and visited my mother's family in Tucson as many as four or five times a year while I was growing up.

The sun already was well up when I reached the Coronado National Forest boundary fence, just above where a house now sits at the end of Ponatoc Road. As I approached the barbed-wire fence, I suddenly heard rocks rolling ahead of me. I climbed the fence and ran to where I could look down into the canyon. Standing perhaps seventy-five yards below me, looking back to see what had startled it, was the first white-tailed deer of any kind that I had ever seen. It had a small rack, but it was a buck. Before it could turn and run off, I brought my rifle up, placed the top of the post in my 2.5X Weaver scope on its shoulder . . . and yanked the stiff trigger. The deer whirled and ran a few yards downhill before collapsing.

My first thought when I reached my first Coues whitetail was that it had a mouselike face. (I've felt the same about every Coues deer I've shot.) It was a beautiful animal, with the wide skull, short nose, and large ears that set this subspecies apart from other whitetails. It seemed to be a lighter gray, almost silver, and had more white on its underparts than the four or five mule deer I'd taken up to then. As I expected, its tail was longer and broader than a mule deer's, and its neck was swollen in pre-rut. What I hadn't expected to see was the auburn color on top of its tail and on the top of its head. The deer weighed perhaps ninety pounds on the hoof, and its small antlers had three points and an eyeguard on each side, which is typical for a mature white-tailed buck in Arizona.

I gutted the deer and tried carrying it, but I hadn't gone far before I realized there was no way I was going to pack that animal all the way to where we lived. Even if I could have, that deer and I would have created quite a sight when I reached civilization. I hid the carcass and my rifle near a two-track Jeep trail and started off the mountain. It seemed to take forever to finally get home. One of Jean's cousins and I returned in his car to retrieve the buck that afternoon.

This was a half-century ago, and we didn't call them Coues deer then. They were desert whitetail, Arizona whitetail, or just whitetail. We can blame Jack O'Connor, a former Tucsonan who was *Outdoor Life* magazine's gun editor in the 1940s, 1950s, and 1960s, for all the hoopla that surrounds these deer now. He romanticized them in his articles and books, calling them "gray ghosts" and declaring them one of North America's top trophies, second only to his beloved wild sheep, of course. (According to O'Connor, nothing came close to sheep hunting.) We also can blame the Boone and Crockett Club for establishing a separate category for *Odocoileus virginianus couesi* in its record books. When the club's first books were published, some scientists believed our little deer were a distinct species. Later, after they decided the Coues whitetail is only one of thirty-eight races of white-tailed deer, the category remained.

I have no idea how many magazine articles have been written about Coues deer hunting since O'Connor wrote the first one, but there must be hundreds. Why the Texas outdoor writers haven't also promoted the hunting of their Carmen Mountains subspecies is beyond me. Their deer are found in similar habitats in a limited range and closely resemble the Coues race in their habits and appearance.

* * *

I used to carry a card in my wallet that showed I was a member of the Record Desert Whitetail Club, one of the most prestigious hunting clubs in the country at the time. It certainly was the toughest to join; neither money nor influence could make you a member. When the club was created by John Doyle, Wes Bramhall, and brothers Jim and Seymour Levy, a candidate had to shoot a white-tailed buck that qualified for the Boone and Crockett Club's record book and then restrict his deer hunting in Arizona to only record-class desert whitetails. The club's annual meeting featured a steak dinner at Doyle's taxidermy shop, where members compared the antlers of the deer they'd taken that year. The hunter taking a buck with the largest antlers served as president for the next year.

Members were serious about hunting only whitetails, and shooting a mule deer was cause for immediate expulsion. Lester Stuart, a heavy-equipment operator, was among the first to go when he shot a mule-deer buck with antlers so wide, heavy, and tall they didn't seem real. Few hunters would pass up a mule deer that would qualify for the Boone and Crockett

Club's record book, especially in southern Arizona's Galiuro Mountains, but it was only a "carp" in the eyes of purist desert-whitetail hunters.

But that was when the Boone and Crockett minimum score for an Arizona whitetail was 90 points after deductions for non-symmetry, so a good hunter who lived in southern Arizona and was willing to pass up lesser bucks could reasonably expect to find a deer that would qualify for the book. When Boone and Crockett increased its minimum to 110 points, it became much more difficult, and the whitetail club did not raise its minimum. When more members strayed and shot mule deer and the club's membership declined, that portion of the rules also was relaxed. The club still exists, its presidents still are "elected" by shooting the largest Coues deer of the season, and its only meeting is an annual steak feast. As far as I know, no hunter has been president for two consecutive years.

I qualified for membership in the 1960s with a 104-point buck I found at the base of the giant monolith that distinguishes the skyline of the Baboquivari Mountains southwest of Tucson. The interesting thing about that deer was that it had a deep trough across the base of its left antler, just above the burr, that could only mean someone had shot that deer before I did that season! I can only imagine how that hunter must have felt when he saw his buck drop like a rock (the only response a deer could possibly make to being struck in an antler by a rifle bullet) and then watched it jump up and run off.

Over the many years that followed my first whitetail, I shot a lot of Coues deer in Arizona. In the beginning, before I got smarter, I hunted them as I did mule deer: I crept along just under the ridges, throwing rocks, hoping to chase bucks out of their hiding places. Later, I rode horses and mules, waiting for the sound of their hoofs to get the deer moving so I could see them and jump off to shoot. Neither method was as successful as making short drives with five or six other hunters, as I did when I hunted the Sierrita Mountains with one of Jean's cousins and his friends.

Someone would drive us to the top of a long, deep canyon, and then we'd spread out from ridge to ridge a hundred or more yards apart and move slowly downhill for a mile or so, always trying to keep the others in our group in sight. When a buck got up, it almost always tried to run uphill, where one of the drivers was waiting to shoot it. It was amazing how many bucks we took from the same spots several years in a row. Eventually, though, I discovered binoculars and spotting scopes and found I could locate many more deer by simply sitting and glassing from a high place.

I have never fallen into the trap of thinking I was smarter than a deer, especially a whitetail. I'm well aware of the studies biologists have done by releasing a single buck into a forested enclosure and trying unsuccessfully to find it again every time they enter the pen. For the most part, Coues deer in southern Arizona live in wide-open, rugged terrain, broken only by patches of ocotillo and oak trees. They seem to prefer steep, rocky places. They have no trouble eluding mere humans, probably because not one of us is the efficient predator some of us think we are. For proof of that, go out in Arizona's whitetail country during the January rut, and you will see more bucks—and larger bucks—than you would have thought could possibly exist on heavily hunted public land. Where were all these bucks during the October, November, and December rifle hunts, when hundreds of would-be deer shooters were scouring the country on foot with long-range rifles and scopes and expensive 15X Zeiss and Swarovski binoculars? These trophy bucks were very close to where you found them in January, that's where.

I remember a hunt when a buck showed me just how smart a whitetail can be. I was walking slowly down a ridge behind the Fort Grant correctional facility for boys north of Willcox, crossing back and forth, hoping to surprise a buck bedded in the head of one of the many little side canyons on each side of the ridge. Something made me look back at where I'd just been, and when I did, I spotted a deer quietly sneaking away from me. It was almost as if it were moving in slow motion. The top of that ridge was so narrow I must have walked within ten yards of that deer, but it waited until I was past it to get up! When I first saw the deer, its tail was tucked between its legs, and its neck was stretched straight out to reduce its height. It was a beautiful buck with heavy, wide antlers, and I shot it.

A similar incident occurred in the Galiuro Mountains, above the Sunset Ranch north of Willcox, in the mid-1960s. Mule deer began moving into that area a decade later, replacing the Coues white-tailed deer, which used to be so abundant in that canyon that their tracks would obliterate those of my little Jeep overnight. It was in the middle of the day, and I was sitting atop a small cliff, glassing every crag and slope in sight with my binocular, hoping to find a bedded buck. I still was a chain-smoker then, and I must have smoked three or four cigarettes before I decided to move on. As soon as I stood up, a heavy-antlered whitetail burst out from below where I had been sitting. Looking back, I'm surprised that I was able to recover from the shock and kill that buck before it got away. It obviously knew I was above it all the time I sat there smoking. The noise I made when I got up must have been more than it could take.

I also remember a white-tailed buck I almost lost. It got up running while I was sneaking along the brushy side of a long, deep canyon on the eastern slope of the Galiuro Mountains, a hundred miles east of Tucson. I could hear rocks rolling and the crashing of brush as it raced downhill on my side of the gorge. I first saw the buck as it ran up the opposite slope about two hundred yards away. Because canyons are v-shaped and not vertical, each jump increased the deer's distance from me. I must have shot four or five times before that buck ran into one of my bullets. I distinctly remember seeing it roll and slide down the steep slope and hearing the bullet slap before I lost sight of it. I have no idea how far it was when I killed it, but it was a long way off.

When I crossed the canyon, the buck wasn't where I expected to find it dead. I made increasingly larger circles until I found where it had slid over a fifteen-foot cliff. When I climbed down to the base of the rocks, all I could find was a little puddle of blood on the leaves under an oak tree that was growing next to the cliff. The ground around the spot wasn't disturbed, and I knew that deer couldn't have gotten out of there without my seeing it. I was standing there, wondering where it might be, when I looked up. It was above me, caught in the tree's limbs, after falling off the cliff onto the tree. I couldn't see it from the top of the cliff, and I wouldn't have found it if I hadn't found the blood. I had to climb the tree and push that deer off the limb to retrieve it.

* * *

I took several desert whitetails off the Santa Catalina Mountains above Tucson, but I remember a hunt up there when I didn't see a deer. I parked at the first wide spot on the Mount Lemmon Highway after entering the Coronado National Forest and began climbing the mountain above me. It was steep, and there were huge boulders and twenty-foot drop-offs I had to get over and around. When I finally reached the edge of an open, grassy basin, I stopped, rested my binocular on my walking stick, and began looking for deer. I saw nothing at first, but I soon could hear someone talking. Sound carries a long way in open country, so it was a while before I found the two young women. They were on a hiking path that led below the place where I was standing. When they were five hundred yards away or so, I could see they weren't wearing shirts or brassieres. They appeared to be in their mid-twenties.

As they walked side by side toward me, I could hear the young women talk about making a casserole, of all things. They were just below me when I decided to let them know they weren't alone on that mountain.

"Hello," I said, as they walked past.

I was standing on a rock twenty or thirty feet above them, with my hands and chin on my walking stick, trying to appear nonchalant about their nakedness. They hadn't seen me until then, and I must have frightened them. It was cruel, I know, but I couldn't let them just walk away. They didn't say a word, but they did take off running. The last I saw them in my binocular was as they left the cover of a tree, where they stopped to put on their shirts.

* * *

For an example of how wily our little whitetail can be, you need only look at a day I hunted with George Parker—a rancher, Mexican desert-

sheep guide, international hunter, and family friend. George served my
brother Tom and me *menudo* (soup made of beef tripe and hominy) for
breakfast at his ranch in Amado, about midway between Tucson and
the Mexican border, an hour before daylight the day the season opened.
We then rode south in his dilapidated Jeep another twenty miles to
what now is Patagonia Lake State Park, using his keys to open perhaps
a half-dozen ranch gates along the way.

The country he took us to had only a few oak trees in the bottom
of wide, shallow canyons. Above the canyons were low, rolling hills
covered with grass. A more unlikely place for a white-tailed deer
in southern Arizona would be hard to find, or so I thought until we
found deer. At least a dozen of them were feeding on an open slope
when I found them in my binocular from so far away we couldn't tell
if any had antlers. The three of us left the Jeep and began a stalk that
took us within four hundred yards of the herd. We arrived in time
to see all the deer sink out of sight in the grass. They obviously had
seen or heard us but chose to hide instead of running off when we
approached them.

George and I decided to stay where we were and send Tom around
the hill and have him advance over the top. We were expecting him
to get a close-up shot at one of the bucks in the group when they got
up. It took perhaps forty-five minutes before we saw him on the ridge.
Using our hands, we signaled that the herd was directly below him.
We had been watching the hillside and were certain the deer hadn't
left. However, we never saw them again. We had Tom walk back and
forth across the hillside, but the deer wouldn't get up unless he stepped
on them, which he didn't. The three of us went home that day without
firing a shot.

As far as I know, the only deer Tom has shot was the buck I found
for him elsewhere in the Santa Rita Mountains the previous year. It
would have stayed hidden if I hadn't gone out of my way to investigate
a shallow cave whose entrance was almost covered by an oak tree. The
little buck was standing in the mouth of the cave (it may have been
cooler there) when I walked up to it. It was almost close enough for me

to touch when it bolted past, ran straight to Tom, and stopped suddenly when it saw him. Tom's second shot put it down.

* * *

As a newspaper's outdoor editor, I hung out at Tucson's taxidermy and blacksmith shops during the hunting seasons, looking for stories for my columns. Newspapers still published photos of hunters with exceptional trophies, and I saw and photographed a great many Coues white-tailed bucks local hunters took during that period. For a while I naively believed I could tell where a buck came from by merely looking at its antlers.

Southern Arizona's whitetails are found on and around so-called sky islands, small but high, rugged mountain ranges that are separated from each other by wide valleys that usually are inhabited by desert mule deer. There is very little movement of whitetails from one island to another, so a case could be made that these deer, isolated from others of their race, would develop characteristics that are distinctive to their home range. The tips of the main beams on many Coues deer taken from one mountain, for example, might come close to touching, while the tips of the antlers of many bucks from another range would be much farther apart, or so I believed. I thought I had stumbled onto an undiscovered fact of natural history until I realized I was guessing the kill sites of only about half the deer I inspected. Tossing a coin would have given me similar results.

* * *

A wildlife biologist will tell you it is impossible for two distinct races of the same species to exist for long in the same location. There are areas where the ranges of two subspecies come together, but the differences between the subspecies of deer in these areas will be blurred. That's why I always was (and still am) skeptical about the stories I heard about "Mexican fantail deer." The fantail supposedly is a miniature race of whitetail that lives among our Coues deer in Arizona and Mexico. While I worked for the newspaper, I saw many small adult whitetails in Tucson's taxidermy shops. I even shot one myself. The eight-inch-wide antlers on my forty-pound buck had five points on each side of its minuscule rack, counting eyeguards. A Game and Fish Department wildlife manager who checked its teeth said it was just over four years old, so it was a mature buck and not a juvenile.

Carlos Gonzales Hermosillo, a hunting outfitter who operates in northern Mexico, is convinced fantails exist and offered to take me to an area in Mexico's Coues-deer country where he said they are regularly taken. Unfortunately, I waited too long to take advantage of his invitation. I no longer can climb the steep, rocky mountains where Coues deer live.

If the fantail is a mythical beast, as I believe, then the only explanation for the half-sized Coues deer that a few hunters take in Arizona and Sonora every year is that they must be dwarfs. The problem is, dwarfism is supposed to be rare in wild populations of animals.

My Quest for Housholder's Big Ten

Chapter 5

Bob Housholder died many years before this writing, but he still is widely remembered as the founder of the Grand Slam Club, the organization for hunters who have collected the four major types of North American wild sheep. Bob was a large and controversial man with a bigger-than-all-outdoors ego. His day job was with the Arizona Highway Department, where I was told he had something to do with acquiring rights of way for new highways. I got to know him well after I became the *Tucson Citizen*'s outdoor editor. I even served as a judge for one of the awards he presented to Arizona's top big-game hunters. Before that, though, I knew him only by his byline while he was editor of a small magazine called *Arizona Wildlife Sportsman*, which I eagerly read from cover to cover every month during the 1950s. Housholder used the magazine to promote an award he created, called the Arizona Big Ten, which he presented to hunters who had taken Coues white-tailed deer, mule deer, elk, pronghorn, bison, desert bighorn sheep, mountain lion, black bear, javelina, and wild turkey in our state.

While I still was in high school, Housholder's articles and photos featuring the award's recipients inspired me to try to collect all ten animals. I had no way of knowing that it was a quest that would take half a lifetime to complete.

* * *

I'd taken three of the Big Ten—mule deer, white-tailed deer, and javelina—when I applied in July 1956 for an elk tag with two of my wife's cousins and one of their friends. We started planning our hunt as soon as our tags arrived in early August. As opening day drew nearer, we decided that Eddie Norgard and I would drive his wood-paneled Chevrolet station wagon and tow a little camp trailer. The other two would follow in a pickup truck. We would pack our camping gear in the trailer; the food would go in the truck. We planned our finances down to the last penny.

After studying maps and talking with people who knew our area, we chose a spot along the Black River called PS Knoll, the remotest part of Arizona's White Mountains at the time, for our camp. When the time came for us to leave town, the guys in the pickup truck called to say they couldn't leave until later that day. They planned to drive north through Safford, which was a shorter distance but a longer drive in hours because of the mountain roads. They wouldn't reach our campsite until the middle of the night, they said. Eddie and I arranged to meet them where we had previously decided to camp with the help of our topo maps.

We got there at sundown, leveled the trailer, and went to bed without supper because nearly all of our food was in the other vehicle. We expected to be awakened by our friends, but they didn't show up that night or for the next four days. We were about three hours from the closest town on bad roads, but we didn't have enough money to buy more food and have anything left for the gas we needed to get home.

It was September, and it rained every day. The station wagon had only two-wheel drive, and it slipped all over the muddy roads on its bald tires, but we managed to keep from getting stuck until the day I shot my elk—the first live elk I'd ever seen. Hunting in timber was new for us, so we stayed close to roads. I was trying to sneak through a place thick with aspens and spruce when I jumped up on one of the many blowdowns and spooked a bull elk that was bedded on the other side of the fallen tree. It was out of there so fast I didn't have time to bring my rifle up. I ran as fast as an excited twenty-one-year-old can run downhill, jumping over and up and down on blowdowns as if they weren't there. When I caught up with the elk in the bottom of the canyon, it had its head behind a pine tree, apparently believing I couldn't see it. My first shot put it down kicking.

When I walked up to my first elk, I couldn't believe its size. It was in the rut and smelled of the urine and semen on its belly. Its body was at least four times the size of any mule deer I'd shot. Its antlers were five feet long, and they were wide and thick, with six points per side. It still is the largest of all the elk I've taken. I was standing over it, trying to figure how we were going to get that huge chunk of meat to the car, when a logging truck drove past me on a gravel road only fifty yards behind the elk!

First I found Eddie and told him about my success, and then we had to check our maps and find the logging road. I guess we both were excited because we buried the wheels of his station wagon in mud while we were turning it around to go after the bull. We were trying to decide what to do when a man drove up. He hooked a chain to our bumper and pulled us out with his truck. Our new friend was interested in seeing my elk, so he followed us to the site, then helped us cut up and load the animal into our station wagon.

Eddie was as hungry as I and didn't want to wait until we found an elk for him. We cooked and devoured a chunk of one of the elk's backstraps, then packed up and headed for home the next morning, still wondering why our friends hadn't showed up. When one of Eddie's tires blew on the way back to civilization, we didn't know what to do. His spare tire was in even worse shape than his other tires. I could see us stranded without a spare in the middle of the desert between Globe and Tucson with our meat getting warmer by the minute if another tire blew. We bought a used tire in Show Low and splurged on a couple of hamburgers, french fries, and Cokes, leaving us just enough for gas to get us to Hayden Junction, where Jean's parents lived. My father-in-law loaned me a few dollars, and Eddie and I made it home without incident.

The first thing we wanted to know when we reached Tucson was if the other two hunters were OK. The only thing we could think of that would keep them from joining us was an accident or a death in one of their families. They were fine, though. Eddie and I were furious when we heard their story. They'd stopped for a beer at a bar in a mining town called Clifton, met two women in the bar, and spent the weekend eating our food and carousing before driving back to Tucson.

* * *

My next elk was a cow that I took five or six years later on my first horseback hunt. I was trying to launch a monthly outdoor newspaper when I got a letter from the U.S. Forest Service, inviting me and other journalists to join a horseback tour of a proposed wilderness site on the Blue River in Arizona and New Mexico. I couldn't go, but my friend Alex Jacome could. When he returned, he enthusiastically described the country he'd seen. More important for us, the Apache National Forest supervisor, a man named George Proctor, invited us to join a group of forest rangers on an elk hunt that fall. A dozen of them applied for tags individually every year and scheduled their vacations for the first week of the season. Those who didn't draw tags went along and worked as wranglers, packers, camp helpers, and cooks.

Alex and I drew tags for their area that same year. The day before the season opened, we met George at the corrals in the Strayhorse Campground, just below Hannagan Meadow on the Mogollon Rim, and were introduced to our horses. They were gentle animals, for which I was thankful. Jacome's mount, we were told, was trained to stand in one place when its rider dismounted and dropped its reins. I remember riding three or four miles in the dark to where our new friends had built corrals and put up several large white canvas tents equipped with sheepherders' stoves. They had packed everything—tents, cooking utensils, food, sleeping bags, and hay and oats for the horses—to the site on horses and mules earlier that week.

Alex and I had bought chaps especially for this hunt. They were batwing style and were made of rough-cut leather. We were afraid their newness would brand us as the dudes we were, so we left them in the sun for two weeks to darken and stiffen, and then we rubbed them with various things to try to make them appear as if we'd worn them a lot. We didn't fool anyone.

Everyone saddled up an hour before daylight and headed in various directions on the season's opening morning. I was told to ride to the head of a certain canyon, tie up my horse, and find a place to sit where I could see across the canyon. I was sitting there thirty minutes later when I spotted movement in an opening on the opposite ridge. I soon found a cow elk facing me in my binocular. It didn't know I was there. My tag allowed me to take any elk, so I placed the cross hairs on the center of the cow and sent a .270-caliber bullet into its chest. The elk collapsed and slid downhill fifty feet like a sack of JELL-O. I was congratulating myself on my great shot when a bull elk with antlers that seemed to reach all the way to its rump appeared at exactly the same spot where the cow had been standing. I'd filled my tag and could only watch that huge bull walk away.

Alex and I had a wonderful time hunting with those forest rangers. At night we played cards, told stories, and drank Bacanora, a powerful Mexican moonshine, from a clear glass gallon jug Alex had brought. In a couple of days we had five or six elk in camp. A tough young man named Rolfe Hoyer took one of them. I remember his name because I was impressed by the fact that he had shot an elk, cut it into quarters, loaded everything on his bobtailed mule, and brought it in, all without help from anyone. When he died in a wildfire in New Mexico seven or eight months later, the forest service named a campground near my cabin in Greer after him.

It was on this hunt that I also met Buck Buckner, then a forest ranger. He now is an Oregon rancher, a recognized expert on the life and works of gun editor Jack O'Connor. Buckner is also an author and editor, and a prominent member of the Boone and Crockett Club.

Alex didn't take an elk on that trip, but he and I had a couple of experiences worth mentioning. After shooting my elk that first morning, I was assigned the task of riding back to where we'd parked our truck and returning with more hay for the horses. Alex decided to bring his rifle and join me, just in case we might ride up on an elk. On our way out, he was bragging about how his horse stood where he dropped its reins.

"You can open all the gates," I said.

His horse did stand at the first two gates. Alex got off when we reached the third and last gate on the trail and dropped the reins, just as he had been doing. This time his horse bolted through the gate and didn't stop running until it reached the corrals at Strayhorse. I didn't know enough about horses then to catch it. It ran off whenever I tried to approach it on my horse, and it wouldn't allow me to get in front of it and chase it back to my partner. Alex walked the final mile or so to the corrals, his batwing chaps flapping. He was angry enough to spit nails.

It was the first time either of us had packed bales of hay on a mule, but we got the job done, thanks to instructions we had received from one of the rangers earlier. We cinched up a packsaddle on the mule the rangers had left at the corral, tied a bale of alfalfa on each side and one on top, and headed back to camp, leading the mule behind our horses. The problem was, the mule kept trying to knock the hay off on every tree within six feet of the trail. We managed to get most, but not all, of the hay to camp.

The other incident involving Alex on that trip happened on our way back to Tucson. He was driving his Chevrolet Suburban down the horrible twisted road that follows the New Mexico border down to the mines at Clifton when a black bear crossed the road and ran up a tree. Alex hit the brakes, jumped out with his pistol, and ran toward it. He was so excited that he left the truck's engine running and didn't put the transmission in park. The Suburban began rolling backward toward a canyon's edge, but I managed to get from the passenger side over the transmission hump to the driver's seat and stop it in time.

Meanwhile, Alex was banging away at the bear with his .357-Magnum pistol, and nothing was happening. He was hitting the bear with every shot, but he couldn't kill it until I loaded his .30-06 and handed it to him.

* * *

My most recent elk was taken five years before this writing. You might say this six-by-six bull committed suicide. I was alone at our cabin that summer, while Jean stayed in Tucson to be near her ailing father, when I learned that Alex Jacome, Eric Sparks, and I had drawn elk tags for a unit just thirty minutes from the cabin. I spent every morning and evening scouting, sometimes alone and sometimes with my friends Bill Mattausch and his son Ben. Bill's summer home is in Eagar, the little town where we buy groceries and gas when we're at our cabin in the White Mountains from May through October.

It's hard to describe how I felt when I missed three shots at a good bull elk on opening morning. The bull was following a cow elk across a clearing when I spotted it through a corridor of juniper trees. I had to shoot offhand. There was nothing I could use for a rest, and I couldn't see the elk when I sat down. At my first shot the bull stopped. I shot and missed two more times before it ran off. I couldn't believe I hadn't hit such a large animal, so I searched for blood. It took three hundred and twenty-five long steps to reach where it had been, which was closer than I thought it was. I probably had shot over that bull. Ben, Alex, and I followed its tracks to where it had crossed a shallow cattle pond, but we found no blood.

It now was about 9 A.M., too late to hunt, I thought. Ben and his brother David, Eric, and I drove into Springerville for breakfast at a McDonald's. It was perhaps 11:30 A.M. when we returned to the hunting area to learn that Alex had passed up a young bull with five points on each antler at first light. It was the only elk he saw on that trip.

We were on a two-track road, driving along the top of a ridge, when Ben and Dave, who were riding in the back of my truck, pounded on the cab and yelled for Eric and me to get out with our rifles. A cow elk was crossing the road two hundred yards behind us, followed closely by a bull. The first shot out of my 7mm Remington Magnum missed, but it turned the bull, and it began running toward us. I fired my next shot when it started to leave the road and turned it again, and it continued running straight toward us. When it was less than thirty yards away, it turned sharply to our left, and I sent a 175-grain Nosler Partition bullet through both shoulders, rolling it end over end. The entire incident took less time than it takes to tell about it. Eric hadn't fired a shot because his rifle was jammed.

We backed the truck up to that bull, gutted and loaded it whole, and were at a butcher shop in Springerville thirty minutes later. The bromide "It's better to be lucky than good" certainly was true that day.

* * *

Next on my Big Ten list was a bison, and I drew a tag the first year I applied. It was 1960 or 1961, and by then I had graduated from the University of Arizona and was working for Tucson's largest department store as its advertising manager. My boss was the sales promotion manager, Ulysses Charles Drayer, a short, gruff man who was my mentor. I had been a student in one of the marketing courses he taught, and he had hired me to assist him under the University of Arizona's work-study program. I had attended classes with Charlie's son, Gary, who was more interested in learning about hunting than in following in his father's footsteps in business. When I drew my tag to hunt a bison on the North Rim of the Grand Canyon, I invited Gary to accompany me. Coincidentally, the turkey season was scheduled to open on the same weekend as my hunt. In those days turkey hunters could buy their tags at sporting-goods stores, which Gary and I did.

No one had told me how Arizona's bison hunt was conducted before we arrived at the corrals in House Rock Valley on the date and time specified in the letter that arrived with my tag. I expected to have to spend a day or two just trying to find a herd. What I didn't know was that this was a shoot and not a hunt. Game and Fish Department employees rounded up the buffalo they wanted removed from House Rock Valley and drove them into a corral. Two tag holders at a time were positioned in the middle of a large enclosure, and a chute was opened, releasing two bison into the arena. The first shooter (who had won a coin toss) chose an animal and shot it. The second shooter got to shoot the remaining animal. The dead bison were hauled to a skinning shed, and two more shooters were brought in. I was horrified, but I was young and wanted to collect a bison. I now wish I'd refused to take part in what was happening.

The game department required tag holders to attend a pre-hunt indoctrination lecture, where we were told that we would ruin too much meat if we shot our bison behind the shoulder. Instead, we should aim for a two-inch spot below the ear and behind the base of the horn. If we hit that spot, we would break the animal's neck and drop it instantly, a Game and Fish Department employee claimed.

Bless the Beasts and Children, Glendon Swarthout's book[1] about Arizona's bison shoot, had been released a year earlier. It told about a group of juvenile misfits who ran away from a summer camp and attempted to stop the "hunt." I'm ashamed to say that at the time I sided with the Game and Fish Department and the state's major sportsmen's groups in believing this was the most efficient and humane way to manage the herd. Bison are not indigenous to our state, and they could be seen and enjoyed by the public here only because hunters paid to keep them around. I was young and foolish enough to believe that if the "experts" at Game and Fish said the best way to "hunt" bison was to shoot them in a pen, then they must know what they are talking about. What they meant, however, was that it was easier for them to manage the "harvest."

Because of the furor the book raised, and despite the fact that House Rock Valley is a long way from anywhere, *Life* magazine and at least one other national publication and every large newspaper in Arizona sent reporters and camera crews there to cover the shoot that year. When it was my turn in the arena, I walked out slowly. I didn't want to screw up with thirty or forty people watching and photographing me.

I had retired my .303 Savage and now was carrying a J. C. Higgins .270 Winchester with a 4X scope. I'd bought it on sale at Sears for $80. Since then, I had written and designed a brochure and an advertising campaign for a Tucson gunsmith named Harry Lawson, swapping my work for his. Harry did some minor metal work on the FN Mauser action and restocked my Sears rifle with what he called his Cochise

---

[1] Swarthout's book served as the basis for Stanley Kramer's award-winning 1971 film and Karen and Richard Carpenter's popular song, both with the same title as the book.

thumbhole stock, using a highly figured blank of curly maple. My bison would be my "custom" rifle's first victim.

When the chute was opened, two bison dashed out and ran around the perimeter of the arena. They stopped suddenly when they reached a spot where several other bison had died that morning. I was the first shooter, so I shot the one with the larger horns when it dropped its head to smell the blood in the sand. A cloud of dirt erupted where I'd aimed below and behind the horn, as instructed, but the bison only shook its head and didn't go down. I could hear the gallery say *"Oooh"* while I worked the bolt, brought another round into the chamber, and quickly shot again. More than half the people watching from outside the corral applauded when my bison collapsed without kicking. Gary photographed me with my "trophy" before a truck drove into the corral, winched up the animal, and drove it to a shed where Game and Fish employees gutted, skinned, and quartered it. I was allowed to keep only the head and hide and one-quarter of the meat. The remainder was sold to raise funds earmarked for maintaining the herd.

I was not proud of what I'd done that morning, and I'm still not. The book, film, and song did what hunters should have done years before Gary and I drove to House Rock Valley—put pressure on the Arizona Game and Fish Department and Commission to make our buffalo hunting a true hunt. Hunters who draw tags now go out by themselves and search for bison that are roaming vast unfenced areas. They may draw only one bison tag in their lifetimes. If their hunts are unsuccessful (as some are), they cannot apply again.

* * *

Gary and I left House Rock Valley the afternoon I shot my bison and drove to Jacob Lake, then on to a place called Turkey Springs. Neither of us had been on the fabled Kaibab Plateau before that day, but we'd found the springs on a topographical map and figured that any place with a name like that had to be a good spot for hunting turkeys. We were about six hundred yards from the springs when we parked our car and loaded our shotguns. We'd walked only a few yards when we saw the heads of a hen turkey and her nearly grown poults moving rapidly through the grass in front of us. Gary and I shot at about the same time, and then ran to where our birds were flopping.

As I would learn over the next half-century, turkey hunting is seldom that easy.

* * *

Arizona is one of the few western states that did not have bison when the first Europeans reached this corner of the continent. Ours were brought here by a remarkable man named Buffalo Jones, a flamboyant former buffalo hunter, showman, and expert in wild animal capture. Charles Jesse Jones rode in the Great Land Rush and served as the first game warden at Yellowstone National Park. He roped a lion, rhino, and various antelope in Africa, and muskox in Canada, but he was best known as one of the saviors of the North American bison. Arizona's herds are descended from animals he bought from private owners in Texas and Canada and shipped to a railhead in southern Utah, where he and two cowboys on horseback drove them overland to his ranch in House Rock Valley on the North Rim of Grand Canyon. His attempt to cross bison and domestic cattle to create a hardier meat animal was a failure, however.

Some of his animals wound up at Fort Huachuca, a U.S. Army post on the Mexican border about ninety miles southeast of Tucson. The post was closed when the bison were released there, and when it was reactivated, the army asked the game department to remove the bison. Some were rounded up and shipped to the agency's two bison ranches, but all the others were shot by hunters—all but one bison, that is.

That animal, a big bull, escaped and wandered around the San Rafael Valley and into Sonora, Mexico, for a couple of years until nearly everyone had forgotten about it. When it reappeared, ranchers began complaining about the beast destroying their fences. Alex Jacome and I were among those who went looking for it when the Arizona Game and

Fish Commission declared it to be an unprotected animal, but it wasn't a hunter who found it. The bull walked into the courtyard at the Little Outfit Guest Ranch and fell into the swimming pool and couldn't get out. Game and Fish was called, and the waterlogged animal was rescued and shipped to the commission's Raymond Ranch near Flagstaff, where it rejoined others from the Fort Huachuca herd.

* * *

Many years after my House Rock Valley bison shoot, I was invited to hunt a bison from a private herd on a ranch near Steamboat Springs, Colorado. Even when bison roamed freely across our prairies, hunting them was not among the most sporting of activities, but my host intended to make the hunts he would be offering more sporting than most. When he asked that I bring a muzzleloading rifle, I planned to use a flintlock I'd built. My friend Lynton McKenzie, who, in addition to being a world-renowned firearms engraver, was one of the most knowledgeable black-powder shooters I knew, thought I needed something better suited for animals as large as bison. Lynton had restored an original .45-caliber Alex Henry sporting rifle made in the early 1800s, and he wanted me to use it.

"It is what an English gentleman would have brought to America to shoot bison with," he said.

I'd shot javelina in Arizona and more than a few deer in Texas with .45-caliber muzzleloaders, and I was concerned that I might need a larger caliber for something as large as an adult bison until Lynton said I'd be shooting .45-caliber bullets weighing 500 grains at somewhere under eighteen hundred feet per second. That's ballistically similar to the .45-70 rifles the old buffalo hunters used.

The hunt was not without some pressure. My host had invited a local club to join us, and its members were told that any bison I shot at and missed or wounded would be fair game. I'd been asked to dress in 1800s-style apparel, but the only thing I had close to that was a wool jacket with bone buttons. My host provided a fur hat and leather chaps. The club members wore everything from breechcloths to Scottish trappers' garb.

To make the hunt as close to the way buffalo hunting used to be, we began by riding horseback around a mountain and into the valley, where a herd was staying at the edge of a grove of quaking aspens. After tying up the horses, the club members spread out and began to approach the herd, while I loaded the rifle and found a place where I expected the animals to pass if they were disturbed. A few minutes later, bison began drifting toward me. When my host pointed to a certain bull, I held where I expected its heart to be, set the rifle's hair trigger, cocked the hammer, and fired.

I had expected the bull to run wildly, as most heart-shot animals do, but that bull dropped in its tracks, kicked a couple of times, and died with all four legs in the air. The problem was, it had fallen in a frozen creek. By the time we rolled it around and skinned it, we had broken the ice, and everyone in our group was soaked halfway up to his knees.

After quartering the animal and loading it on mules, we rode back to the outfitter's house, where the club had set up a teepee, and gorged ourselves on buffalo backstrap. It was as close to an authentic buffalo hunt as it is possible to have today.

Pronghorn and Bear: Numbers Seven and Eight

Chapter 6

I drew a pronghorn antelope tag the year after taking my bison and turkey. The Arizona Game and Fish Department was reintroducing antelope to southern Arizona, and my permit was for the first hunt on a newly established herd north of Willcox. There were only ten tags, and I was lucky to have drawn one of them. According to the map the agency sent me, the center of the area the antelope were using in that unit was a place called the Eureka Ranch. Its owners were expecting us, the letter said, and would not restrict access.

I'd seen a few antelope while hunting mule deer near Prescott, but I had no idea how to go about hunting one, except for what I had read in books and magazines. I arrived at the ranch believing I would have to shoot at distances of four hundred yards or more. I had asked Wilbur Minderman—the husband of my mother's older sister, and a wonderful man who had grown up chasing cattle on horseback—to accompany me.

I was driving my ten-year-old Hudson, and it didn't have four-wheel drive, of course. We couldn't take it far in that rocky terrain, but we did make it to a place where we could erect my little tent the afternoon before opening morning. We chose the site because it was next to a mesquite tree, the only tree in sight, and because we could see at least three or four miles in any direction from that place. That tree was probably no more than six feet tall. We could see small groups of antelope from our little camp, so I went to sleep believing I'd have my buck hanging in that tree soon after the season opened the next morning. It was not to be.

We had no trouble finding pronghorns. Getting close enough to shoot one was a different matter. There was absolutely no cover, and I was in the wrong place every time other hunters chased herds toward us. I was disappointed when Wilbur and I walked back to our camp for lunch. I had taken a couple of Hail Mary shots at antelope too far off and wasn't lucky. (Today I know better than to shoot wildly at game. My only defense of what I did in those days was that I suffered the enthusiasm of youth.)

At noon Wilbur and I were in camp, sitting on rocks and eating something, when an antelope buck suddenly appeared out of nowhere and ran between us and the tent! I jumped up, grabbed my rifle, and got off a poorly aimed shot before it was out of range. The rest of the afternoon was just as frustrating as that morning, and we went to bed early. Just before dawn, Wilbur woke me up and asked me to drive him to Tucson. He had had one of the first heart bypass surgeries in Arizona a few years earlier, and he wasn't feeling well. We broke camp in the dark and were heading for home thirty minutes later.

It took three hours to get Wilbur to Tucson, another couple of hours to talk with my wife and Wilbur's wife and learn that his doctor believed Wilbur's discomfort was not serious, and another three hours to get back to my campsite—alone. The hunt was only three days long, which meant I had only a day and a half left, but it was September, and the sun in southern Arizona didn't set until after 8 p.m. I parked the Hudson, walked a mile or so and climbed a hill, and found five or six antelope looking up at me on the other side. I should have taken my time, sat down, rested my elbows on my knees, and killed the only buck in the group, but I was young and tried to shoot offhand, and I missed. The herd didn't stick around. I emptied my rifle without hitting that buck.

I was sitting by my fire at sundown when two hunters drove up in a military-surplus Jeep. They wanted to know what I'd seen that day, and when they realized I was alone on that vast flat without a four-wheel-drive vehicle, they invited me to ride with them to a new area the next day. I quickly accepted.

It still was dark, but I was ready to go when they returned. We drove to areas I couldn't have reached on foot, and then crossed a wide, deep canyon called Paddy's River. Once atop a plateau, we parked the Jeep and went off in different directions on foot. We still were in sight of each other when an antelope buck jumped up from where it was bedded in a shallow arroyo. It was less than a hundred yards away, staring at me as if it had never seen such a creature. Again, I should have sat down. Instead, I shot offhand and missed. Incredibly, that buck stood frozen. I shot again and missed again. When the buck finally bolted, I swung my rifle like a shotgun and sent the animal rolling. I'd fired most of a box of ammunition to get my first pronghorn antelope.

I shot many antelope in Wyoming and Arizona after that, but my best buck was one I took in Arizona west of Flagstaff, near the little town of Seligman. My cousin, Bob Dixon, lived in Flagstaff and had a pilot's license. As soon as we learned we had been drawn, Eric Sparks and I rented a single-engine airplane so Bob could scout from the air for us. By the time we arrived at a Seligman hotel at noon before opening day, Bob had found three or four good bucks he wanted to show us. One was with a small herd of does very near the historic Highway 666; the other buck was hanging out by itself in a recently subdivided but still unoccupied section of land two or three miles away on the opposite side of the road.

Eric liked the horns on the second buck when we drove out to look at the two antelope that afternoon. Its horns were tall, at least eighteen inches long, and they stayed thick all their length, but its prongs were short. We immediately named it the "two-by-four" buck because it seemed to be wearing two pieces of dark lumber on its head. The horns on the buck I chose, as we later learned, were 17½ inches long and had normal prongs.

A half-hour before first light, Bob and I were where we had seen my buck at sundown. Eric and one of Bob's friends were waiting for light where we'd left Eric's buck. Bob and I spotted the little herd during the first light of dawn and were trying to move closer when one of the does spotted us and took the herd away. Disappointed, Bob and I turned around and started walking toward my truck. The sun still wasn't up and the light was poor. We were about halfway to the vehicle when six or seven antelope suddenly appeared about eighty yards away across a shallow canyon. It had to be the same group we'd tried to stalk.

I searched the herd with my rifle's scope, found the buck, and asked Bob if it was "my" buck. I fired the instant he said yes. My 7mm bullet broke both shoulders, and the antelope dropped instantly. Bob was surprised that I had shot so quickly offhand. I no longer was a young man with little experience in shooting game. By then, I'd hunted on five continents and had killed more than a hundred game animals. I'd also spent two summers competing in a silhouette league in Mexico, shooting forty to fifty rounds of centerfire rifle ammunition offhand each week. It was not as tough a shot as he thought it was.

It was a beautiful buck, and Bob photographed me with it as the sun was just starting to peek over the horizon. It made a beautiful photo.

We spent the next couple of days trying to get Eric close to his two-by-four buck. When the short antelope season ended, we had followed it at least ten miles from where we had first seen it.

✳ ✳ ✳

After my first antelope came a black bear. Until then, I had not really had to push myself to the limits of my physical ability on any of my hunts. Although I had climbed rocky hills and carried white-tailed bucks off steep slopes, I was able to do this at my own pace. This was something I couldn't do when I hunted my bear.

I spent four years hunting without a guide or dogs before deciding I could hunt the rest of my life without bumping into a bear or having one come to my varmint call. I'd hunted in some of Arizona's best bear country: Black River Canyon (once), Mount Graham (three times), and the Chiricahua Mountains (twice). When I realized I needed professional help, I booked a bear hunt with an interesting young man named Jim Bedlion. His day job was as a fire-control officer for the U.S. Forest Service, but he spent every spare minute running hounds on the San Francisco Peaks, Arizona's tallest mountains, above his home in Flagstaff. A friend of mine had taken a bear with him a week earlier but neglected to tell me what to expect. He should have said this was an endurance test, not a hunt.

It still was legal to use bait to hunt bears in Arizona, but Jim didn't bait in the ordinary sense of the word. He had "bait stations" at a dozen sites along a road that ran around the peaks. At each site he dug a two- or three-foot-deep hole, which he filled with suet and scraps of meat, then rolled rocks or logs over the hole to keep coyotes and foxes from reaching the bait. Before leaving, he'd sweep the ground around the hole so he could check for bear tracks and try to figure how big the animal that had made them might be. An hour before daylight, he'd drive the road and check each site with a flashlight.

We found a big bear's tracks at the base of Doyle Peak the first morning. I was amazed at how that bear had thrown the heavy log Jim had rolled over the hole the previous evening. My hunt began when Jim went back to the truck and released four or five hounds, just as it was getting light enough to see. The hounds immediately found the scent, and the chase was on. We were on foot around eighty-five hundred feet elevation. The peaks above us were at least two thousand feet higher, and that's exactly where the chase took us. I was slim and young (just a few days past my thirty-seventh birthday), but I had spent almost all my time sitting at desks. Jim's job had kept him outdoors. I was out of breath and close to exhaustion when I reached the summit where Jim and Don Johnson, a Flagstaff policeman who was Bedlion's assistant, were waiting for me.

Far below us, in what Jim and Don called the Inner Basin, we could hear the dogs barking treed. I checked to see that my .357-Magnum pistol was loaded and joined my companions in slipping and sliding down the hill toward the barking dogs. Before we got there, however, we suddenly heard two shots fired quickly.

"Someone shot your bear," Jim said, when the dogs returned to us a few minutes later.

Here's what apparently happened:

The dogs treed the bear close enough to a road for someone to drive up, see the bear, and shoot it. He (or they) had enough time to load the bear into a vehicle and drive away before we could get to it.

Only small bears visited Jim's baits that night, so we didn't release the dogs the next morning. I returned to Tucson that afternoon. I was not a happy camper, and I spent the next week calling taxidermists in Flagstaff and Phoenix to see who had brought bears to them when they opened on Monday. No large bears—such as the one that had made the tracks we followed on Saturday—were reported, though.

A toothache suddenly erupted about the same hour I arrived at Jim's home the next Friday afternoon. It was so painful that I called Jean to ask her to call our dentist and have him call a Flagstaff drugstore and prescribe a painkiller.

"Just go to an emergency room at the hospital up there," Jean said.

I stubbornly insisted that she call the dentist. When she did, he told her to tell me to go to a hospital emergency room, a fact she's never forgotten. The ER doctor gave me a supply of pills and sent me away. I returned to Jim's house in time to help him and Don load the dogs. We were chasing a bear at first light forty-five minutes later. The pills must have helped because my toothache was gone.

Knowing the bear would run uphill, I didn't try to follow the hounds. Instead, I just kept plodding up the mountain. I was almost at the summit when I heard the dogs chasing the bear nearby. In a minute or two they were barking treed just two hundred yards below me. When I got there, I found a dark shape the size of a washing machine perched on a pine limb only about six or seven feet from the ground. A couple of dogs were jumping up at the bear and snapping at it; the others were all around the tree, trying to climb it. I'd hunted with dogs before and knew that if I didn't do something, that bear would catch its breath, jump off that limb, and run away. I didn't want to chase it one inch farther, so, without thinking, I ran at the bear, yelling and waving my arms. It was so steep that my momentum took me all the way to the tree. *That was a stupid thing to do,* I told myself when I stopped.

Fortunately, Mr. Bruin had decided to climb the tree instead of leave it; otherwise, that bear and I might have collided.

After I recovered, I climbed the hill until the bear in the tree and I were about the same level, sat down, and waited for my guides. The bear had long, reddish-brown hair, and the more I looked at the small hump on its shoulder, the more it reminded me of a grizzly bear. I knew it was only a brown-colored black bear, though. The last grizzly bear in Arizona was killed in the early part of the twentieth century, not far from my cabin in Greer.

After Don showed up, followed by Jim, the three of us watched the bear a few more minutes. They then caught and tied up their dogs because they didn't want a wounded animal to maul them. When my guides were ready, I sat down, took careful aim with my pistol, and shot the bear square in the chest. Nothing happened, so I shot it again. And again. The only response I got from the bear was a loud roar each time I shot it. After I'd emptied my pistol, I asked Jim for his .44-Magnum revolver and literally knocked that bear out of the tree with its heavy bullet. That bear was dead before it hit the ground. Jim and Don released their dogs and allowed them to chew on the animal for their reward. It was the first time I'd seen something like that. I was amazed they didn't rip the hide off my bear.

It was a big bear, and Arizona law required that we pack out every scrap of its edible meat. Even after gutting the bear, it was all the three of us could do (even on the slippery pine needles that covered the ground) to roll, push, and drag the carcass downhill to where we could reach it with the truck. In Flagstaff we stopped traffic when we weighed it on scales outside a sporting-goods and liquor store on the town's main street.

This happened in 1973, and I have forgotten how much the bear weighed, but it was more than three hundred pounds, which is larger than the average bear in our state. I do remember inspecting the carcass when we skinned it. I wanted to see why I couldn't kill it with my .357-Magnum revolver. All five shots had hit it, but only one bullet reached a lung. The other four bullets stopped in the bear's thick fat and didn't reach its vitals. The .44-Magnum round broke both shoulders before exiting.

I don't know why our laws require hunters to salvage and utilize bear meat. The only way we could eat that animal was to cook the meat thoroughly, then place it on a rack and cook it some more. Even after the fat was rendered, that bear's meat literally dripped grease.

* * *

As a newspaper outdoor editor producing two columns and a features page with a variety of articles and photos every week, there were times when I had to scramble to find material. So I was ready when Tom Waddell called. He was a wildlife manager for the Arizona Game and Fish Department and was conducting a research project on black bears.

"If you can get up here before daylight Saturday, I should have a bear or two for you to photograph," he said.

"Up here" was Riggs Lake atop Mount Graham, one of southern Arizona's sky islands. To reach Riggs Lake I'd have to drive about a hundred miles east from Tucson to the community of Safford, then take a narrow, winding road to the top of the mountain. It took me three hours to get there, but it still was dark when I reached the camp trailer Tom had parked near the lake. A propane lantern inside the trailer was lit, indicating he already was up. Tom was not alone, as I had expected him to be. A personable young man wearing jeans, a roper's buckle on his wide belt, and a straw cowboy hat was sitting at the table in the trailer, tying trout-fishing flies. I've forgotten his name, but Tom claimed the guy had caught enough trout to feed both of them during the week they'd been on the mountain.

"What I've been doing," Tom explained, "is catching bears, weighing them, pulling a tooth to age them, and fitting them with radio collars. It should help give us an idea how many bears we have, and where they go."

It sounded good to me. After more coffee than I needed, Tom announced that he would drive his companion and me to the head of a canyon and let us out. He then would drive to where the road crossed the canyon a couple of miles below and walk up the canyon to meet us coming down.

"I've got baits and snares in four cubbies in that canyon, and we should have a bear in one of them," he said.

The sun was not yet up when Tom dropped us off and drove away. I was carrying a camera bag full of gear. The cowboy had a pump-action 12-gauge shotgun over his shoulder. It was loaded with rifled slugs, just in case a bear didn't want to be messed with, he said.

We had been walking downhill for about ten minutes when I asked if he worked for the Arizona Game and Fish Department.

"Nope," he said.

"The forest service?"

"No."

There was no state-owned land or U.S. Bureau of Land Management land on the mountain, and I was curious about his employer.

"The U.S. Fish and Wildlife Service?"

"Nope. I'm a convict."

I knew that there was a minimum-security prison nearby and that the Game and Fish Department had an arrangement where it used model prisoners to do various jobs at a ranch the agency owned near Safford.

"Really? What are you in for?"

"Murder."

The shotgun on his shoulder suddenly grew to bazooka size.

"What happened?"

"I got into a fight with two brothers in a bar in Willcox," he said. "They beat me up pretty bad before I shot one of them."

When I said two against one sounded like self-defense, he said because he'd left the bar and returned with a handgun, a jury found him guilty of premeditated murder.

"I'm getting out early," he said. "But first I have to go to a halfway house."

What could I say? We didn't talk much after that. About a mile down the canyon we found Tom sitting on a log, waiting for us.

"Take a look over there," he said, when we got nearer.

I guess I must have forgotten why I was there because a bear was the last thing on my mind when I walked around a pine tree and an angry bruin lunged at me. A steel cable on one of its rear feet stopped it suddenly at what seemed merely inches from where I stood. I hadn't seen the bear because it was in a "cubby," a baited cave Tom had made of logs and brush to force the bear to step into the snare's noose.

My companions thought my walking up to the bear was the funniest thing that had ever happened on Mount Graham or in all of Arizona, for that matter. When I recovered from the shock, Tom handed me an air pistol, and I shot the animal with a dart filled with a tranquilizing drug. I photographed Tom and the convicted murderer setting up a tripod and weighing the drugged bear, drawing a blood sample, pulling a tooth, and fitting the animal with an ear tag and a radio collar. The little bear weighed only about a hundred pounds, and large patches of its hair were missing. It had a nasty case of mange, Tom said.

Tom didn't want to leave the sleeping animal exposed to other bears and predators, so we found a place to sit and waited a safe distance away until it woke up and walked off. It was the only bear Tom caught that day, but it helped me fill another outdoors page with text and photos.

Two years later, Tom called and said he had caught the same bear, and it not only had gained more than a hundred pounds, but it also no longer had mange.

✳ ✳ ✳

I had more experiences with black bears in Arizona after that, and two involved a mule I once owned. Jenny was a huge animal that looked as if she should have been pulling a plow in Missouri instead of wearing a saddle. I was told a ranch owner had used Jenny when she was younger to carry steel fence posts to places that couldn't be reached by Jeeps. Later, she carried tourists up and down the Grand Canyon's Bright Angel Trail. She was old, but a better animal for hunting in our rocky and steep terrain would be tough to find. I built a trailer to transport her, and she would readily walk in and out of it—until the day

Alex Jacome got impatient when she stopped to look inside the trailer before stepping on the ramp. When she stopped, he hit her rump with the knotted end of her lead rope. From that day on, I had to coax her into that trailer.

The thing about mules is, or at least that mule, they will not do anything they think might hurt them. As you've seen in a dozen movies, you can ride a horse over a cliff. You would have to blindfold Jenny and shove her off the cliff with a tank to get her to do that.

I gave Jenny her head when I hunted with her. I'd point her in the direction I wanted to go, and she would find the best way to get us there. I remember getting hung up in a patch of manzanita on a steep and rocky slope. A horse would have panicked in such a spot, but that mule simply backed up and found a way around the brush. Jenny paid no attention when I tied the rear legs of javelina together and hung them from my saddle horn. I'd ride back to camp with the "pig" flopping against her belly and shoulder. I packed out a whitetail by cutting slits in its belly skin to hang it from the saddle horn and riding out with it on my lap. Nothing seemed to bother that mule until I asked her to pack out a bear.

I was hunting a whitetail near Stockton Pass between Fort Grant and Safford when I rode up on two young men who had killed a bear and wanted me to help them get it to a road. Because Jenny had carried my deer and javelina, I expected to have no problems. Was I ever wrong!

She started behaving strange when I rode up to their dead bear, so I got off and led her around it, and then had her step over it. Eventually, she seemed to calm down. I'm not a cowboy, and I had never packed out a bear, but it seemed to me that the best way to do it would be to drape the bear over the saddle and tie its legs to the cinch rings on each side. Jenny kept shying away every time the two hunters tried to lift the bear up on the saddle, so I took off my jacket and used it to blindfold her. That worked for a while. She stood still while the bear was loaded and its front legs were tied to a ring. The two men had started to tie up the bear's rear legs on the opposite side of the saddle when the mule shook her head violently and knocked me down. One look at the bear on her back was all it took. She spun around, bucked, and took off running with the bear hanging off one side of the saddle. A hundred yards or so later, the bear fell off when its paws slipped out of the ropes.

I chased that mule for at least a mile before I found her with a stirrup caught in a tree stump. Her eyes were as large as baseballs, her teeth were bared, and her ears were folded back against her head as I approached. Somewhere along the way she had broken off a rein. (I can't explain why I didn't find it when I followed her.) I was holding the remaining rein when I unhooked the stirrup and found I couldn't control her with just one rein. There was nothing to do except jump on and ride her back to camp. It was a terrifying ride I will never forget. She was an old mule, but she didn't stop running until she reached her trailer.

She was her gentle self again the next morning, so I jerry-rigged a rein from a piece of rope and rode out again. Every time I pointed her toward the canyon where she'd seen the bear, she danced sideways. I don't think I could have dragged her there with an eighteen-wheeler.

My other experience with Jenny and a bear took place a year or so later. I was hunting on Chitty Creek, a roadless area under the Mogollon Rim, not far from the New Mexico border, when I rode up over the dam of a large, nearly empty water hole and spooked a big bear on the opposite shore. I jumped off, yanked my rifle out of its scabbard, and used the saddle as a rest to shoot from. Jenny was never bothered by gunfire. Honest to gosh, that mule held her breath and didn't move while I aimed at and shot that bear. The bear roared when the bullet struck it, and then it ran into the brush.

I followed the blood trail for at least a mile before getting off Jenny and looking for that bear on foot. I eventually lost its trail. I've wounded and lost very few animals, and I felt bad each time, but I don't know how I would have packed out that bear if I'd found it. Jenny certainly would not have carried it, even if I could have loaded it on her back by myself.

71

TWO MONTHS ON HORSEBACK FOR A LION

CHAPTER 7

The black bear I shot with a handgun on one of the peaks above Flagstaff was the eighth Arizona species I'd taken, leaving only a mountain lion and a desert bighorn sheep to complete my quest to take all of my state's big-game animals. I applied every year with several thousand other hunters for one of the hundred or so desert sheep tags our state issued, and while I waited optimistically, I got serious about hunting a mountain lion. Using a varmint call while hunting deer under the Mogollon Rim and in the Santa Rita Mountains, I did manage to call in a lion on two occasions, but I didn't kill either of them. I was as surprised as they must have been when they suddenly appeared, and they turned and were running as soon as we made eye contact. I didn't have time to shoot at the first cat, and I missed two shots at the second as it ran down a canyon.

I also spent a few days in known lion country, blowing a varmint call in the hopes that a lion would come to it, but all I brought in were bobcats, foxes, and coatimundis.[1] I must have had a natural skill for calling coatis because I called in many small packs of these raccoonlike creatures. There are a lot more of them in southern Arizona's oak-grassland habitat than most people realize. It was fun to watch them run around with their tails erect. They have always reminded me of monkeys.

[1] There reportedly are four varieties of coatis found from the southwestern United States to Central and South America, and those in Arizona are the largest. The coatis my granddaughter Natalie Greene and I saw pestering tourists for food in a parking lot at Iguaçu Falls, Brazil, were much smaller than ours.

Hunting only on weekends, I then spent a total of fifty-seven days over three years—nearly two months of my life—on horseback, following the hounds of three different houndsmen, before I finally took my lion. I began by hooking up with a man named Gene Clayburn. He was not a professional guide, but he liked to run his hounds and wanted company. He and I shared expenses and followed his dogs all over the Chiricahua, Sierra Ancha, Baboquivari, Catalina, and Santa Rita Mountains and chased a lot of lesser game. We even chased a few lions, but I never had an opportunity to take one with him.

The funny thing about Gene was that he spent more time on foot leading his horse than he did in the saddle in some of Arizona's roughest and steepest mountains. At first I would get off my mount and try to follow him on foot, but when I couldn't keep up, I stayed on my horse, except in the worst places.

Gene liked to hunt a place he called Lion's Kitchen on the ridge between Brown and Thomas Canyons in the Baboquivari Mountains, twenty miles north of the Mexican border southwest of Tucson. He called it that because we sometimes found Coues deer that had been killed, partially eaten, and covered with dirt and brush by lions there. It's still one of the better places in southern Arizona to find a mountain lion.

Gene had a buckskin gelding called Sam that I became attached to the first time I rode it in the mountains. It was an old, gentle, surefooted animal, and it didn't panic in brush or rocks as some horses do. I felt safe on that horse, so I bought it from Gene. I enjoyed riding Sam and hunting with Gene, even though we never caught a lion. We spent some interesting days together, dragging our mounts through brush and across shale slopes, and riding up hill and down dale because neither of us knew where to find the horse trails that cattlemen have made in every mountain range in our part of the country.

We also spent a miserable night trapped on a cold and windblown ridge. It was the last day of the year, and a rancher had called Gene to say a lion had killed one of his calves the previous day and probably had returned to the kill site that night, so the trail should still be hot. It was our opportunity to break my lion jinx, so we loaded our horses and Gene's dogs and went hunting. Jean and I were invited to a New Year's Eve party that evening, and I told her I'd join her at the party if I got home late.

What was intended to be a half-day hunt was a disaster. The lion's scent took Gene and me, along with a friend named Richard Kane, up Brown Canyon, through Lion's Kitchen, and then along the ridge above Thomas Canyon all the way to the base of Baboquivari Peak. We had reached the point where we had decided to turn around and follow our trail back if the dogs didn't bump the lion in the next half-hour. We had ridden the same trails on previous hunts, and it had never taken us more than four or five hours to make the loop.

Unfortunately, it didn't happen that way this time. Richard's horse was a handsome and expensive black quarterhorse that had little experience with rocks and rough mountains. It panicked as the three of us were leading our animals across an especially nasty shale-covered slope. It jerked the reins out of Richard's hand and tried to bolt uphill, but it was too steep, and when the horse began sliding on the shale, it reared up and rolled backward down the slope. In the excitement Sam broke away from us, and so did Gene's horse, but they made it to the top of the ridge. We could only watch in horror as Richard's horse rolled end over end downhill for two hundred yards, falling off a couple of ledges along the way. We could hear a hollow *thunk* every time the horse's head bounced off a rock.

The three of us slid down to it, picking up Richard's camera, food, rifle, and an assortment of items from his saddlebags that were scattered across the hillside. The horse was unconscious and wrapped around a tree above another ledge when we reached it. The saddletree was broken, and Richard could lift up a bloody triangular flap of skin about the size of a folded napkin on the horse's rump. When we got to the animal, it woke up, lifted its head, and then slammed it on the ground, knocking itself out again. I was sure we would have to shoot

74

that horse where it had landed. There was no way we could get it up where it was. Gene took one look at the situation and said, "One more fall won't hurt it."

Gene had broken his left arm a few weeks earlier, and it still was in a cast, so he had Richard tie his horse's neck to the tree with a long rope. Then the three of us sat down and pulled on the horse's rear legs while using our feet to shove the front part of that horse off the ledge. After it hit the end of the rope and fought to stand up, we released the rope, and the horse found its footing and stood there below us, shaking. Richard then packed all his gear on the horse and led it off the mountain, while Gene and I went looking for our mounts.

I found Sam on top of the ridge, not far above where Richard's horse had panicked. Gene's horse was feeding a hundred yards away. Before I climbed on Sam, I noticed a piece of wood jammed between the skin and the hoof of its left front leg. I pulled it out, thinking I'd gotten all of it. I hadn't, though, and a piece of that stick eventually worked into a joint and caused Sam to go permanently lame.

Sundown was just minutes away, and it would take at least an hour to get back to our truck. Forget what you've heard about horses being able to see well in the dark. Ours couldn't. We rode them until they refused to take another step, leaving us in a bad spot. The knifelike ridge we were on dropped almost straight down for forty or fifty feet to the south of us. To the north was a steep slope covered with shale and a series of ten-foot-tall ledges. It was so dark and it was such a dangerous place that we couldn't move very far to look for firewood, even if we'd had a flashlight, which we didn't. There wasn't a lot of wood on that rocky ridge, anyway.

Gene and I spent the night trying to stay warm. The wind had blown the snow off the ridge, but it was so cold our saddle blankets soon were frozen stiff. We had taken off the saddles and turned them on their sides, and tried taking turns using them as a windbreak. We even tried hugging each other to share our body heat. To make matters worse, Gene's dogs barked treed most of the night. They'd caught a lion below us, and there was no way we could get to them.

Long before daylight, I thought I saw someone with a lantern walking up our ridge. The more we watched the light, the more certain we were that whatever we were watching was moving toward us. Just before dawn, we realized we had been watching a star on the horizon from our perch on that high ridge. Gene's dogs joined us after we'd saddled up and started off the mountain at first light. The lion they'd treed probably had jumped from the tree and escaped, but it also was possible that they simply had grown tired of waiting for us to show up and had left it.

I learned much about the lives of mountain lions from Gene's dogs. I would watch as they took a scent trail to the edge of a cliff, and I could visualize the cat standing there, surveying its kingdom. I learned how to tell when there is a lion in an area by the tracks and scratches it has left behind. In southern Arizona, at least, lions travel the spines of our mountain ranges, marking their territory by defecating and urinating in certain saddles and then covering what they've done with dirt, as a house cat uses a cat box. They also sometimes scratch trees, just as a house cat scratches furniture, and leave some of their hair in the bark. Like a "honey hole" for largemouth bass, such places are used by lions for generations.

I also learned that, despite what some who have not done it may say, hunting these cats with hounds and horses is sporting and downright physically challenging in my part of the world. Too much can go wrong, even when the dogs have been put on a hot track. Lions can get into places that humans, horses, and dogs cannot go. And even with experienced hounds, the scent can easily be lost.

Gene and I found deer and porcupines killed by lions. We even found a yearling lion that had been partially eaten by a larger male. We rode horses in places most people wouldn't believe a four-footed animal with a human on its back could go. We found Indian ruins few have seen and came upon illegal border-crossers in places it was hard to believe anyone could have reached on foot. We also encountered a sow black bear and its cubs on the western slope of the Santa Catalina Mountains at a time when the Game and Fish Department was convinced none existed on that mountain. We did everything except catch a lion.

The only lion I saw while hunting with Gene was running in front of the dogs in a canyon at least five hundred yards below us. It ran to the base of a fifteen-foot bluff and jumped up on it as easily as our house cat jumps on a table. The dogs piled up at the bottom of the cliff, and although we led them around the cliff and put them back on the track, they lost the cat. The sun had "burned off" the scent, Gene said.

I had written a few columns in the *Tucson Citizen* about my unsuccessful lion hunts, and in each one I campaigned for making lions full-fledged game animals and abolishing the bounty the Arizona Livestock Sanitary Board was paying for lion scalps. I didn't realize how controversial the issue was until Gene warned me not to tell the rancher my name when we hunted Horseshoe Canyon in the Chiricahua Mountains in the southeastern corner of Arizona.

"These guys want to see every lion killed," he said. "They don't want the bounty ended. They want it doubled. You're not very popular with them."

When Gene moved to Oklahoma, I spent a weekend with another houndsman. We never saw the lion his dogs caught. The scent trail we were following abruptly ended atop a cliff, where the dogs were running around with their noses up, barking treed. The lion obviously had found a hiding place somewhere in the jumble of rocks on the side of the cliff below us and wouldn't budge. We reluctantly had to pull the dogs off and ride away.

A week or so later, Ollie Barney, a southern Arizona rancher, building contractor, and our state's most successful lion hunter and hunting guide at the time, said he would get me a lion if I were willing to ride with him when he explored new country. He would charge me half of his regular fee when I shot my lion.

On my first weekend with him, we rode around and through a terribly rough canyon called California Gulch, on the Mexican border west of Nogales. We found lion tracks right away, but they were old, and Ollie wouldn't let his dogs run them. I was impressed. With Gene, no tracks were too old, and we followed more than one cold trail. After two days of riding in and out of that rugged canyon, my hunt was over, and I drove back to Tucson. An hour after I left, a customer who was paying Ollie's full fee arrived in his camp. The next morning he shot one of the largest mountain lions ever taken in southern Arizona.

Next, Ollie and I hunted the Santa Rita Mountains near an abandoned mining town called Helvetia, hoping to catch a lion that had killed a calf earlier in the week. By then, I had traded Sam for my mule, Jenny. She was a great mount for hunting deer and javelinas at a slow pace, but she was old, and she tired quickly when we tried to keep up with Ollie's hounds in steep terrain. We had followed them off the kill nearly to the top of the mountain when she started breathing deeply and began stumbling. Ollie was in much better shape than I was, so he continued on foot after we tied Jenny to a tree, and I climbed on his horse. The scent of that lion took us into some incredibly rugged places, but we never caught the cat. Ollie's dogs were willing to continue, but we were exhausted. He called them off the track, and we picked up Jenny and returned to Tucson. Another client of Ollie's eventually killed the lion.

A couple of weeks later, Ollie and I were in the Baboquivari Mountains in the same area I'd spent so much time with Gene Clayburn. Unlike Gene, Ollie didn't try to go everywhere his dogs went. The mountain had a network of horse trails Gene and I didn't know about. We stayed on those trails while the dogs tried to unravel the tracks a lion had left below us a couple of days earlier. We never found a hot track, though.

The next weekend we released Ollie's dogs in Peppersauce Canyon on the northeastern slope of the Catalina Mountains, just fifteen air miles or so from the million-dollar homes in the foothills above Tucson on the other side of the range. Although the dogs hadn't found a lion track yet, they seemed more enthusiastic than they'd been the two previous weekends. We rode our horses up a primitive mining trail to the top of Oracle Ridge and then headed south toward Rice Peak. We hadn't gone far when Ollie halted his horse and pointed to a set of tracks in the dust.

"There's a female lion here. You want it?"

What a question. Of course I wanted it.

Ollie's dogs had run over the lion's track on the sunlit trail without catching its scent. When Ollie called them back and sent them into the shady side of Canyon del Oro, they bayed the lion in just a few minutes. Ollie knew what he was talking about. My lion was a mature female, and it was on the ground fighting the dogs when we approached it.

Shooting it with the Winchester carbine Ollie had fitted with a .44-Magnum barrel was anticlimactic after all those days I'd followed hound packs through, over, and around the most rugged canyons of six mountain ranges.

A few months after I shot that lion, Arizona's governor signed a bill making the mountain lion a big-game animal under the jurisdiction of the Game and Fish Department and ending the bounties the Arizona Livestock Sanitary Board had been paying.[2] I doubt that my columns had made much difference. Times and public attitudes were changing all across the country, including Arizona. We no longer were a rural state. By far, the majority of our citizens lived in the urban areas of Phoenix or Tucson, and they had learned all they knew about wildlife from watching public television. The state already had moved to protect the occasional jaguar that wandered north out of Mexico. On the federal level, the U.S. Marine Mammal Protection Act was just two years away, and the Endangered Species Act would follow a year later. Groups such as Alice Harrington's Friends of Wildlife and Cleveland Amory's Fund for Animals already were campaigning to abolish hunting.

---

[2]Arizona's mountain lion population increased significantly over the next four decades, and lion are being seen again in such places as the Kofa National Wildlife Refuge north of Yuma, where they were not known to exist from around 1940 to 2000. There now are seasons and bag limits on mountain lions, and tags are required to hunt them anywhere in Arizona.

After taking my lion, I lacked only a desert bighorn sheep to have collected every big-game species in my state. I had no way of knowing it would be many more years before I finally drew a sheep tag in Arizona's annual hunting lottery.

Author at age seventeen in 1954: skinny as a straw and six feet four.

Dude ranch owner Jack Jackson, then Arizona Wildlife Foundation president, bought the first subscription to author's newspaper, the Arizona Outdoor News. *Tucson, 1965.*

Author's mother was eighty-nine when they visited Italy with his daughter and granddaughter in 2002.

From left: Author (age five), his brother Jerry (age three), and their father a week before the bombing of Pearl Harbor. Yuma, Arizona, 1941.

In the late 1950s, an article in Outdoor Life *magazine about calling predators led the author to order a call from a mail-order supplier. This big coyote came to his .303 Savage the first morning he tried it. Tucson, Arizona.*

A photographer was paid to photograph author and his first mule deer, but lens glare ruined the photo. Aguila, Arizona, 1948.

Horses made southern Arizona's remote mule-deer country more accessible to author and his friends. North of Willcox, Arizona, circa 1990.

Mary Knagge, one of Tucson's top mule-deer hunters in the 1970s, took this mule-deer buck on the Arizona Strip.

The sharp-pointed plants around author's legs are called "shin daggers." He shot this javelina with a recurve bow about a mile from the Mexican border. Near Patagonia, Arizona, 1985.

Author and wife, Jean, inspect one of his javelinas. Tucson, Arizona, circa 1980.

This young desert mule-deer buck was taken with a .45-caliber muzzleloader built by the author. Near Sierra Vista, Arizona, circa 1992.

The author staged this photo to illustrate a Tucson Citizen *newspaper article in the 1980s depicting*

something that happens every year in Coues deer country.

Getting a javelina off a mountain can be work, although the animals usually weigh no more than fifty pounds. Near the Mexico–Arizona border, 1985.

The Coues white-tailed buck George Parker shot in 1947 took first place in the Boone and Crockett Club's annual awards competition.

Ed Stockwell, a beekeeper in Arivaca, Arizona, was a teenager when he shot the world-record Coues white-tailed deer while hunting near the Mexican border.

A game department check station in the 1970s. This area near Patagonia, Arizona, was gunwriter Jack O'Connor's favorite spot to hunt Coues deer.

Shooters received only one-quarter of the meat from their bisons in the 1960s and were told where to shoot their animals. House Rock Valley on Grand Canyon's North Rim.

A careful stalk brought bison within range of a muzzleloader that had been built in the nineteenth century. Near Steamboat Springs, Colorado, early 1980s.

Packhorses brought the bison quarters out. Near Steamboat Springs, Colorado, early 1980s.

Author's grandson, Logan Greene, shot this big Merriam gobbler at age eleven near the family's cabin. Arizona's White Mountains, 1999.

Author's best Arizona pronghorn was taken west of Flagstaff, circa 1992.

A really big bear left these tracks in Arizona's White Mountains, 1980s.

This cinnamon-colored black bear was shot with a handgun atop one of Arizona's highest peaks. Near Flagstaff, Arizona, 1970s.

This adult Arizona black bear was photographed during a deer hunt in an area closed to bear hunting.

There are larger mountain lions, but the author was happy to take this mature female after following hounds across Arizona's roughest terrain for fifty-seven days. Santa Catalina Mountains above Tucson, 1970s.

The author found these Salado Indian cliff dwellings while hunting lion on the White Mountain Apache Reservation in the 1970s.

Another view of the Salado Indian cliff dwellings, found while hunting lions. White Mountain Apache Reservation, Arizona, 1970s.

When the author photographed this herd, feral burro threatened Arizona's desert game. Kofa Mountains, 1954.

This desert bighorn ram with a chipped horn ended a thirty-nine-year quest to take Arizona's ten species of big-game animals. Little Horn Mountains, 1993.

This bull elk was shot as it ran past author at thirty yards. From left: Ben Mattausch, Eric Sparks, and author. Springerville, Arizona, 2002.

Desert bighorn sometimes seek the shade of caves during Arizona's warmest days. Kofa Mountains, early 1960s.

Waiting for opening-day fog to lift in sheep camp. Little Horn Mountains, 1993.

Desert sheep hunting is an optics game, and the more eyes, the better. Little Horn Mountains, 1993.

Much of Arizona's sheep country can be glassed from a vehicle. Little Horn Mountains, 1993.

Doug Campbell, author's friend and winner of the first NRA-sponsored Silhouette Competition matches in the United States, hosted the author on deer hunts at his ranches in Texas. (NRA press release photo)

This Columbia black-tailed deer was the best buck seen in a day-and-a-half hunt. California, 1985.

This buck is not the ten-pointer author wanted, but it will do. Michigan, circa 1992.

The author and Governor Ed Herschler shot these bucks near Lander, Wyoming, 1982.

There was no shortage of Columbia black-tailed deer where author hunted. Northern California, 1985.

No one knew how to determine the age of this bull, but all agreed it was an old animal in its last years. 1987.

A good pronghorn buck taken on author's first trip to Lander, Wyoming, 1981.

Author (third from left) with Craig Boddington (fourth from left) and David Petzel (fifth from left) at the One Shot Antelope Hunt's bullet-blessing ceremony. The author's outdoor writers team won the annual event. Lander, Wyoming, 1982.

From left: Astronaut Wally Schirra, Arizona Game and Fish Department supervisor Tom Spalding, and author. Near Tucson, Arizona, 1989.

A nine-day storm kept outfitter Rick Furniss (left) from getting author home on time. Note duct tape on Super Cub's door. Hart Lake, Yukon, 1988.

Peter Zidek (left) and Sonny brought author's moose to camp in a snowstorm. Hart Lake, Yukon, 1988.

Yukon Outfitting's Hart Lake Camp was comfortable, even after storms left fourteen inches of snow on the ground. Yukon, 1988.

Author's second bull was shot from a boat. Little Marten Lake, Northwest Territories, 1989.

Author packs the cape and antlers of his first bull to the lake. Little Marten Lake, Northwest Territories, 1989.

Author's Cape buffalo took seven shots from a .458 Winchester Magnum before it went down. Zimbabwe, 1983.

Victoria Falls was named Mosi-oa-Tunya, "The Smoke That Thunders," by the Kololo people living in the area in the 1800s. Zimbabwe, 1983.

Professional hunter Rob Martin (left) and outfitter Fanie Pretorius. Westwood Wildlife Safari block, Zimbabwe, 1983.

Rob Martin's crew loaded author's buffalo bull by digging a trench to make the Toyota's bed the same level as the ground. Zimbabwe, 1983.

Author was in the trees in the background when he shot his first sable antelope. Zimbabwe, 1983.

When this herd of elephants blocked the road, the author's professional hunter parked his Toyota and waited for them to leave. Another elephant behind them spotted the vehicle, however, and it charged. As the PH drove through a gap in the herd, the author snapped an out-of-focus photo of the angry animal as it chased them. Zimbabwe, 1983.

Author's southern greater kudu may have lost the ivory tip of one horn by fighting another bull. Zimbabwe, 1983.

Alex Jacome, author's longtime friend and hunting partner, took this springbok ram on Rooipoort Estate near Kimberley. South Africa, 1983.

A bedded southern greater kudu bull sleeps, unaware that hunters have decided to look for another kudu with longer horns. Zimbabwe, 1983.

A huge crocodile was hiding in the reeds where the outfitter wanted to launch his fishing boat on the Zambezi River. Zimbabwe, 1983.

Solitary dagga *boys often are the oldest buffalo bulls in an area, but many have damaged their horns while fighting. Zimbabwe, 1983.*

This springbok was running when the author shot it—a shot that surprised not only himself but also his hosts. Near Kimberley, South Africa, 1983.

Scratches on these rocks were made by the glaciers that covered southern Africa thousands of years ago. The animal designs were chipped into the rock by indigenous people. Near Kimberley, South Africa, 1983.

Author's first gemsbok was taken on the Rooipoort Estate. Near Kimberley, South Africa, 1983.

Something must be wrong when meat-eating animals ignore tourists in open vehicles at night. Sabi Sands, South Africa, 1983.

Morning rush hour brings a traffic jam in Kruger Park. South Africa, 2002.

This Cape buffalo with freak horns adorned the wall of the director's office in Kruger Park. South Africa, 1983.

Zulu women in brightly colored clothing lined the sides of roads across Zululand. South Africa, 1983.

Ostrich have no teeth, but this bird tried to pull off a thumb. South Africa, 1983.

This cheetah had posed for so many photos that it ignored tourists and vehicles. Mala Mala, South Africa, 1983.

Mafunyani, one of Kruger Park's Magnificent Seven, died of natural causes. South Africa, 1983.

Zulu rondavels. South Africa, 2002.

Zulu women were waitresses at a resort when they weren't wearing their "traditional" dress. South Africa, 1983.

The "Big Hole" is where Cecil Rhodes made his fortune in diamonds. Only about a third of the pit can be seen here. Kimberley, South Africa, 2002.

Kimberley's historic DeBeers building still houses the company's offices. South Africa, 2002.

Above: The trophy nyala bull author shot in Zululand after a morning of walking stooped over.
Below: A nyala cow in the thick brush, which is where these elusive Southern African antelope spend many of their daylight hours. Note the difference in the appearance of the sexes. The cows are red and smaller; the bulls are gray-brown and have long hair on the neck, belly, and back. *South Africa, 1986.*

Author took the blesbok above and the steenbok below on the Rooipoort Estate while collecting birds and small animals for SCI's International Wildlife Museum. South Africa, 1986.

Author took black wildebeest (also called white-tailed gnu) on DeBeers property near Kimberley. South Africa, 1986.

Author's first of many warthogs. South Africa, 1983.

From left: Henri van Aswegen, C. J. McElroy, and author. Mumbwa West, Zambia, 1994.

This Lichtenstein hartebeest was the author's first antelope in Zambia, 1994.

The buildings at van Aswegen's comfortable camp were built with local materials. Mumbwa West, Zambia, 1994.

Tracks of a big lion were found the first day of the hunt. Mumbwa West, Zambia, 1994.

The author poses with his puku while C. J. McElroy looks on. Zambia, 1996.

The author and his first Chobe bushbuck. Zambia, 1996.

C. J. McElroy and author with the lion. Mumbwe West, Zambia, 1994.

A pair of impala rams taken from a herd with two quick shots, and the meat was given to a San Bushmen village. Botswana, 1998.

Sandy Cox and his son with author and a red hartebeest. South Africa, 2002.

The horns on the author's Zambia sable were nearly as large as those on a bull he had shot ten years earlier in Zimbabwe. Zambia, 1996.

Author took this Crawshay defassa waterbuck on his second trip to Zambia, 1996.

C. J. McElroy shot this Crawshay defassa waterbuck with author's rifle. Zambia, 1994.

Author's first zebra became bait for his lion. Zambia, 1994.

The author took this Limpopo bushbuck with a running shot. Northwestern South Africa, 1997.

When in China, do as the Chinese do. . . . Beijing, 1990.

Beijing's Tiananmen Square, the Gate of Heavenly Peace. The Forbidden City is at the end of the square.
People's Republic of China, 1990.

Ulaanbator, a city of nearly one million people, had a resident herd of elk. Mongolia, 1990.

The hunting party and trophies taken during the seven-day hunt. Mongolia, 1990.

Lynton McKenzie (left) with antlers from his bull elk, the largest taken by the twelve hunters. Author holds antlers from his record-class Siberian roebuck. Mongolia, 1990.

From left: Local guide, driver, and interpreter with author's 6x6 elk, taken on the last day of the hunt. Mongolia, 1990.

Taking a break to stretch on the return trip to Ulan Bator. Note how the elk antlers were transported on the vehicles. Mongolia, 1990.

Many believe Iguaçu Falls is the world's most spectacular. The arrow marks a boat. Border of Argentina and Brazil, 2004.

Author's red deer stag, taken on the North Island. New Zealand, 1989.

A Desert Ram Makes It Ten

Chapter 8

There are no words to describe how I felt when I called the Arizona Game and Fish Department's number in Phoenix, followed instructions, and reached the hotline that would tell me how I'd fared in the 1993 drawings. A computer-activated voice said, "You . . . have . . . drawn . . . a . . . permit . . . to hunt . . . bighorn sheep. . . ." I couldn't believe what I'd heard, so I dialed the number again. It had taken thirty-nine consecutive years of applying, but I finally had what I needed to hunt a desert sheep.

I had grown up in the heart of Arizona's desert bighorn country, and I had seen enough sheep to know they aren't God's smartest animals on four legs. They sometimes will come running to a truck's horn or the sounds a two-cycle gas engine makes. Pardon the pun, but I've seen them in situations no self-respecting whitetail would ever be caught dead in. The problem is, I really didn't know how to hunt them. It had taken too long to draw that tag, and I would never draw another. I couldn't take the risk of not being successful.

I learned about Larry Heathington by a fortunate coincidence. I was Safari Club International's publications director when Pete Cimellaro, Larry's former partner in a big-game guiding business, drove down from Phoenix to visit SCI's wildlife museum. When he stopped by my office, I mentioned I'd drawn a sheep tag. The next day Larry called me. He had talked with Pete and offered to guide me at half his usual fee if I would write a magazine article about the hunt. It was something I couldn't refuse. I told Larry I wanted to tag along when he scouted my unit. I also asked if two of my friends—Boris Baird, a retired U.S. Air Force pilot, and Fritz Selby, a retired teacher and Realtor—could join us on the hunt. I'd invited them to hunt with me long before Larry called. He agreed to charge them a nonhunter rate that barely paid for their food.

I worked up a special load for my 7mm Remington Magnum and shot my rifle until I knew exactly where it was shooting out to three hundred and fifty yards. If I stayed calm, I wouldn't embarrass myself.

Heathington was a chain-smoker (as I also was then); he was opinionated; and four-letter words flowed nonstop from his mouth. I liked him from the instant we met. He had left his job as a policeman in Phoenix, I think, to become one of Arizona's few full-time hunting guides at the time. He guided hunters to every type of big-game animal Arizona offers, but his specialty was and is desert sheep.

Larry, Boris, and I made only one trip into my sheep unit before the hunt, and it was only to check the area's road system. We got hung up in brush along a dry river a couple of times but eventually found the best way to gain access. I had a feeling I'd been there before, and then I realized this was one of the places where a couple of high-school friends and I had looked for wild burros in the early 1950s. Larry and I had driven to it from the north off the highway that links Phoenix, Quartzite, and Blythe; more than forty years earlier, my friends and I had reached it from the Welton and Gila Bend side on the south. At that time there were supposed to be feral burros all over the place, but I saw no burros then or on this trip. Larry said it had been at least twenty years since the last burro was seen there.

Today "wild" burros are protected under the U.S. Wild Free-Roaming Horses and Burros Act of 1971, but when I was going to high school in the early 1950s, the Game and Fish Department and the U.S. Fish and Wildlife Service urged hunters to kill them on sight. The overpopulated feral animals competed for food and water needed by mule deer and bighorn in that arid country, they claimed. I knew wildlife managers who bragged about shooting five hundred or more burros in the course of their work. The Yuma Rod and Gun Club even held annual barbecues featuring pit-cooked burro meat.

At any rate, after we'd decided on the best route into the unit and found a place for our camp, we set up our spotting scopes and began looking for sheep. If I hadn't been there, I would not have believed the distances from which Larry could spot them. One ram was more than two miles away, according to my topographical map. We watched its blurry image in our spotting scopes for an hour as it fed and moved around in a clump of paloverde trees beneath a cliff. Later, we drove up on five or six ewes in the middle of a two-track road that led into the Kofa National Wildlife Refuge. When we found the shell of a long-dead ewe's horn while looking for firewood, I took it as a good omen. Until that day I'd expected we would have to spend days searching before we found our first sheep.

Things went downhill after we returned to Tucson. Three weeks before the hunt opened, someone stole my nearly new pickup truck and a Jeep Wagoneer owned by *Safari* magazine's manuscripts editor, Elaine Cummings, from the parking lot at Safari Club International's headquarters. Locked inside my truck were two 35mm Nikon camera bodies with three expensive lenses, a Smith & Wesson .357-Magnum pistol, two walkie-talkies, my Swarovski 10X50 binocular, an assortment of mechanic's tools, and my prized desert-sheep tag. Farmers Insurance Company wrote checks to replace the truck and everything else except the pistol and radios.

I still was writing outdoor columns for the *Tucson Citizen* and knew almost every Game and Fish Department employee, so I didn't relish having to ask for a duplicate tag. I was jokingly told that never in the history of Arizona's sheep hunting had anyone lost a tag, and there was no precedent for issuing a duplicate. They eventually sent me home with a new tag after they'd had their fun. I also was able to buy a new truck and binocular before the hunt, but my troubles were only beginning.

Fritz, Boris, and I left in two vehicles for our campsite the day before my hunt began. Larry already was there with two other people: his assistant guide and a young woman he'd hired to cook for us. They had set up two large white canvas tents. One was for cooking and eating; the other had cots for Larry and his assistant and also served as a place to store food and gear. The cook had her own tepeelike sheepherder's tent. There also were two ten-by-something wall tents. I took one; Boris and Fritz had the other. It was a wonderful camp, but it attracted Air Force pilots like a fat wallet attracts some women. The Coleman lanterns we burned for a while each night lit up our four tents and made them glow like huge fluorescent lights, attracting fighter jets from a military base outside Yuma. They obviously were holding nighttime exercises because every half-hour they'd noisily swoop down to get a better look at us from just a couple of hundred feet up.

The desert bighorn sheep hunt that I'd waited thirty-nine years for couldn't start on the season's opening day. We awoke to find a rare fog covering the desert, and it never lifted all that day. Everyone in camp spent opening day in the dining tent, getting to know each other. I've forgotten the assistant guide's name, but he was obsessed with sheep hunting after having taken a ram in a nearby unit a couple of years earlier. I remember him saying he had a farm in another state but returned to Arizona every December to help Heathington guide other hunters. The cook had worked in moose- and sheep-hunting camps across Canada before moving to Arizona.

The fog lifted during the night, allowing us to head out before daylight for a spot that Larry wanted to check. We found no sheep there, and we were hurrying to another vantage point, hoping to get there before the sheep bedded, when our left rear tire suddenly blew. I'd loosened all of the wheel's lug nuts and was waiting for Larry to throw down a spare tire off the roof of his camper shell when his Hi-Lift jack slipped off the bumper, catching my left arm between the top of the tire and the opening in the truck's fender. It was like being caught in a dull guillotine, and the two long bones in my arm snapped instantly. My left hand was hanging at an awful-looking angle.

Fritz took charge immediately. First he found an empty dog-food sack in Larry's truck to support my broken arm, and then he got a sack of ice from the ice chest and told me to lay my arm on the ice to reduce the risk of infection. He then wrapped everything in duct tape to create a makeshift but serviceable splint. We were at least forty-five minutes over a rocky trail to the highway, and an hour from there to Phoenix, but we stopped at camp long enough to get me a couple of pain-dulling pills that Fritz kept in his shaving kit for emergencies.

We left Larry and his assistant behind to scout while we were gone and headed for Phoenix with Boris driving his Bronco. The pills didn't take effect until we reached pavement, and even then they didn't totally block my pain. The closest hospital was in West Phoenix, another hour away. It was a Saturday, and a broken arm apparently wasn't considered a serious injury in an emergency room filled with victims of gunshot and knife wounds. One of the nurses asked if I had taken any drugs, and I said I'd swallowed two OxyContin pills two hours earlier. She looked at me as if I'd been injecting heroin. She had me crawl up on a gurney, then rolled me to a corner where I immediately was forgotten. Twenty to thirty minutes later, a different nurse parked another gurney next to mine. I couldn't see who was on it, but he moaned constantly until he suddenly made a loud, gurgling noise. I knew he had died because he didn't make a sound after that. This was confirmed by a nurse who checked on him thirty minutes later.

By now, the effect of Fritz's painkillers was gone, and the pain was growing increasingly worse. Just when I thought I wouldn't be able to endure it a second longer, a doctor walked up.

"Are you one of the guys who were hunting sheep?" he asked sternly.

Damn, I thought. *The way my luck has been going, this guy is probably an antihunter.* Many doctors are.

"Yes," I said, tentatively.

"We're going to fix you up as quickly as we can," he said. "I've applied for a tag for fourteen years, and I know how important it is. We'll operate tonight and get you out of here by noon tomorrow if you don't develop a fever."

That's exactly what he did. I woke up after surgery with two steel plates in my arm and a cast from above my elbow to my wrist. My wife, daughter, and son-in-law were standing above me. They had driven up from Tucson to see me.

149

Fritz, Boris, and I were on the road and back in camp before sundown the day after we'd left. Doing ordinary things was difficult without the use of my left arm, but Fritz treated me as if he were my mother. He helped me dress and undress, and took care of anything else I needed. The pain pills the hospital gave me worked, but whenever I dozed off, which was often, I would have the most horrible nightmares I've ever experienced. When I realized what the pills were doing to me, I took only Tylenol.

I was afraid I wouldn't be able to shoot when we finally found a ram, so Fritz helped me practice getting my rifle to my shoulder while resting it over my cast. I decided I might be able to shoot if a sheep gave me enough time to get ready.

We hunted every day for the next six or seven days, and we saw only one large group of ewes with a ram. They were within range, but the ram was young. Its thin and widely flared horns reminded me of those on Dall sheep.

Walking around in Arizona's sheep country with only one arm is not as easy as it might seem. On some steep and narrow trails I walked backward so I could use my right hand to grab rocks and brush. There was no way I was going to fall and have to go home. On the twelfth day of the season, we found Pete Cimellaro waiting in camp when we returned after sundown. His client had taken a ram in another unit, and Pete was there to help us. According to Larry, Arizona's sheep guides work together to keep a one hundred percent hunter success rate for professionally guided hunts. We could have as many as six other guides helping us if my hunt continued much longer, he said.

The first to arrive was Bill Hook, an experienced desert-sheep hunter who had heard about my broken arm from Larry's wife. So the next morning Larry, Fritz, and I went one way while Boris, Bill Hook, Larry's assistant, and Pete went another. When we met at noon for lunch, Pete reported that they had found a mature ram feeding on a cone-shaped peak. The three of them had watched it from a distance with their spotting scopes. Its horns weren't as heavy as those some rams carry, but it was a decent ram, Pete said. More important, it was in a place I could reach with one arm. I needed only one look through the spotting scope to say I wanted that ram.

Larry and his assistant, Pete, and I left Hook, Fritz, and Boris behind while we made the stalk. We stayed in the bottom of a wide arroyo that ran past the bottom of the peak the ram was on, moving from one old ironwood tree to the next. We were in sight of the ram during most of the stalk, but it apparently didn't feel threatened by us. When we reached a point directly below and out of sight of the ram, we started straight up the hill toward the ledge and stopped when we were below where we'd last seen the animal. We hadn't heard the ram leave, so it had to be bedded nearby.

I quietly removed the sling from my arm, rested the cast on Larry's backpack, and got into position to shoot with only my right arm. We had been there a few minutes, waiting for something to happen, when someone coughed. The ram leaped to its feet no more than thirty or forty yards above us and began racing around the peak. My first shot made it stagger, and I quickly jacked in another round, shot it again, and saw it wobble before going down. It must have been dead on its feet from the first shot.

I look more tired than happy in most of the photographs Pete and Larry took of me with my ram, but I assure you I was elated. I finally had taken all ten of Arizona's big-game species. When I was younger, I'd fantasized about posing with my bighorn while holding up all of my fingers and thumbs, but with my left arm in a cast, it was not to be.

Three men I hadn't seen before were in our camp when we returned after dark. Larry knew what he was talking about. They may have been competitors in the sheep-guiding business, but they were friends who had driven one hundred and fifty miles to help Larry find me a ram. We celebrated that evening. Cimellaro even wrote a poem to commemorate the occasion. He made certain to mention the angle was so steep that my second shot had exploded the ram's testicles from below.

Larry and his crew took down our camp the next morning, Boris and Fritz left in Boris's vehicle for Tucson, and I drove to Yuma to get my ram checked by a Game and Fish Department wildlife manager, as required by state regulations. When I left, I felt confident that I'd have no trouble driving with one hand, but I should have asked Fritz to drive me. I couldn't scratch or blow my nose. To drink water I had to pull over and hold the bottle between my knees while I tried to remove the cap with my good hand. I made it to Yuma, only to learn that the wildlife agency's office was closed. I had driven a hundred miles out of my way and now had no choice but to continue on to Tucson. I reached home in time to call the agency there and make an appointment for someone to check my ram that evening. Jean drove our grandson, Logan Greene, and me to the local Game and Fish Department office, where Jim Heffelfinger drilled a hole in one of my ram's horns and inserted a numbered metal plug to indicate my sheep had been taken legally.

I was exhausted by the time I crawled into bed that night, but I'd completed a goal I'd set a lifetime earlier.

The letters to the editor poured in after I wrote a newspaper feature article about my hunt. Two people accused me of being so dumb and inept I couldn't change a tire without getting hurt. Most wanted to know how I could kill one of God's beautiful creatures. Another claimed I should be jailed for killing an extinct animal. One man, who didn't sign his letter, said he was going to follow me to my "killing ground" and murder me with "a telescope-sighted sniper rifle" the next time I went hunting. It was not the only death threat I had received in twenty-eight years of writing outdoor columns for that newspaper, but this guy seemed to be more serious than the other writers. I told the paper's publisher, who called the sheriff (my home is outside the city limits). A deputy read the letter, listened to my story, and politely let me know there was no way I could be protected if someone really wanted to kill me. I spent the next month checking my back trail and carrying a pistol in my truck.

I am grateful the creep didn't try to make good on his threat.

Expanding My Horizons beyond Arizona

Chapter 9

My first hunting trip outside Arizona was to the Texas Hill Country, but how I came to go there is a story in itself. Beginning in 1967, Alex Jacome and I got involved in a shooting sport called *metalicas siluetas* across the border in Nogales, Sonora. It required competitors to shoot centerfire rifles offhand, without slings or other aids, at steel, animal-shaped targets one hundred to five hundred meters away. The rifles were required to be something a hunter would use, which meant the special equipment developed for Olympic shooting was prohibited. Although not mentioned in the rules, shooters chose calibers such as .270, 7mm, .308, and .30-06. Recoil could be brutal from anything larger when shooting twenty to forty rounds in a morning. Anything smaller, such as .243 or .257, didn't have the energy needed to knock the heavy sheep and javelina targets off their pedestals.

We had no problem taking our rifles and ammunition across the border. The top Mexican general in Sonora was a member of *Club de Cazadores y Tiradores, Nogalenses* (the Nogales Hunting and Shooting Club), which hosted the shooting matches, and whenever a Mexican immigration official noticed our rifles in Alex's vehicle, we merely mentioned that General Lemon Lepe had given us permission to cross. Things are much stricter now. Mere possession of even a single cartridge in Mexico without an official government firearms license will bring a jail sentence.

Southern Arizona's and northern Mexico's best marksmen outclassed us, but Alex and I enjoyed the camaraderie, the shooting, the food, the mariachi music, and the Cuba libres that were served throughout the matches.

I was shocked the first time I saw a bartender serving rum at the club's shooting range in a long canyon on the western edge of the city. Everyone knows guns and alcohol do not mix, but at that range everyone policed each other, and the rangemaster was especially strict. The first time I competed, for example, a stern-faced Mexican walked up to me as I was placing my rifle in a rack along the wall of the range's ramada.

"Please open the bolt, señor," he said, without smiling.

There were no exceptions. Rifles were kept in racks with their bolts open until a shooter was called to the line. No one else was allowed to go near them. If someone drank too much, or broke any rule of safety, he was escorted off the range.

I surprised myself (and everyone else) one day by tying a Mexican with the day's top score. Winners in such situations were determined by sudden-death shoot-offs in the afternoons, so I watched my opponent closely while club members brought out the *cabrita* (barbecued goat meat, frijoles, and tortillas). When I saw him drink a Cuba libre, I felt safe drinking one, too. I soon would learn how dumb that was.

Our match started with both of us missing all five of the metal chicken targets at one hundred meters. We then both missed the five javelina at two hundred and fifty meters, the five turkeys at three hundred and eighty meters, and the five sheep at five hundred meters. We were the day's best shooters, but we both had missed twenty consecutive shots!

I had brought only forty rounds of ammunition with me, so I had to borrow a box of reloaded .270 Winchester cartridges from someone. As I did for my ammo, the other shooter had developed the load especially for his rifle. It worried me that I couldn't check where the ammo would shoot out of my rifle, but I stepped up to the shooting line anyway and waited for the signal to load a single cartridge into my rifle's chamber.

Someone honked a truck's horn, and the range boys, who had been hiding behind barriers at each row of targets, stood up. When they ducked down and waved white flags, the horn was honked again. The Mexican and I started at the bottom again, and again we each missed the five chickens. Next came the pigs. I missed the first one, hit the next, and then missed the last three. My opponent missed all five, and I was declared the winner. Someone asked me to give a speech—in Spanish—which I did, but badly.

The lesson I learned that day is how little alcohol it takes to impair a person's coordination. My opponent and I had swallowed less than an ounce of rum each, and under other circumstances we each would have knocked over a few targets with our first twenty shots. Instead, I won by missing "only" twenty-one consecutive shots.

When Alex and I returned to the range the next week, the club's members had a special trophy waiting for me. It was a replica of a rifleman standing by a chamber pot. Its plaque declared that I was the club's champion "near misser." Inside the pot was a small brown lump of ceramic. I still have that trophy.

Winning that match was a fluke because some very good shooters competed each week. One of them was Bob Jensen, the owner of a sporting-goods store and a frequent winner of one-thousand-yard Palma matches around the world. Another was Roy Dunlap, a Tucson gunsmith and author of *the* book on his craft. Still another was Victor Ruiz, the personable owner of a liquor store on the Mexican side of the border and a skilled amateur gunsmith who liked to convert semiautomatic .22 rimfire rifles to full automatic.

More important, there also was Doug Campbell, who won the first U.S. national championship when the National Rifle Association and the Tucson Rifle Club brought the sport of silhouette shooting north of the border. Doug grew up and lived in Tucson, but he owned ranches in two counties in Texas, and when he invited Alex and me to hunt deer there with him, we didn't hesitate to accept.

Alex and I left Tucson in the late afternoon on the designated day that fall and drove through the night, arriving a half-hour after sunrise at Doug's Blanco Verde Ranch, a couple of miles outside the little town of Lampasas. We'd stopped only to buy one-hundred-dollar Texas nonresident hunting licenses in El Paso and to eat a midnight meal in a town called El Dorado. (Texans pronounced it "Doe-ray-doe" and not

"Dohr-ah-doe," the proper Spanish pronunciation. They also murdered the words *Colorado* and *Llano*.) Alex and I passed our time during the last couple hours of the long trip trying to count the deer we saw along the road. We stopped after three hundred—and we didn't count about two dozen road kills. I'd hunted all my life in Arizona, where our best whitetail habitat might have one or two deer per square mile, and I can't remember ever seeing more than three or four road-killed deer in all my time here. After seeing all those deer, it was easy to see why the Texas game department estimated there were seventy-five deer per square mile across the Hill Country's Edwards Plateau at the time. That's a deer for every eight and a half acres!

A white-tailed doe bounded across the dirt road as we left the paved farm-to-market road and started up the long drive to a little house, where we found Doug waiting with three of his friends from Dallas. The place was divided into four rooms—a small bedroom, a bathroom, a kitchen, and a living/dining area. Doug's only furniture was a dining table, six chairs, and six cots. We and our baggage took up virtually all of the remaining space. With that many men in a space that small, each of us tried to be the first to fall asleep. Those who didn't were kept awake by world-class snoring and wind-passing.

I'd been hospitalized with a heart condition and released only a few days before Alex and I left Tucson. Although I felt fine, Jean wasn't sure I should go. My cardiologist gave his blessing when I explained that the most strenuous physical activity I might experience would be climbing into a deer blind. Doug was concerned about my problem, so he had called the Texas Parks and Wildlife Department and learned "handicapped" hunters could legally shoot from a vehicle, and that's what he wanted me to do.

When it was time to go hunting, Doug drove me to his mother's ranch in Burnett County, and the four others went to two of his ranches. As I was climbing into his truck after opening the main gate, Doug said I needed to load my rifle and get ready to shoot. We then drove no more than a few hundred yards before we came upon a group of perhaps fifteen or sixteen deer. I didn't see a buck among them, but I had tags for two does, so I opened the door, got out, and shot the largest animal I saw. I wanted to field-dress it, but Doug said that chore could wait, and we temporarily left the doe where she had fallen.

I shot my second Texas deer—another doe—just five minutes later, when we drove up on another group of deer in another pasture. Doug wanted to look for the one buck my license allowed, but I felt two deer were enough for one day. We would be there for a week, and I didn't want to end my hunt before 8 A.M. the first morning. I waited until two days later to shoot a three-point buck (an eight-pointer in Texas) with wide antlers.

By the end of the week, the five of us—Doug didn't hunt while we were there—had fifteen deer hanging in Doug's barn. I had never experienced anything like that anywhere else I had hunted deer. There were two or three ground blinds with corn feeders on Doug's properties, but the most productive way to hunt was just to find a place to sit in a thicket and wait for a deer to come along. On future trips I read paperback novels and looked up at the end of every second or third page. By the time I'd gone through a couple of chapters, there often would be a deer staring at me from fifty to seventy-five yards away.

An interesting thing happened once, when I didn't bother to hide. Instead, I was sitting at the edge of the water on the dam of one of Doug's cattle ponds when a forked-horn buck appeared across the pond and dropped its head to drink. I easily could have shot it—it was only forty yards or so across the pond—but I had only one tag left, and I wanted to use it on a larger buck. After a minute or two, the deer's head jerked up, and the animal stared at me. The wind was in my face, and I held myself absolutely still.

The little buck stomped its feet and snorted, but when I didn't move, it trotted a few yards closer to me. It did this again, and when I still didn't move and it couldn't decide what I was, it slowly and cautiously approached me until it was only a long step away. I couldn't believe it when the buck actually moved forward and sniffed my boots before running off. It stopped about fifty yards away and stared at me again. I sat there in wonderment.

Just when I decided I wouldn't tell anyone what had happened that morning because nobody would believe me, Doug stepped out from behind the trees a couple of hundred yards away, smiling his Robert Douglas Campbell signature smile.

The buck that sniffed my stinking boots and ran away made me the brunt of jokes that evening, and I happily joined in on the fun. I'd experienced something no hunter could dream of experiencing, and I'd had a witness.

Magazine articles frequently say the two smallest whitetail races are the Key deer of Florida and the Coues deer of Arizona, New Mexico, and northern Mexico. Those authors apparently had never heard of the miniature whitetails of Central and South America, where whitetails are even smaller than the Florida Key deer. They certainly had never hunted in this portion of the Hill Country, where a field-dressed "big buck" seldom reached sixty pounds. So-called trophy bucks were nonexistent. The antlers on even the best bucks had thin, fairly short tines and were neither tall nor wide. It didn't matter to me. I enjoyed the experience of hunting them.

Although they were much smaller than our Arizona whitetails, the Hill Country's deer seemed to have longer, slenderer bodies and faces. Their ears were smaller and rounder, their coats were darker, and they had slicker, shorter hair. The biggest difference between the two races, though, was in the taste of their venison. I have never eaten deer meat that tasted better than that of Hill Country deer, and I'm certain it was because of their diet. Doug's ranches were covered with oak, walnut, and pecan trees, but, more important, the entire region was so badly overgrazed by cattle, goats, deer, and various "exotic" game animals that ranchers were forced to put out supplemental feed for their livestock. It was not unusual to see three or four deer at a cattle feeder, even in the middle of the day.

Alex and I hunted on Doug's ranches for at least seven or eight years before a year came along when Alex couldn't go. I then invited another friend, Buddy Bristow, to accompany me. Buddy was regional director of the Arizona Game and Fish Department's southeastern region then. (He later became director of state wildlife agencies in Arizona and Virginia.) He also was an experienced and enthusiastic amateur wildlife photographer. When Doug heard this, he proudly showed us a snapshot of a crane he'd photographed with an inexpensive point-and-shoot camera at one of his ponds. We politely praised it, even though the crane's image was only a small, light-colored spot in the center of his print.

Buddy changed Doug's life forever when he opened his camera box and brought out the large-format Hasselblad camera and lenses he'd brought on the trip. From that day on, Doug began acquiring skills and equipment that would make him one of Arizona's best-known wildlife photographers. His work (bylined Robert Campbell) frequently appears on calendars and postcards and in *Arizona Highways* and other major magazines, and is featured at galleries across the United States.

Texas hunting licenses also served as hunting tags. Perforated strips could be torn off and attached to four deer and four turkey, the state limit for both species then. At the end of the year, a successful hunter would be left with only about a third of the license he'd purchased. The strips were so small we had problems keeping them attached to our kills, so most hunters simply stuffed them in the ears of their deer. As you can imagine, strips and ears sometimes became separated, and this is what happened the first year Buddy hunted in Texas. We returned to Tucson after driving across two states without knowing that we had six deer and only five tags. We would have had a lot of explaining to do if a law-enforcement officer had stopped us.

I hunted on Doug's ranches for five or six more years. Buddy took his two teenage sons, Bret and Kirby, on at least one trip, and my son-in-law, Robbie Greene, was along on another. The way we hunted changed after I bought a CVA caplock muzzleloader on sale at a gun shop on a whim for about $50 and shot a yearling buck with it. If I'd been hunting with a centerfire rifle, I would have waited for a larger buck, but when it stopped about fifty yards away, I couldn't resist taking the shot with my new black-powder rifle. When that little deer whirled and ran about thirty yards and dropped, it opened a new world for me. I soon was reading everything I could find about muzzleloading rifles, including Joe Kindig Jr.'s wonderful *Thoughts on the Kentucky Rifle in Its Golden Age.*

From there, I went on to build a flintlock long rifle from parts ordered from a Dixie Gunworks catalog and a slab of walnut Doug and I had cut on his ranch. I patterned the rifle from a photograph in Kindig's book, and then used it to take three deer on Doug's ranches. Buddy caught the bug, too, and we eventually shot all our deer with muzzleloading rifles we had assembled ourselves. After using my flintlock that first year, I put it away and built two caplock rifles, which I used for the rest of my muzzleloading career in Texas and Arizona.

Buddy and I shot a lot of deer with our muzzleloaders, but it didn't take long to learn that round balls were not the best projectiles for these deer. About half of the animals we shot with round balls ran a long way before dying. We were fortunate that we were able to find all of them. When hit with large-caliber minnie balls or cast bullets, our deer usually dropped on the spot.

One of the things that bothered me on our trips to Texas was the number of deer we found caught in barbed-wire fences. We couldn't drive very far on a country road without seeing a deer hanging by a front or rear leg from a fence. They must have died horrible deaths. I found several fence-kills on Doug's ranches over the years I hunted there, and Alex was with me when we found a deer hung up in a fence and still alive. It was a buck with good antlers, and either of us would have shot it under other circumstances. Instead, we spent at least ten minutes working with sticks to get enough slack in the twisted strands of wire to free the buck's leg, all the while it was struggling and bleating pathetically. Both of us expected the deer to run off when we freed it, but it was so exhausted that it couldn't stand up. It obviously was terrified to have two humans handle it, but it wasn't strong enough to escape us. We watched it for a while, then left it alone to recover while we hunted elsewhere.

We found the buck dead, apparently from shock and exhaustion, when we returned later that day to check on it. It hadn't moved from the spot where we'd left it.[1]

As my workload at two jobs increased, I eventually stopped going to Texas. I began my day on the copy desk at the newspaper at 4 A.M. By noon I was at my desk at Safari Club International. Most days I was home before 7 P.M. I could work ahead of schedule and take long weekends off, but finding seven or eight consecutive free days became increasingly tougher. Later, when my work schedule eased, my friends (except for Whitey Devries, who still is hunting there) also had stopped hunting on Doug's ranches for one reason or another. I have many great memories from the years I hunted there. Thanks to the generous Texas limits and Doug's generosity, I may have shot as many as fifty deer in Texas.

Just thinking about how they tasted makes me want to hunt them again. I remember a trip when Doug and I drove to Texas together. He had breaded and fried the backstraps of one of his little deer for us to nibble on as we drove. I'm ashamed to say that I nibbled more than Doug did. I ate nearly all of that meat with very little help from him. It was gone before we reached the New Mexico border. There is no better eating than a breaded and fried Hill Country deer's backstrap, unless it is a pot-roasted haunch of Hill Country venison.

✳ ✳ ✳

There have been only two other places where I saw anything approaching as many deer per square mile as in Texas, and one was on a private ranch in California that could be reached only in a small aircraft. The ranch had belonged to the family of the man who called to invite me to hunt there. I found the way his family sold the land to

---

[1]Alex and I also found a mule-deer doe caught by its front hoof by the top two strands of a barbed-wire fence on Arizona's Kaibab Plateau. It still was alive, even though coyotes had eaten a large portion of its rump during the night. We saw one of them run away when we drove up, and were attracted to the deer by its pitiful bleating.

be very interesting. Instead of selling the place outright, a corporation was formed that allowed the sale of thirty or forty "interests" in the entire place. The sales contracts allowed the family to continue living there and draw salaries. A dozen or more chaletlike luxury cabins were built in secluded and scenic settings for visiting interest holders, and chef-prepared food was delivered to their doors. Guides with horses and Jeeps would take them hunting in season if they desired. A fully equipped butcher shop with a walk-in freezer processed the game they and their guests killed. There was a corporate meeting room that also was used for small banquets and parties.

After the infrastructure was completed, the old roads leading into the ranch were closed. To reach the place, interest holders could charter a flight or fly their own planes and find a Jeep waiting for them on the runway when they landed. The shares were expensive but probably worth it to the wealthy people the ranch attracted. Everything was first class. I doubt that a more secluded spot to hold a business meeting or escape from city life existed in California. This was before cell phones became popular, and my host proudly said there were no telephones there. If someone truly wanted to get away from it all, it was the place.

I flew on American Airlines from Tucson to Los Angeles in September 1985, and then on to the ranch in a four-seat Cessna piloted by one of the ranch employees. We had to buzz the airstrip twice to run off a dozen Columbia black-tailed deer so we could land and taxi up to where a Jeep was parked. Between the airstrip and the lodge we saw another dozen deer and a semi-tame flock of Merriam's turkeys that had been introduced to the ranch. My host said arrangements were being made with the California Fish and Game Department to introduce tule elk also. No one I talked with that weekend was happy that legislation to extend total protection for California's mountain lion had passed recently. There were too many lion, all claimed. Could be, but too many lion obviously hadn't hurt the deer population on that ranch. I saw several hundred during the day and a half I hunted there.

I had arrived on a Friday afternoon and was scheduled to leave Sunday afternoon. I didn't have enough time to look for a trophy, so I shot the largest mature buck we saw by Saturday afternoon. It looked exactly like a mule deer, but its body was about half that size. Its tail resembled a whitetail's that had been dyed black on top. My guide kept apologizing that we weren't seeing the trophy bucks he knew were there. The rest of that day and Sunday morning I hunted feral hog. Family groups of six to eight of them were everywhere. I had to laugh (to myself) when my guide pointed to a sow and four or five of her nearly grown youngsters.

"That's a Russian boar," he said about a brown-colored hog we were watching with our binoculars.

He claimed each of the animals in the herd was a different race, even though all of them had the same mother. This is a biological impossibility, of course.

We used our binoculars to find the boar I eventually shot. It was feeding at the edge of a water hole in a canyon about three-quarters of a mile below a road that ran along the ridge above the airstrip. My guide said that it probably would run away before we got there if we tried to drive the Jeep down the road that led to it. So I left him on the ridge and walked down the canyon as quietly as I could, trying to keep my scent from reaching the lone animal. I was able to approach within fifty yards and shoot it with my .257 Roberts, and when I did, the boar flopped and fell off a ledge into the pond. It was starting to sink when I waded to it and pulled it out.

I'd been told to watch the weight of my luggage because we'd be flying in the little Cessna, so I'd left my street shoes at home and wore my hunting boots during the entire trip. They still were wet when I got off the plane in Tucson that evening.

* * *

The most deer per square mile to be found anywhere in North America have to be at places such as The Sanctuary, about sixty miles north of Grand Rapids, Michigan. The Sanctuary was built by a group of investors led by developer Pat Bollman, who would later serve a term as SCI president. Bollman began by erecting a deer-proof fence around one square mile of timbered land and then asking Michigan's state wildlife agency to count the white-tailed deer inside it. After The Sanctuary bought those deer from the state, no other animals were ever released into the enclosure.

The deer herd has grown to the point where hundreds must be culled every year to keep the closely managed herd at the number The Sanctuary's managers want. This is done by shooting excess females and "management" and "cull" bucks. But it is The Sanctuary's so-called gold medal bucks that attract hunters from all over the globe, and they are the reason The Sanctuary is in business. Gold medal hunters pay $8,000 to $12,500 for a four-day hunt in the peak of the rut for bucks with antlers measuring 150 to 220 Boone and Crockett Club points.

When I was invited to join a group of outdoor writers hunting at The Sanctuary on a junket hosted by Realtree, Browning, and The Sanctuary, I wasn't sure I should go. I didn't know how I'd feel about shooting a deer on a game farm. Eventually, though, I bought an airline ticket to Grand Rapids. I'd shot a "northwestern" whitetail in Wyoming, but I also wanted a "northeastern" whitetail, which I had not taken on hunts in Illinois and Minnesota. I justified my decision by telling myself I'd hunted behind wire (on much larger properties) in South Africa, and although Doug Campbell's deer were free-ranging, most deer hunting in Texas takes place inside high-fenced properties.

When we gathered at The Sanctuary's lodge that first evening and were told we could shoot any buck we saw, I made a pledge to myself to shoot only a "ten-pointer," a buck with four long tines and an eyeguard on each antler.

It proved to be easier said than done, although many such bucks were there. The rut had ended a couple of weeks earlier, and the trophy bucks that had survived the gold medal hunts were not dumb. I saw perhaps eighty or ninety bucks during the four days I hunted in The Sanctuary, but nearly all were younger than the four and one-half years it takes to grow trophy antlers. It wasn't hard to judge the ages of the larger bucks. Crews of wildlife-management students and other volunteers lined up after the fawning season and walked across the place, catching and tagging each fawn they encountered. The year I was there, the four-and-one-half-year-old bucks wore small, blue plastic tags behind their ears, and they didn't move out of the thickets until well after sundown.

My guide and I found the ten-pointer I wanted the third evening I hunted. It was peeking around a tree inside a thick grove of trees, watching our blind from about two hundred yards away. I could clearly see in the fading light all of its long tines in my binocular and riflescope, and the rack was wide. It did not give me a clear shot at its body, though. When it was too dark to see, the guide and I walked back to the truck and returned to the lodge.

We were in the same blind the next evening, watching smaller bucks walk out into the open to feed. The big buck did not appear until at least twenty minutes after sundown and only a few minutes before it would be too dark to see anything. It was in approximately the same place, peeking around another tree, staring at the blind. It obviously knew that the little house on stilts was a source of danger. I was watching the buck in my scope as the light was fading, wondering if I should try shooting it in the throat, the only shot it would give me. This was my last chance. I was scheduled to leave for Grand Rapids and travel on to Tucson the next morning. Before I could get into position to shoot, my guide tapped my shoulder and pointed to our right, where a buck with high and wide antlers had stepped out into the open. I didn't hesitate. I swung my rifle, found this new buck in my scope, and shot it. It ran about thirty yards and died at the edge of a swamp.

Although it was an "eight-pointer," I was happy with it. The rack was wide and the tines were long. One antler even had a bump that an eastern deer hunter would say made my buck a "nine-pointer."

Was my shooting a deer at a place such as The Sanctuary really "hunting?" I think so. I could have killed a buck every morning and afternoon I was there, and if I had, there would be no need to ask myself that question because I would know the answer. It would have been killing, not hunting. But I had searched for a special animal, and it had eluded me.

* * *

"How would you like to hunt an elk this weekend?" was the question I heard over the telephone.

Would I? Of course I would, but what was the catch?

"My client bought five elk licenses from the Jicarilla Indians," Eric Sparks said. "One of the guys couldn't show up. His tag is yours if you want it."

Sparks still was practicing law in Texas when he called. I had met him at the One-Shot Hunt in Wyoming, and I was flabbergasted that he had thought of me because I didn't know him well. There must have been dozens of other people he could have called. I didn't question him, however. I met him and three other men at a hotel in Dulce, New Mexico, two days later. We were the only hunters on the reservation at that time, and each of us was assigned a tribal member to guide us. I couldn't believe my good fortune.

There was no problem finding elk. All five of us took six-point bulls in three days of hunting. I passed up three or four small bulls and missed a far-off bull before I killed mine. It was an old animal with long antler beams, but one of its tines was broken and the others were short. Nobody knew how to determine its age, but we all agreed that it was an old animal in its last years. How I shot it is worth telling.

I've forgotten the name of the young man who helped me, but I couldn't have had a better guide. I've never met anyone who was as enthusiastic about elk hunting as he was. He was a proud member of the Rocky Mountain Elk Foundation, and the walls of his house were plastered with photos of elk he'd cut from magazines. He knew how to find elk on his reservation, too. After I missed that far-off bull, I had him drive me to the end of a long ridge and let me out. I then slowly walked a mile or more to where he was waiting for me with the truck. I saw nothing on my jaunt, and I still was feeling bad about missing that bull earlier in the day. It was the last day of my hunt. My guide wasn't worried. We walked to a spot a half-mile away, and he pointed to where he wanted me to sit. The spot overlooked a break in a fence where he said elk crossed regularly.

"I'm going to make a loop around that hill, and if we're lucky, I'll push a bull to you," he said.

I'd been sitting on that little knoll long enough that I was having trouble staying awake when I heard rocks rolling. I barely had enough time to grab my rifle from where I'd rested it against a tree, flick off the safety, find the better of the two bulls in my scope, and determine that it had wide, long antlers. It was in view only an instant, but I was able to get off a quick shot before it was out of sight in the brush. The distance to the elk when I shot was only about forty yards.

I wasn't sure whether I'd hit it or not, so I stayed where I was for five minutes to allow the bull time to go down, in case I'd only wounded it. I was getting up to track it when my guide trotted up.

"What did you shoot?" he asked.

"It looked like a good bull. It ran through there after I shot," I said.

We found the elk dead a short distance inside the brush. My bullet had entered behind the left shoulder and exited through the opposite shoulder. If anyone ever needed proof that elk are tough, he need only look at that animal. Hit like that, it should have piled up on the spot. Instead, it ran at least seventy-five yards before dropping.

Wyoming's One Shot Antelope Hunt

Chapter 10

The One Shot Antelope Hunt in Lander, Wyoming, is the best known and most prestigious of the many so-called celebrity hunts that copy its format. A challenge in 1939 between hunting buddies Harold Evans of Lander and Harold Dahl of Golden, Colorado, became the first One Shot Antelope Hunt in 1940. It has been held every year since then, except for the World War II years of 1942 to 1945. I first heard about the hunt in 1969, when Arizona Governor Jack Williams competed in it. The newspaper articles I'd read about participants having to use just one shot to kill their pronghorn antelopes intrigued me. At the time I had no idea I would ever see Lander or be elected president of the One Shot Hunt's Past Shooters Club.

What led to my association with the One Shot was a call from Boris Baird, then president of the Safari Club International chapter in Tucson. He'd called the local outdoor editor (me) for help in finding someone to guide a group of men from Wyoming who wanted to hunt quail while visiting Tucson. I often got such requests, but I usually gave them the name and telephone number of someone else.[1] I don't remember why, but this time was different. I told Boris I'd see if I could get Dr. Don Saelens, a dentist and bird-dog fanatic, and some of his like-minded friends to take them out with their dogs. Don was not

---

[1] I remember a call from a man who wanted a guide to take him dove hunting in Mexico. "Bill, this is Kevin Costner," he said. At first I didn't believe he was the star of such films as *Waterworld* and *Dances with Wolves* and said to myself, *Sure, and I'm Brad Pitt.* I'm glad I didn't voice my doubts because the caller really was Costner.

a professional guide, but he usually hunted quail at least once a week during the season to train his dogs.

In addition to the three men with dogs, there were three hunters from Wyoming—Don Taylor, Jack Brody, and Glenn Wadsworth— and Harold Mares from Wisconsin, plus Tucsonans Larry Hughes, Don DeLuca, Boris Baird, and me. I'm not a bird hunter, but I enjoyed the day. The dogs handled well, and there were plenty of quail.

Larry Hughes, a retired FBI regional supervisor in a Midwestern state, held the post of ramrod at the One Shot. Meeting him that day led to our friendship, and he invited me to attend the event as his guest in 1981. Alex Jacome and I flew from Tucson to Lander with Boris Baird in a single-engine aircraft he had borrowed from a friend. The flight was uneventful, except when Boris switched from one wing's fuel tank to the other in midair. Alex was asleep when Boris warned me that he intended to drain one of the tanks. We were somewhere over Utah when the plane's engine sputtered and then stopped. The sudden silence woke Alex, and when he saw the propeller wasn't moving, he wanted to know what was happening.

"We're all going to die," Boris said.

Light aircraft have a long glide ratio, so we were in no danger. Boris switched to the second tank and restarted the engine, and we landed without incident in Lander an hour later.

The three of us attended the nightly banquets, watched the initiation ceremonies, and heard each team member tell why he had or hadn't shot his antelope with one shot. I was impressed with a ceremony where someone read a list of names of past shooters who had died during the previous twelve months. As each name was read, the chief of the Wind River Shoshone Indian tribe jacked the lever of a Winchester carbine and allowed a cartridge to fall to the floor. *When I go*, I told myself, *I'd like to be remembered that way, too.*

I was surprised to see that a friend, George Parker from Amado, was a member of one of the competing teams. Although I didn't realize it then, a kidney disease that would eventually lead to his suicide a year later was causing him to sit down whenever he could. I seldom saw

George on his feet that week. One of George's team members was Eric Sparks, a lawyer who would become one of my hunting partners after he moved his practice from Midland, Texas, to Tucson.

One Shot events begin on the Wednesday before the Saturday opening of Wyoming's pronghorn antelope season with shooting contests and a welcoming banquet, followed by more events and dinners held the next three nights. Everyone gets together for a pre-hunt breakfast long before daylight on Saturday and then heads out to the various hunting areas. The Wyoming legislature had set aside seventy-five tags for the hunt, and, as a past shooter, Larry was able to assign his tag to me and convince a friend to give Alex his tag. He also arranged for a couple of his local friends to take us hunting.

The day before the hunt, we drove out to scout the area Alex and I would be hunting, and a story that would plague me for many years was born. We were parked on a high ridge, and I was sitting in the truck, using my binocular to watch a herd of antelopes about a half-mile away, when Boris walked up.

"Have some M&M's," he said.

Not thinking, I kept my binocular on the animals and stuck my hand out the window, stuffed the rounded things he handed me into my mouth, and bit down. What I'd popped into my mouth definitely were not candy-coated peanuts. Nearly everyone has heard the grammar-school joke about rabbit droppings being smart pills. Well, I was smarter after that incident, and I can truthfully say I now know what pronghorn pills taste like—a blend of sage and alfalfa.

* * *

I had never seen so many antelopes in a single day as I did on my first hunt in Wyoming. I remember trying to approach on foot a herd of at least two hundred animals. It was a waste of time, of course. With that many sharp eyes watching me in that wide-open terrain, there was no way I could get within five hundred yards of the herd. I did manage to shoot a lone animal with good horns by around 9 A.M., though. It was standing about two hundred and fifty yards away when my first shot dropped it.[2]

As soon as my animal was in the truck, we drove to a camp alongside a little stream and met Alex, who had killed a buck. Larry and his friends were there also. Tom Bandy, a longtime One Shot Hunt supporter, was hosting his annual brunch featuring sage grouse baked in Dutch ovens. There must have been thirty or forty people there, and I was introduced to each of them. They made me feel as if I'd known them for years. I had met Wyoming cattle buyer Jack Brody in Tucson, and now I met his family, as well as many other people I would come to know well. Among them were Larry's wife, Jane; her daughter Gail; and Gail's husband, Dick Remaly. There also were country-western singer Hank Thompson and his wife, Ann, and auctioneer and rodeo announcer TV Jones.

I had no idea Larry and his friends were watching me as a potential candidate for a One Shot participant, but I must have passed the test because Larry invited me to put together a three-person team of outdoor writers and send a challenge to Wyoming Governor Ed Hirschler the next year. As a mere newspaper outdoor editor, I wasn't much of a celebrity outside Arizona, so Boris, with the help of his friend, gunwriter Gary Sitton, hooked me up with *Petersen's Hunting* magazine editor Craig Boddington and *Field & Stream* magazine editor Dave Petzal. The three of us comprised the 1982 Outdoor Writers Team.

Each team member was assigned to a "greeter," whose job was to see that his shooter showed up for all the events. My greeter was Bill Gustin, a local Realtor and a tall, good-natured fellow. Bill drove me to the motel where team members were staying and introduced me to my teammates, who had arrived before me. Although I'd talked with them on the telephone, this was our first face-to-face meeting. I also met some of the other competitors. I already knew Bob Jantzen, who

---

[2]You can forget what you've read and heard about having to shoot pronghorn antelope at extremely long distances. I must have killed more than a dozen over the years I hunted them in Wyoming and Arizona, but this was my longest shot. Most of them were much closer.

had been director of the Arizona Game and Fish Department before he was appointed the Reagan administration's director of the U.S. Fish and Wildlife Service. He was competing on the "Interior Department Team" with his boss, Secretary of Interior James Watt.

Members of the various teams spend a lot of time together during the week of their initiation, and I found Watt was not the crazed anti-environment fanatic that media were portraying him to be. He was a lightning rod for the Reagan administration, so his participation in the One Shot Hunt drew print and broadcast reporters from all over the country. One of them gave Watt a baseball cap bearing the dried skull of a rattlesnake, fangs and all. He wore it for a while, until someone reminded him that all the venom might not have been removed when the little skull was cleaned.

The One Shot Hunt competition consists of eight three-man teams. When hunting, each shooter is accompanied by a member of another team, as well as a driver, a guide, and a scorekeeper, who uses a stopwatch to record the official shooting times. Wyoming Governor Ed Hirschler was my opponent; our guide was the county sheriff, a man named Pee Wee. I've forgotten the names of the driver and scorekeeper, but Bill Sniffen, the editor of Lander's only newspaper, was along to report on Hirschler's hunt.

We began by driving in two pickup trucks about three or four miles past a dying uranium-mining town and stopping at the edge of a gravel road while it still was dark. Pee Wee said he already had flipped a coin and the governor had won the right to shoot first. (I didn't say anything, but I suspected the governor always won the toss.) I would follow in the second truck. My time would begin the instant the governor fired his rifle. I could not shoot without my guide, Pee Wee, so I would have to leave my truck and jump into his vehicle. Before we started, though, I had to promise Pee Wee that I would never tell anyone where we were hunting. There was a reason for this, I soon learned. There were antelopes everywhere in Pee Wee's secret spot. I suppose we must have seen five hundred or more during the forty-five minutes we were there.

At exactly a half-hour before official sunrise, our two trucks drove off the gravel road and followed a two-track trail through the sagebrush into the hunting area, with my truck staying about a quarter-mile behind the governor's. Hirschler got out a couple of times and aimed at various antelopes with the commemorative Winchester carbine someone had given him, but he didn't shoot, for one reason or another. Finally, about thirty minutes and six or seven antelopes later, he shot a buck with one shot about fifty yards from his truck. My driver roared up to Pee Wee's truck and slammed on the brakes, enveloping us in dust. Before we were completely stopped, I was out the door with my rifle, and I jumped into the sheriff's truck. Pee Wee drove as if his truck were an Indy 500 race car and caught up with the herd as it came around the side of a small hill.

"Can you shoot from here?" he asked, as the confused animals milled around after seeing us again.

I didn't bother to reply. I leaped out, quickly found a spot to sit down, and dropped the herd's largest buck with the first shot from my .257 Roberts. The scorekeeper recorded my official time as a bit over four minutes. This was not a trophy hunt, and I had not taken a trophy buck I would have looked for under other circumstances, but I had done what I'd set out to do: I'd taken a pronghorn with one shot.

Hirschler was an experienced politician, so he had our drivers take us where James Watt was hunting. I posed for a photo with the secretary of the interior and his antelope, which he also had killed with one shot, and then everyone headed back to Lander in a four-vehicle caravan. Hirschler, Watt, another shooter, and I rode in a Chevrolet Suburban at the front. We stopped at every ranch house along the way for Hirschler to get out and talk with constituents. Inevitably, he'd drag them to our vehicle to introduce them to Watt, a fellow Wyomingite and a popular figure in that state. The problem was, Watt was a Republican and Hirschler was a Democrat. I could sense that Watt was uncomfortable about being forced to help Hirschler campaign.

Back in Lander, I learned that Boddington and Petzel also had killed their bucks with one shot each. Our aggregate team time for three one-shot kills was a record twenty-six minutes. At the Saturday evening victory banquet, Boddington explained that as outdoor writers we could do no less. Anyone who read what we wrote knew we never missed, he told the audience.

* * *

As a result of the friendships made in Lander, Alex Jacome, Larry Hughes, Whitey Devries, Boris Baird, Doug Campbell, my son-in-law Robbie Greene, and I hosted what we called the Arizona Pig and Quail Hunt in Tucson each January for several years. This was before there were drawings to issue tags to hunt Arizona's javelina, so our guests who wanted to hunt them during the month-long archery season bought their licenses at a sporting-goods store. Country-western singer Hank Thompson and astronauts Wally Schirra and Ron Evans were among the celebrities who attended our hunts.

We used Whitey's motor home for our base camp when we hunted. We had three dinners. The first featured pit-barbecued javelina and was held at our home. The second was a Mexican-style buffet hosted by Alex and Suzie Jacome. The victory dinners were held at various restaurants. We had great times during those hunts, but we discontinued them when Arizona stopped selling javelina licenses over the counter.

One of the things I remember from our pig and quail hunts was the time Ron Evans and I were alone in my truck, driving up a steep two-track trail after a morning of quail hunting. It was one of those clear Arizona blue-sky days when the full moon can be seen in the middle of the day. I was about to comment about how big the moon seemed when Ron suddenly said, "You know, every time I see it I have a hard time believing I've been up there."

Ron was always great company, and until that moment I'd forgotten he was the command-module pilot for Apollo 17 on NASA's final manned mission to the moon. Wally Schirra was a high-profile extrovert who was always swapping jokes and going into his "José Jiménez" mode, and those qualities, as well as being one of the seven Mercury astronauts featured in the book and movie *The Right Stuff,* had made him a household name. But Ron held the record for the most time in lunar orbit and had logged a record 301 hours, 50 minutes in space.

Whenever Ron and I were together, however, our talks always were focused on hunting and our families. I wish now I'd encouraged that always-smiling guy to tell me more about his time with NASA. I was shocked, as was everyone who knew him, when he died of a heart attack at age fifty-seven in 1990.

✳ ✳ ✳

With sponsorship of Larry Hughes and Harold Mares, I moved through the chairs in the Past Shooters Club until I was elected its president in 1990, the fiftieth anniversary of the One Shot Hunt. The club had been holding its annual banquets at the Elks Club, Lander's largest facility for such events; but it was small, and its kitchen was inadequate for the number of people who turned out for our banquets. My predecessors had investigated several other sites but found nothing better, so we set out to help the town expand the Elks Club site. Dick Remaly led a fund-raising campaign that asked past shooters for cash donations, while Eric Sparks sought items for our auction. Between them they raised more than the amount needed for the project, and it was completed in time for that year's One Shot. Soon after that, Lander's officials obtained the site and declared it the city's community center.

I returned to Lander many times after that, and shot an antelope on all except the three trips on which I opted to give up my tag and guide my friends Fritz Selby and Paul Casey and a friend of a friend from South Africa. I've lost count of how many Wyoming antelopes I killed, but I do remember the last two bucks I took there.

Eric Sparks and I were in two rented vehicles and decided to drive in different directions on opening morning. Eric's vehicle was still in sight when I came upon a herd of ten or twelve antelopes running flat out across the two-track road about one hundred and fifty yards in front of me. I jumped out of my truck and, without thinking, found the running buck in my scope, pulled the cross hairs at least twenty feet in front of the animal, and shot it through both shoulders. At the time I didn't know whether I'd hit it or not because the recoil had caused me to lose sight of it. I watched the herd run up a hill at least six hundred yards away and stop to look back at me. A check with my binocular showed every animal in the group was a doe, which meant the buck had to be down somewhere between them and me. A few minutes later, I found a spot of white in the sagebrush and walked over to a very dead pronghorn.

I had pulled off my greatest-ever shot at a running big-game animal, and there was no one there to see it!

The Past Shooters Club holds a contest for its members during the hunt, with points awarded according to the size of their antelopes' horns and the time they register their bucks in town. Mine was a good buck, and I was the second member to check in. Someone else shot a larger buck and won the trophy, though.

My last Wyoming antelope was taken in a unit I hadn't seen until that year. I'd been staying alone in our cabin in Arizona's White Mountains while Jean was in Tucson when I realized it was only a week before the third Saturday in October, the annual opening of Wyoming's antelope-hunting season. It took me two days to drive to Lander, but I arrived in time for a Past Shooters past-presidents' meeting on Wednesday. As I've already mentioned, of the seventy-five licenses set aside for the One Shot Hunt, twenty-four are issued to that year's team members, leaving fifty-one licenses for past shooters and their guests.

Larry Hughes said there was a time when there were fewer would-be hunters than licenses, and, as the hunt's ramrod, he'd have to find people to buy them. By the time I became involved in the club, there were more people who wanted to hunt than there were licenses available. To issue the licenses equitably, a system evolved, and it worked this way. Past shooters who applied for licenses and had proof they had been rejected had priority over past shooters who merely showed up. Third in line were guests of past shooters. I fit into the second group and didn't know when I left Arizona whether I'd get to hunt or not. I was lucky, though, and was issued a license.

The problem was, my license was for an area I'd never seen, and the hunt began the next day. As soon as I had my tag in my hand, I headed for the unit and tried to locate the biggest concentration of antelopes. I drove around until it was too dark to see, and the only wild creature I found was a coyote. I couldn't believe this was Wyoming!

The next morning I left the pre-hunt breakfast not knowing where I was going. On the way to the unit I decided to follow the same route I'd taken the previous day because I now knew the roads. I told myself there was no way I could spend two days in Wyoming's antelope country and not see a buck. By 9 A.M., after three hours of driving and glassing without seeing an animal other than cattle, I was thoroughly disgusted and was driving back to town. It eventually dawned on me that the reason I hadn't seen other hunters was that the season had opened in that area a week earlier. I was almost to the highway when I stopped to glass an area where I hadn't driven, and I spotted an antelope running back and forth along a fence about a mile away, trying to find a place to crawl under the barbed wire. When I drove closer to get a better look, I could see that it was a buck with heavy horns. After parking my truck in a gully, I went after the buck. It still was trying to find a way under the fence when I crawled up to about a hundred yards of it. At my shot it whirled and ran fifty yards before going down.

I saw dozens of antelopes in my unit along the highway on the drive back to town. If I hadn't spent all my time in the center of the unit, I might have seen a lot more.

* * *

Many of the people I knew from the One Shot Hunt—Larry Hughes, Wally Schirra, Ron Evans, Hank Thompson, Don Taylor, Glenn Wadsworth, George Parker, Gary Sitton, Basil Bradbury, Bob Jantzen, Ed Hirschler, Roy Rogers, Harold Mares, Fred Huntington, Art Werner,

Don Nolde, Norm Christiansen, Bill Moon, and deputy Pee Wee—have died since my first trip to Wyoming more than a quarter-century ago. I cannot think of the One Shot without seeing their faces and thinking about the ceremonies in Lander, when cartridges fell to the floor as the names of the Past Shooters who died that year were called. May there be vast plains covered with herds of pronghorn in every direction and no shortage of flat-shooting rifles where they have gone.

A Big Moose and a Lot of Snow

Chapter 11

I had wanted to hunt a moose ever since I was old enough to buy a hunting license, but the opportunity didn't present itself until Rick Furniss invited me to hunt on his Yukon Outfitting concession near Hart Lake in Canada's Yukon Territory. I arrived in Whitehorse early on the first day of October 1988, one day after my fifty-second birthday, to find no one at the airport to meet me, though Rick had said someone would be there. I tried calling his office after I checked into a hotel but only reached his answering machine. In case Rick or one of his men showed up while I was gone, I left word at the hotel desk that I was going to walk around town.

This was during the off-season for tourists, so there was little traffic on the Alcan Highway or on Main Street. About half the people who arrived on the flight from Vancouver with me were carrying gun cases and sturdy duffels. Like me, they were clean-shaven and shiny, a vivid contrast to the bearded hunters who'd finished their hunts and were boarding the turnaround flight as I claimed my gear. Unlike towns in Texas and Wyoming, there were no banners above the street to welcome hunters, but there certainly should have been. This was where virtually all big-game hunts—no small industry there—began in Canada's Yukon Territory. Hunters from all over North America and Europe arrived in Whitehorse and flew off in bush planes that took them still farther north. They spent money while they laid over, too. Even at the 1988 exchange rate, meals and lodging were not cheap.

I eventually found myself standing next to weathered pilings that once had been a pier on the Yukon River, trying to imagine what it must have been like when thousands of Yukon Gold Rush "stampeders" passed this spot on their way to the gold fields around Dawson City, some five hundred miles away. For me, at least, the feeling of a boomtown still lingered in the community of seventeen thousand people. When I saw bearded trappers on the streets with backpacks and rifles slung over their shoulders, no one had to tell me that this was where adventures in one of North America's last remaining wilderness areas were launched.

My long walk also took me to a bank, where I got Canadian currency; to the Department of Renewable Wildlife Resources, where I bought hunting licenses for moose, wolf, and wolverine; and to the Hudson's Bay store. At a taxidermy shop I met a man who had driven his pickup truck and utility trailer all the way from Prescott and was returning to Arizona (a seven-day drive, he said) with the frozen moose meat he and another hunter had taken with another outfitter. For dinner I ordered halibut steak. The waiter said it had been caught the previous day off the coast of Alaska and flown to Whitehorse overnight. I cannot describe how delicious this fish can be when it hasn't been frozen.

I had arrived two days early to have time to shop for the cold-weather clothing I couldn't find in Tucson and make certain my baggage and rifle caught up with me, so I spent the next day reading a book, waiting for someone to call me at the hotel. On the morning I was scheduled to leave for Rick's hunting camp, I still hadn't heard from him, but there were piles of hunters' gear stacked in the hotel's lobby when I went for an early breakfast. The deserted coffee shop was supposed to be open, and after waiting ten minutes, I walked into the kitchen and found the waitress sitting on the cook's lap! It was 6:45 A.M.

I'd planned a leisurely breakfast, but it (after the red-faced young woman finally brought it) was interrupted by the taxidermist I'd seen my first day in town. Although he hadn't told me this when I'd met him, I was scheduled to leave for Rick's camp in just a few minutes with several other hunters. It was embarrassing that they had to wait for me to change into warmer clothing, repack my duffel bag, put my rifle in a soft case, pay the hotel, and arrange to have my street clothes, suitcase, and hard rifle case put in storage until I returned.

The taxidermist explained that he was an expediter for Rick and other outfitters who had camps scattered across the Yukon, northern British Columbia, and the Northwest Territories. The outfitters and their guides trailed strings of horses to their hunting concessions and built their camps in July and August. They did not come out until the end of the season in mid-October, so the taxidermist communicated with them via notes transported by bush pilots.

I was surprised when the taxidermist drove past the airport because I assumed that we'd fly to camp on a plane with wheels. Instead, he took a turnoff that led to the river and drove up to a dock where an ancient, twin-engine de Havilland Beaver with floats was tied. I was more careful than usual when loading my gear and climbing into that airplane. Everything, including the floats I had to step on to reach the plane's door, was covered with ice, and, although I can swim, I suspected that hypothermia could make falling into the river fatal, even with the brand-new Hudson's Bay wool pants and shirt I was wearing.

The pilot wanted to distribute the weight, so I got a front seat next to him. The others on this flight—a Frenchman and a man from Florida—were smaller than I was. It was one time I felt fortunate to be larger than most men. They would get their first views of the Yukon's spectacular wilderness from the tiny windows in the back, while I would see the show from a picture window. The takeoff, my first from water, was beautiful, much like putting a powerboat up on plane and then leaping gracefully into the air.

Our flight took us over the Ruby Range, a series of low but steep mountains known for Dall and so-called Fannin sheep. I watched out the window, trying to find a sheep, but I saw none. I did see my first grizzly bear, though. About forty-five minutes after leaving Whitehorse, the pilot circled a lake, landed on the water, drove up to a short pier, and cut the plane's engine. There were tents near the water, and on a tall pole flew the red maple-leaf flag of Canada. The place was surrounded by snow-covered peaks. I'd always thought Lake Tahoe near Reno and the Grand Teton range near Jackson Hole were North America's most beautiful spots, but it was only because I had never been this far north. The scenery was awesome. I had started to reach for my gear when the pilot stopped me. The other hunters were getting off there, he said. My destination was a camp at a higher elevation a short hop away.

It was noon by the time we reached Hart Lake to find the surface of the lake frozen. Believing it couldn't be too thick, the pilot tried bouncing the plane's floats on the ice to break it up. Failing that, he headed south again. I cannot describe how disappointed I was. The plane was noisy, but I was able to hear the pilot talking with Rick on the radio. Rick would fly me to the camp in his Super Cub, the pilot said.

Sure enough, Rick and two men I'd seen at the hotel were waiting for me when we returned to the pier in Whitehorse. One was a giant of a man who must have weighed more than three hundred and fifty pounds. He towered over me. Rick apologized for not letting me know about the taxidermist, but he had been having problems ferrying hunters and supplying his camps. He said we'd be able to land at his camp on his Super Cub's fat tires. I had flown in several types of single-engine aircraft, but I had never seen a Super Cub until the four of us drove up to an unpainted barn covered with gray, weathered wood. Inside was a little airplane that looked as ancient as the barn. Honest to gosh, its skin and the plastic windows were patched with duct tape. There was no airstrip that I could see, and I wondered how Rick was going to fit all of us inside his tiny plane, to say nothing about getting that plane up in the air. Rick didn't seem concerned. We would be ferried to camp in three trips, he said.

We rolled the plane out of the barn, and the big man, a contractor from upstate New York named Frank Kineke, climbed inside, sat on his bag, and gripped a strut above him as Rick started the engine. The takeoff took fewer than forty or fifty yards. The other hunter, Tom Pettiette, and I read paperbacks during the hour or so before Rick returned and landed in a space less than half the length of a football field. Tom climbed inside, and I watched him and Rick fly away. When Rick returned, he said it was too late to fly to my camp, so we would fly to Mayo, an Indian village with a small motel, where we spent the night.

We were airborne again the next morning after eating breakfast in Mayo's old-fashioned diner. There was open water on Hart Lake this time, but Rick landed on a small area that had been cleared of brush. At this camp there were three plywood shacks, as well as another flagpole with the Canadian flag. Waiting for us were Rick's wife, Nancy, and their two young children; Kineke and Pettiette; a hunter who was scheduled to fly back to Whitehorse with Rick the next day; and two guides. The hunter said he'd spent eight days there and hadn't seen a moose larger than one he'd taken on a previous trip. After lunch, he and a guide named Bill rode out to take another look at one of the bulls he'd passed up. They returned after dark, and Bill reported that the bull, although a good one, wasn't what the hunter wanted.

I was impressed with Rick and Nancy's camp. The three small cabins (each perhaps fourteen feet wide by eighteen feet long) were made of two-by-two and two-by-four lumber and quarter-inch-thick sheets of plywood. The cabin for hunters and guides had platforms with foam pads for beds built along the walls, and there was a small wood-burning stove in a corner. Another cabin served as the dining room and kitchen, and had bunks in the space above the table for Nancy, two-year-old Allison, and five-year-old Jamie. The third cabin was used for storing an assortment of things, such as saddles, tack, grain, our food supplies, and chain saws for cutting firewood. There also was a large tent (I never looked inside to see what it contained) and a corral.

Everything had been flown to the lake in a Beaver and Rick's little plane, which was the reason for using scaled-down materials. Although the cabins were not insulated, the little stoves and all those human bodies in the small spaces kept us warm enough—until we went to sleep and the fire in our stove burned down, that is. After I found my boots frozen to the floor in the middle of the night, I kept a small log under my bed to break the boots loose. Rick had ingeniously fitted the seat in the camp's outhouse with a four-inch-thick piece of Styrofoam. Even though the place wasn't heated, the seat never got cold.

About an hour before daylight, we were called to breakfast. The super-cold air hit me as soon as I stepped out the door, even though I was wearing long underwear, wool pants and two wool shirts, a down jacket, two pairs of wool socks, and fleece-lined, rubber-bottom boots, all purchased at the Hudson's Bay store. I had also brought along a lightweight plastic poncho I'd packed with my gear on a dozen trips and had never needed. When Rick saw it, he immediately deemed it worthless and loaned me a heavy rainproof coat with a hood. Rain and snow were forecast all week, he said. I would have been in terrible trouble without Rick's coat.

There were eight men, a woman, and the two children in the dining cabin that morning, which meant there was barely enough room to turn around. Nancy had been up long before us and prepared eggs that Rick had brought with him, moose steaks, and homemade bread and butter. (I was so impressed with the bread that I took her recipe home and tried making it myself. My bread was not as good as hers.) One of the guides had eaten first and left to find our horses. The camp had a small corral, but the horses were fed only a small portion of oats and then were hobbled and allowed to find their own grass and scrub willow around the camp each night. It was too expensive to fly in enough hay to feed a dozen horses.

My first thought when the guide returned leading six horses was that they were better suited for pulling beer wagons. Their hoofs were as large as dinner plates. I asked him which was my horse, and he pointed to one that was larger than the others.

"Is there a ladder I can use to climb aboard?" I asked, only half-joking. I'm tall, but I had to stand on my toes to see over the back of that horse. I'd never ridden a horse as large as those in Rick's camp. Someone said they were Morgans.

For some reason the guides would not allow me to saddle my own mount. I tried to explain that I owned two horses and a mule and knew how to saddle them.

"That's what we get paid for," one of them said.

I couldn't argue with that.

Pettiette and the guide named Bill rode off to a spike camp fifteen miles away, while Kineke and his guide Sonny, my guide Peter Zidek, and I rode off in another direction. I soon learned why Rick used big horses. Their big feet and sturdy limbs were exactly what were needed when crossing patches of spongy tundra. Until then, I didn't know that this pillowlike vegetation grew in clumps surrounded by ice, water, and mud. A smaller horse might have broken a leg, but these animals were raised in muskeg and knew how to place their big feet properly. Even so, I was ready to jump off if my horse slipped or sank into the mud.

The four of us followed a trail for at least five miles until we came to a river, where Frank and Sonny left us to try to find the bull the hunter had passed up the previous day. Peter wanted us to check the remains of a moose a client had killed a week earlier. He and his hunter had boned the carcass, but there would be enough meat and offal left to attract wolves, he said. We were approaching the site when Peter pointed to several ravens perched on a tree on the ridge above us.

"The wolves are there," he said. "The moose is right below the birds, but they won't go near it when the wolves are there."

I suspected that was the case when I first saw the ravens. In Africa, seeing vultures in trees usually means there are lion on a kill under them.

Peter and I got off our horses, tied them up, and started walking to a knoll so we could glass the kill site. I'd walked perhaps fifty yards when he said I probably should take my rifle, just in case we jumped a good bull. I was halfway back to my horse when four moose—a bull, two cows, and a calf—jumped out of their beds and stopped to watch me. I moved as slowly as I could to my horse and was easing my rifle out of its scabbard when the four animals spooked and went crashing through the brush. I jerked the rifle to my shoulder and was ready to shoot the bull as it ran away when Peter stopped me.

"Wait! We can do better than that," he said. "There are bigger bulls here."

I watched the moose run across a wide valley and up a steep ridge before stopping. The only moose I'd seen before that day were of the Shiras race—the smallest of all the world's moose—in Yellowstone National Park and near Lander, Wyoming. I couldn't believe how large my first-ever Alaska-Yukon bull moose was. Its antlers seemed huge. I was impressed with its color, too. I would never use the word "beautiful" to describe a Shiras moose. They always seemed to me to be only one color—black. The coat on this bull was several gorgeous shades of brown, and it had a light-colored "saddle" on its back. Only its legs and belly were black.

I hated to let that bull get away, but I listened to my guide. If he said there were larger bulls around, I had to believe him. I shouldered my rife, a .30-06 Model 70 Winchester with a 3-9X Leupold scope, and followed Peter to the knoll. Wolves had found the kill. There were three of them, and one was a glossy black. Peter and I carefully moved within three hundred yards before I sat down and snuggled my elbows inside my knees, found the black wolf in my scope, and missed! The little pack was gone in an instant.

Those three animals were the only wolves we saw in the nine days I hunted there. We saw no wolverines, either, but we did see Dall sheep, and there were huge flocks of ptarmigan everywhere. The ptarmigan already were in full winter plumage, and it hadn't snowed yet. We could see their conspicuous white shapes from a mile away with our binoculars.

The next morning Frank and Sonny left us and rode to a spike camp twenty miles away. Peter and I went looking for the moose the earlier hunter had passed up. We didn't find it, but we did find a herd of four or five bulls, and one was considerably larger than the others. The only problem was, it had only one antler.

Peter had immigrated to Canada from Poland, where he had worked as a gamekeeper.

"In my country that's a fine trophy," he said. "We like nontypicals and freaks."

Maybe so, but I didn't want to shoot a moose with just one antler. The more I watched it, and the more Peter urged me to shoot it, the more I was tempted. I finally decided that a taxidermist wouldn't be able to find a mate for the single antler that bull was wearing.

Nature called in the middle of that night, so I slipped into my boots and pants, pulled on a coat, and stepped outside. It was snowing heavily, and I'd left my little flashlight under my bed. I found my way to the outhouse, but getting back to the cabin wasn't easy. Snow already had covered my tracks while I was occupied, and it was so dark I couldn't see the cabin fifty yards away. I'm here today because I headed in the right direction and found the cabin that night.

There were more than eight inches of snow on the ground when Peter returned from walking a mile in the dark to where the horses were feeding (he still wouldn't allow me to saddle my horse), and we rode off to a group of hills we hadn't hunted yet. To get there we had to cross the upper end of a beaver pond. I watched Peter's horse slip and fall when it tried to jump onto the bank at the only place we could cross. Fortunately, Peter saw the wreck coming and jumped onto the bank. I was ready when my horse approached the same spot, and I stayed on when it lunged out of the water, so we got onto dry land without any problems.

I wasn't ready for what happened next, however. Just minutes later, a small bull moose suddenly ran out of the willows and stuck its nose in my horse's rump! I surprised myself by staying in the saddle while my horse bucked and ran to higher ground. The moose was still standing there when we rode off. Later, I was too busy congratulating myself on my equestrian skills to pay attention when my horse stumbled on a downed tree buried in a pile of loose snow, and I fell off. I might have been hurt if I'd fallen off that tall horse anywhere else, but I landed on a pillow of fir limbs covered with snow. I climbed back on the horse, grateful that Peter hadn't seen me get dumped.

A couple of things happened after that first snowfall. For one, the snow made white ptarmigan tough to see, and the birds stayed hidden until our horses almost stepped on them. Then they'd explode noisily out of the snow and startle our horses and us. For another, the snow must have done something to the moose to send them into hiding. We saw only a few cows during the next couple of days. We did see two grizzly bears and a herd of Dall sheep. We spotted the bears on a hillside across a wide valley during one of the many times we stopped to glass for moose. We rode up on the same herd of sheep two days in a row. As with our desert sheep, these were not the smartest of animals. One ram ran up to us and stopped when it was only spitting distance away, just to get a better look at us. And, finally, that first snow brought winter to Hart Lake. It snowed off and on during the day, and then it snowed all night.

Peter and I were awakened on my eighth night in camp when Frank and Sonny stomped into our little cabin.

"I got my moose!" Frank yelled.

He had killed it late that afternoon and had returned to the main camp because it was closer than the little tent they were using for their spike camp. Sonny kept an extra sleeping bag in the cabin, but Frank's only bed was a six-hour horseback ride away. He had no choice but to put on all of his clothes and try to sleep on a foam pad without blankets. He was up all night feeding the stove. I didn't need my little log that night.

Pettiette also had killed a moose, and he and his guide rode into camp early the next day. Nancy said she'd talked with Rick on the radio and learned the Beaver was on its way to fly them out. She told me that Rick would return two days later to get me. My hunt was winding down, and the bull we'd seen that first day was growing larger in my mind. Peter and I left camp after lunch.

Fortunately, my luck changed when we found a good bull in its bed at the head of a small canyon that afternoon. We tied up the horses and crawled in the snow over a crest within a hundred yards or so of the bull without it seeing us. I was on my belly, ready to shoot, when Peter whispered that he was going to whistle to get it to stand up. I said I wasn't going to wait. My first shot missed the bull's heart by a couple of inches; my second shot—fired when it tried to get up—struck a mere inch from the first, and the bull collapsed in its bed.

In Poland, Peter said, it was considered unsporting to shoot an animal in its bed, and I should have waited for the bull to get up. I told him American hunters had no such tradition. I'd hunted eight long days and waited all my life to shoot that moose, and I wasn't going to take any chance of losing it.

I knew moose were big, but I wasn't prepared for the size of a really big moose when I walked up to mine. Its antlers were five feet wide and, with its head, were so heavy that Peter and I couldn't move them for a good photo. We had to photograph the animal as it fell.

Before leaving the site, we took time to prepare things so Peter and Sonny could pack out the meat, antlers, and cape the next day. I was surprised that Peter didn't gut the animal. Instead, he slit the hide along the backbone and removed the backstraps, then cut off the hindquarters, leaving only the ribs, neck, backbone, and entrails. I was surprised at how little meat was left on the carcass. There were no trees to hang anything from, so we piled the quarters and the cape and head on top of the highest brush to make it harder for wolves to get to them, and then rode back to camp. We had worked two hours on that moose, and before we left the carcass, the floatplane flew over us, heading back to Whitehorse. Kineke and Pettiette could have seen us if they'd been looking out the window.

Expecting to start my trip back to Tucson the next morning, I packed my gear before going to bed that night. We woke up to find fog so thick the other two cabins and corrals were only indistinguishable shapes. There was no way anyone could fly in that weather without instruments and help from a control tower, and there was neither in Rick's little plane nor at Hart Lake. Sonny and Peter somehow managed to ride out in that soup and find my moose and bring it back.

With Rick's last hunt over, Bill and Sonny gathered up the horses, packed their camping gear and food, and started out leading the horses—eighteen of them in a string, tied nose to tail. According to Peter, it would take them a week to reach the end of the road near a town 120 miles away, where trucks and trailers were waiting for them. Along the way they would camp for the night in the snow wherever sundown found them.

Peter, Nancy, Nancy's children, and I waited eight more days for Rick to return. We tried playing cards; I read all of my paperbacks and all of those left behind by others; and I smoked all of my cigarettes, then smoked every butt in the ashtrays. Sonny had left a package of cigarette papers behind, so I went looking for a tobacco substitute. Coffee burned, but it kept falling out of the paper. Tea leaves were better, but not much. I had to keep relighting them.

I should have enjoyed a week of doing nothing while waiting for the weather to clear, but I was worried about my work back in Tucson. A *Safari* magazine deadline was approaching, and someone else would have to put together an outdoors page at the *Tucson Citizen* for the first time since I'd started working there twenty years earlier. My craving for a cigarette made me incredibly nervous. It would have been a good time for me to quit smoking, but I wasn't ready or smart enough for that. When Nancy reached Rick on a radio, I asked her to have him call Jean and let her know where I was—and bring me cigarettes when he finally was able to fly to our camp.

Being stuck in the middle of the Yukon provided an opportunity to learn more about Peter. Just five years earlier, when he was forty years old, he and his wife and their two children had fled from Poland into Hungary, then on to West Germany, and then to Ottawa, taking only what they were wearing and what they could carry. None of them spoke a word of English when they arrived in Canada, but all now spoke it fluently. Both Peter and his wife had been foresters in their homeland. They had left it because they disagreed with the Communist regime's conservation practices. He found guiding hunters for moose, Dall sheep, and caribou was a lot like hunting red deer, "elk" (moose), and roe deer in Europe. In his spare time he now made extra money by carving wildlife scenes on belt buckles and jewelry made from the antler burrs of caribou and moose. They were quite good.

I cannot describe how it felt when I awoke and saw a patch of blue sky on the eighteenth day after I'd left Whitehorse. I gathered my gear, and Peter and I climbed to the ridge that Rick used for an airstrip. He and I walked back and forth, stomping the snow to compact it for Rick's landing. We were watching when his little plane appeared from behind a cloud and came in for a landing. We also saw him use up our entire stamped-out runway and hit loose snow. The little plane's tail went up, and its nose and propeller went down, coming dangerously close to hitting the snow. I'd seen a plane crash on landing during a fishing trip at Punto Chivato in Baja California many years earlier and was relieved to see Rick and the plane were not hurt.

"I get terrified once a year, and that was it. I don't know if I'm going to be able to get us out of here," he said.

All I said was, "Hi, Rick. Did you bring my cigarettes?"

He not only had brought cigarettes, but he also had collected the things I'd stored at the hotel.

I puffed on the first cigarette so fast it quickly had a hot, inch-long, glowing red tip. We then loaded my bag and rifle, said good-bye to Peter and Nancy, took one last look at the antlers and meat of my moose, and flew off the ridge without any problems. After we were airborne, Rick said the snow had delayed Bill and Sonny, and he was going to drop groceries and cigarettes to them. Twenty minutes later, we found the two guides leading the horses through the bottom of a canyon covered with deep snow. There was no rear seat in Rick's plane, so I was sitting—without a seat belt—on my luggage, holding a bag of supplies for the guides, when Rick banked the plane. When we circled and were over the guides again, I forced the top half of the two-piece door partly open with my shoulder, held onto a strut with my left hand, and dropped the bag with my right. Words cannot describe how that sudden blast of freezing cold air felt.

Thirty minutes later, we were landing in Dawson City, where Rick had used his radio to ask the commercial flight to Vancouver to wait for us. My original ticket had expired, so I bought a one-way ticket to Vancouver. I hadn't bathed or shaved in fourteen days, a fact of which I'm sure the other passengers were well aware. We reached Vancouver late at night, and it must have been a long trip for them. I found a taxi and asked the driver to take me to the nearest hotel, which he did. It was an ultra-modern, posh place with lots of glass and marble in its lobby. The young Asian man at the desk took one look and a sniff at me and asked what I wanted. He must have thought I was a destitute, homeless beggar because he looked down his nose and said his rooms were v-e-r-y expensive. I handed him a credit card and said I didn't care what it cost.

The shower in my room felt so good that I spent a half-hour in it. The bed and its fresh-smelling sheets were so wonderful that I slept until noon before heading back to the airport, where I unsuccessfully tried to exchange my nonrefundable "super-saver" ticket for a flight to Tucson. (My travel agent got me a refund later.) I was home that same evening.

A couple of months later, Rick shipped the antlers and cape of my moose to my friend and taxidermist Nouri Tajbakhsh in San Antonio. The mounted head now hangs in our cabin, and every time I see it after being gone for a while I think of that long Yukon hunt.

Has Anyone Seen Our Caribou Guide?

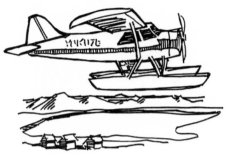

Chapter 12

My next trip to the far north came a couple of years after my Yukon moose hunt, when I hunted central Canada barren-ground caribou in what then was the Northwest Territories. The trip was arranged by Tudor Howard-Davies, whom I'd met in South Africa when he was editor of *Magnum* magazine. Tudor was working for Jerome and Halina Knap's Canada North Outfitting, and he set up two hunts for me before he was diagnosed with cancer and returned to his homeland to die. One was this hunt for caribou; the other was in New Zealand.

The flight from Tucson to Yellowknife seemed to take forever. I began by flying to Las Vegas, changing planes, and then flying nonstop to Edmonton, where I cleared Customs and was issued a permit for my .30-06. I then boarded a smaller plane that had been partitioned to separate passengers from the cargo packed into the front of the cabin. We were over Great Slave Lake, making our final approach for landing, as the sun was rising in the east. Counting layovers in Las Vegas and Edmonton and a brief stop in Calgary, I had been traveling more than twenty-four hours. I've flown from Tucson to Johannesburg in less time.

I was interested in seeing Great Slave Lake because I'd known an Arizona woman who owned fishing resorts on the Colorado River and at the lake. Her ads in outdoor magazines showed photos of anglers holding big striped bass caught in the river and lake trout taken from the lake in front of her resort in the Northwest Territories.

What I hadn't expected to see on the shore above the lake were the huge gold mines—eight separate open pits, four tailings ponds, and at least a hundred buildings—an ugly scar that spread over more than two thousand acres.

Tudor had said Bill Tate, the owner of Raven Outfitters, would meet me at the airport, but this was yet another example of things not happening as planned. I claimed my baggage and waited forty-five minutes, then took a taxi to the hotel where Tudor had reserved a room for me. I was almost asleep when Bill Tate called and apologized for missing me at the airport. Something had come up, he said. He was in the dining room downstairs. Did I want join him?

Bill Tate could joke about anything, which made him fun to be with. He introduced me to a California oil executive who would be the other half of my two-by-one (two hunters, one guide) caribou hunt. Bill and I were interested in the satellite photograph of our hunting area the oilman had brought. In Arizona, where there are no natural lakes, we call five-acre ponds "lakes," and that photograph showed more water than land.

"There are so many lakes up here that no one has ever tried counting them," Bill said. "I've thought about selling lake names like they do with stars."

After breakfast, Bill took us to a wildlife department office, where we bought our hunting licenses. The Californian and I each bought two caribou tags, as well as wolf and wolverine tags, just in case we encountered them. Bill then gave us a tour of Yellowknife's booming downtown area, where shoppers were going in and out of modern stores filled with merchandise. Even now, years later, I have never seen so many high-rise buildings under construction at the same time in one city as I saw that day. Bill said Asian investors had discovered Yellowknife and were buying everything in sight.

We met again early the next morning at a dock on the lake. The Californian and I would fly to the camp in an ancient floatplane carrying supplies and baggage. Two other clients and two guides would follow an hour later in a newer plane. Our plane was an Otter, and it was larger than the Beaver I'd used in the Yukon. Even so, there was very little room for the Californian and me. Every spare inch was occupied by a box or a bag of something needed at our camp.

As we lifted off, it occurred to me that the first pilot to take off his plane's wheels and attach floats must have been one gutsy guy. He didn't know for certain if the plane would get airborne, of course, but what really mattered was that he absolutely had no idea what might happen when he went to land it on the water. To pass the time on this flight, I pondered how elated he must have felt after making the first takeoff and landing in a floatplane. It must have been one of the important achievements in aviation, yet no pilot I've talked with since I returned from Canada knew who the first floatplane pilot was, nor did he have any idea where to go to find his name.

I had a better idea of the Northwest Territory's terrain after seeing the Californian's satellite photo, but I didn't realize just how flat the country would be until we flew north of Yellowknife. It reminded me of the American Midwest, except that there was more water than land. I was watching closely as the pilot circled Little Marten Lake, set the plane down on the water, and taxied up to a sandy beach. I'd seen dozens of caribou from the air within a mile of the group of tents that would be our camp for the next week.

It was drizzling when the Californian and I got out of the plane, and we helped the woman who was waiting for us—our cook—stow gear in one of the four wood-sided wall tents and the supplies in another. After the Otter flew away, we were alone in the middle of Canada with not another human besides the three of us within a hundred miles.

As promised, another floatplane taxied up to the beach ninety minutes later, and Bill Tate, a French couple, and two guides got out. One of the guides had been drinking in the back of the plane and had arrived falling-down drunk. He staggered and then announced, in slurred speech, that he was going to hunt the caribou he'd seen while they were landing. Wouldn't you know it? This drunk had been hired to guide the Californian and me.

"You can't hunt the same day you've been in the air," I reminded him. "It's against the law in Canada."

"Yes, I can. I'm an Indian, and I can do anything I want here."

I decided there was no use trying to tell him that he wasn't being paid to hunt. He was too drunk to care, and I had been around my father enough to know I'd get nowhere by arguing with a drunk.

The man, whose name was Charlie, was having trouble attaching a sling to his rifle, so I did it for him. Charlie wandered around a few minutes before throwing his rifle and a small backpack into one of the three long plywood boats Raven Outfitting had assembled at the site weeks before the caribou hunt started. It took him several more minutes to start the boat's outboard motor, but he eventually took off, heading across the lake.

It was the last we saw of Charlie.

Bill, the other guide, and the cook were getting gear and groceries in order while the French couple, the Californian, and I got settled into our two tents. I was expecting the same miserable weather I'd experienced in the Yukon and had bought a new down sleeping bag, warm clothes, and rain gear for this trip. But it was a month earlier and much warmer than when I'd last hunted in that province. It was now late August in the Northwest Territories, and I slept in my bag without zipping it up. The days were long; there still was daylight when everyone went to bed at 10 P.M. We had blue skies, gorgeous days, and cool but not cold nights the entire week. I woke in the middle of that first night and went outside wearing only long underwear and socks. I'd seen the Northern Lights in the Yukon, but the aurora borealis display that night rivaled the light show at Disneyland. It covered the entire night sky and bounced and changed colors every time I blinked. I made it a point to go out every night I was in that camp.

Charlie hadn't returned when we woke up, and he still was missing when the Californian and I finished breakfast and were ready to go hunting. I climbed an esker (a low ridge pushed up by glaciers during one of the ice ages) and spent a few minutes checking the lake with my binocular. A light-colored object on the shoreline about a mile away was a boat! Charlie must have spent the night there and still was sleeping off all the alcohol.

The French couple and their guide left in a boat to hunt farther up the lake while Bill, the Californian, and I took another boat and went looking for Charlie. I suspected something was wrong when we found his cap floating in the water about halfway across the lake. His boat was on its side on the beach and had at least a foot of water in it. Charlie's rifle and backpack still were stuffed under the seats. The only tracks in the sand had been made by caribou and not by a human or a bear. To make certain Charlie hadn't made it ashore, the three of us hiked in a big circle, hoping to find him or his tracks. We didn't. We did see a caribou calf with a broken leg, though. Bill said its mother had probably abandoned the injured animal and followed the herd, heading south. We were tempted to shoot the calf to keep it from being eaten alive by wolves, but it was illegal to do so. We reluctantly left it and walked back to the beach. We'd found no sign at all of Charlie.

The three of us poured the water out of Charlie's boat and got it floating again. Bill then drove it back to the camp, where he and the cook called the Royal Canadian Mounted Police on a radio to report that Charlie was missing and had probably drowned.

We had come north to hunt caribou, so that's what the Californian and I did. Walking in the muskeg wasn't too bad on higher ground, but the marshy areas were something else. We sank to our knees whenever we stepped into a muddy spot, so we avoided such places whenever we could. About a half-hour out of camp, we spotted a herd of at least fifty caribou feeding on an esker on the opposite side of one of the many small lakes. It took us almost an hour to work our way around the water and reach where we'd last seen the herd. We were fifty yards apart as we carefully advanced over the top of an esker and were ready to shoot when we came upon the animals in a depression on the other side. A few were bedded, but they all were on their feet the instant they saw us. I knew nothing about judging the antlers on caribou, especially when they're covered with velvet, as these were. One of the bulls seemed to have heavier antlers than the others, so I killed it. Unfortunately, I had spooked the herd before the Californian could shoot.

The caribou ran only a quarter of a mile before stopping on another esker to look back at us. I'd read in stories that they were curious to a fault, so I tried something. I raised my rifle over my head, holding it parallel to the ground with both hands, and began walking around, bending my body, hoping to look like a caribou with tall antlers. When the Californian saw the caribou were returning to get a closer look, he also tried to imitate a caribou. When they were about fifty yards out, he shot one of the bulls.

We were two air miles from camp but less than a quarter-mile from Little Marten Lake. We decided to gut, skin, and quarter our animals, then carry the pieces to the water, where we could retrieve them with a boat the next morning. It still was daylight when we reached the camp, but I was so pooped I went to bed without eating.

We were returning to camp with our two caribou in a boat the next morning when a single-engine Cessna with floats flew over us, then turned and circled above us before landing at our camp. The Royal Canadian Mounted Police were there to find out what had happened to Charlie.

"Are you aliens?" one of them asked, as we pulled the boat with our caribou onto the beach.

"No. We're Americans," I fired back. His pompous attitude had struck me wrong.

"You're not allowed to hunt without a guide," he said.

"We have a guide," I said. "It's your job to find him."

It was some time before things got better. There were three Mounties, and for a while they were playing good cop, bad cop. Everyone in camp was grilled before they were satisfied we hadn't murdered our guide and fed him to a bear or the fish. After that, their demeanor changed drastically. They now were friendly guys, eager to share our food and drink. I was interested in inspecting the bedrolls they rolled out on the ground a short distance from our tents. I'd never seen anything like them. They were eight inches thick and must have weighed at least twenty-five or thirty pounds each. Sleeping bags need to be thick in the winter in subarctic Canada, but these really were too warm now, they said.

The French couple killed two caribou that day, and the one taken by the woman was the largest in camp. That fact obviously wasn't taken well by the husband. They had shot two muskox farther north the week before, and hers would rank second or third in Safari Club International's record book. Both of them were shooting .375 H&H Magnum rifles. Although that's a time-tested caliber for Africa, and it can be quite useful in Alaska's brown-bear country, it isn't needed for muskox and is overkill for caribou. The husband missed his first caribou that day and couldn't believe it was his fault. He had no idea how to adjust a riflescope, so he asked me to check the rifle's zero. My first shot hit about an inch and a half high when I fired at a large black dot on a cardboard box I had set up about a hundred yards away. It would be close enough to kill a caribou out to two hundred or two hundred and fifty yards by holding on the middle of the animal, I said. The man still couldn't believe it wasn't his rifle's fault that he'd missed, so he had me punch two more holes in the box. The woman asked me to check her rifle, too, but was satisfied when my first shot went where it should.

The Californian and I spent the morning in camp, waiting for a guide Bill had arranged to be flown to our camp. To pass the time, I assembled a little four-piece fishing rod I'd brought and caught a five-pound lake trout on my first cast with a red-and-white metal spoon. I caught five or six more in the next fifteen minutes, and all of them were the same size. The cook prepared them that evening, and we shared them with the Mounties.

The supervisor of "our" Mounties arrived early the next morning, took one look at where his men were camped, and ordered them to move a quarter-mile away. They were not permitted to fraternize with "suspects," he said. He didn't mind them commandeering one of Bill's boats to drag the forty-mile-long lake with grappling hooks and an electronic fish-finder, however. They reported finding big schools of lake trout with the fish-finder, but they didn't find Charlie. They still were searching for him when we left for Yellowknife several days later.

Our new guide arrived in another plane an hour after the Mounties had begun their search. I was relieved to see he was sober. He told us later that he did not drink alcohol and was saving money to go south and attend a university. He was a nice enough young man, but he wanted the Californian and me to shoot every caribou we saw. He couldn't understand why we were interested in antlers.

"You can't eat them," he said.

I shot my second bull that morning. As with my first, it had a tall rack and double shovels. We were heading up the lake when we saw it feeding near the edge of the shore with a dozen other bulls. Our new guide shut down the outboard as soon as we spotted it. The bull I selected was about two hundred yards away, and to shoot from a rocking boat I wanted to get closer. It must have taken twenty minutes for a breeze to push us within fifty yards of the animal. There were three of us in an open boat with absolutely nothing to hide us from the caribou, but they paid no attention to our boat. They obviously were not looking for danger to approach them from the water. When we were close enough, I shot the bull, and it plunged into the lake, then turned around, climbed the bank, and ran a short distance before dropping in the tundra.

Our new guide took over after we photographed my caribou. He first removed its cape, head, and antlers, then skinned the rest of the animal. The back skin was laid out on the tundra and used for the meat that he expertly removed from the carcass. When only a skeleton and guts remained on the ground, he wrapped the meat in the back skin and tied it into a bundle that ingeniously used the hide skinned from the legs to make straps for a backpack. He then slipped his arms into the legs and placed a tumpline tied to the package on his head. He didn't stop until he reached the boat, even with more than a hundred pounds of meat on his back. I was impressed.

We were in camp, eating lunch, when the French couple arrived with their guide. The woman was excited, but not about both having taken their second caribou that day.

"They're coming," she said. "A hundred Indians."

There weren't that many, but there may have been forty or fifty of Charlie's friends heading our way. They'd heard the Mounties talking on the radio about the search for their friend. They had followed a series of waterways to get to Little Marten Lake in every type of small boat imaginable. They didn't bother to stop to talk to us, though. They pulled their boats onto the beach in an inlet across from us and began to party even before they'd set up their camp. They sang, drank, and played radios loudly most of the night.

As soon as it was light enough to see again, they declared war on every caribou within two miles. I stayed in camp with the French couple, and the Californian went out with our guide and shot a trophy bull at the far end of the lake. While he was gone, I made friends with the couple. Among other things, he was a member of the board of a European automaker, owned part of the company that farms salt in Scammon's Lagoon in Mexico's Baja California, and was the mayor of his town in France. He was so grateful when I helped him remove his tight boots and sighted-in his rifle that he promised to send me a case of champagne, which he did. It arrived at my office in Tucson the same day a letter from his wife reached me. A heart attack had killed him two days after he shipped the champagne.

The antlers of all of our caribou were in velvet, and I was interested in seeing how our guides would prepare them for shipping. They used knives to strip the hairy skin, tied ropes on the antlers, and tossed them into the lake. The cold water drew blood from "green" antlers and helped harden them, they said. It worked. Anyone who sees the bull I had mounted would never know its antlers were in velvet when I shot the animal. (I hung the antlers of my other bull outside on my cabin.)

On our last day in camp the Californian and I took a boat to the far end of the lake, where it drained through a series of waterfalls and rapids into another lake. We cast Mepps spinning lures and Z-Rays into the whitewater and allowed them to work through the rapids and into a big pool. We had strikes on nearly every cast. If an arctic grayling didn't grab our lures in the whitewater, a lake trout would strike them as soon as they washed into the pool. I've never experienced anything like it. It was exciting, but fishing really isn't my thing, and casting and pulling in fish every time soon grew boring. I sat down and watched the Californian until he, too, decided he'd had enough. We had kept a small bucket of fish for the camp. We'd also brought a piece of aluminum foil, which we used to wrap a lake trout and roast it over a small fire. There was no wood, so we burned the largest dried tundra stems we could find. I usually don't like eating fish with bones, but even without salt, pepper, or forks, that was among the best fish I've ever eaten.

✳ ✳ ✳

Bill Tate called me the next May. A group of his clients—the first to fish Little Marten Lake that spring—had found Charlie's body in the same rapids the Californian and I had fished.

"Were his pants unzipped?" I asked.

When I was a newspaper reporter, a member of a search-and-rescue team told me that a large percentage of the drowning victims he pulled out of lakes were found with their flies open. As Charlie may have done, they drank too much, stood up in the boat to urinate, and fell overboard. Their clothes and shoes hindered their swimming, and they either got tangled in moss and weeds or hypothermia got them. There were no weeds in Little Marten Lake, but the water was only a few degrees above freezing.

"I don't know about that," Bill said. "But I thought you'd want to know that his friends went back and built a monument for Charlie. It's on the inlet where you camped."

I would be willing to bet the plaque they placed on that monument doesn't mention the real reason Charlie drowned.

Africa! I Wanted to Pinch Myself

Chapter 13

My first-ever sightings of elephant spoor included round, dusty prints the size of the lids of small garbage cans, spaced five feet apart, and piles of alfalfa-colored dung as large as basketballs. These were scattered across the two-lane tarmac road that led to a hunting concession an hour's drive from Victoria Falls. I wanted to pinch myself. I was in Africa!

Just before turning onto a dirt road, Stephanus "Fanie" Pretorius, the outfitter for my first African safari, stopped the Land Rover so that his wife, Joyce, and I could watch a herd of sable antelope in the thick brush a few yards off the road. The young bulls stared at us and allowed me to take several photographs. Fanie and Joyce must have seen thousands of sable antelope during their lifetimes along the Zambezi River, but I was thrilled. I took it as a sign that the first herd of antelope I encountered in Africa would be the most beautiful animals on the continent.

We went through a wire gate across the graded road and drove up on a group of Africans who were repairing a culvert. One of the four workers was armed with an AK-47 automatic rifle, which Pretorius said the men carried at all times because of the possibility of encountering dangerous game. Even a greenhorn visitor knew that an automatic rifle and military ammunition were not appropriate if an inexperienced shooter had to stop a charging elephant or buffalo, nor would this firearm be likely to make a hungry lion immediately change its plans for dinner.

Zimbabwe's revolution against white rule had ended just twenty-eight months earlier, and the African majority now controlled the country. The end of colonialism had not brought good things, however. News reports in South Africa in 1983 told of unspeakable atrocities by government troops in Matabeleland. As had happened after America's Civil War, a few scattered groups of guerrillas had become outlaws. The similarity ended there. In Zimbabwe they were using tactics and weapons given to them by North Koreans, Chinese, and Cubans before the collapse of Ian Smith's Rhodesia in 1980.

We waited while Pretorius spoke with one of the men in his language. When he returned, we learned that a half-hour earlier a cow elephant with an injured foot had walked across the road exactly where we were parked. This was the Africa I had read about and dreamed about. I always knew that I would see and experience it one day. Here it was, finally, just as I had imagined.

I was in Zimbabwe thanks to C. J. McElroy, the founder of Safari Club International, and SATOUR, the South African Tourism Department. When I took over *Safari* magazine a few months before this trip, Mac said I needed to get to Africa so I would understand what the club's members and the magazine's authors were writing about. He first arranged for me to hunt an elephant and a bongo in Zaire (now the Democratic Republic of Congo) with a safari company managed by Adelino Serras Pires, whom I later would come to know very well. The U.S. State Department and the Centers for Disease Control in Atlanta both suggested that travelers visiting Zaire undergo an assortment of inoculations. I had taken all the shots and was packed and ready to leave the next morning when I received a telegram from Brussels warning me not to leave home. The government of Zaire had suddenly banned all hunting, it said.

Mac, who often said he envied no one except someone on his first African hunting safari, then arranged a week-long hunt for me with Pretorius's company in the Matetsi region of southwestern Zimbabwe. At the same time, SATOUR was inviting journalists on two-week junkets to South Africa, all expenses paid, including first-class airfare.

My first safari cost me the price of a room at the Victoria Falls Hotel for two nights and the government trophy fees for the animals I shot.[1]

So in June 1983 I flew from Tucson to New York and then on to Johannesburg on South African Airways. I was so excited that I stayed awake during the nineteen-hour flight from New York. I was thrilled when I finally saw the narrow strip of beach on the coast of what then was called South-West Africa (now Namibia) below me. I felt what an Olympic medal–winner must feel when standing on a platform while his or her national anthem is played. I had reached my lifelong goal. I had arrived!

When we landed at Jan Smuts International Airport, I had no trouble clearing my two rifles—a .458 Winchester Magnum and a .30-06, both super-grade Winchester Model 70s. I had bought them especially for my first safari. The people at SATOUR had said that I should take a taxi to the Carlton Centre Hotel in downtown Johannesburg, where a room was waiting for me. During the drive to the city, the taxi driver, a black woman, asked if I'd like to see Soweto. When I said I was tired after traveling halfway around the world and wanted to take a shower and get some sleep, she told me all her fares from America wanted to see Soweto.

Under apartheid, Soweto was where black citizens who worked in Johannesburg were forced to live. U.S. media portrayed it as an awful place. That was not entirely accurate. True, much of the town consisted of brown shacks thrown together with scavenged cardboard and sheet metal. But there also were large, freshly painted, modern homes with manicured gardens. I was told on another trip that the largest and best-maintained home in Soweto belonged to Winnie Mandela, wife of Nelson Mandela, who would become South Africa's first democratically elected president in 1994. In 1983 Mandela still was imprisoned on Robben Island, after being sentenced to life imprisonment as a terrorist in 1964.

---

[1] The receipts I kept show I paid trophy fees totaling $1,100 for a buffalo, sable, and kudu in Zimbabwe and a gemsbok and springbok in South Africa on this trip. As I write this in 2008, the trophy fees for the same five animals would exceed $10,000.

The Carlton Centre was a modern high rise. Out the window were tall buildings rising twenty or more stories. Below the hotel was a three-level underground shopping mall with dozens of shops. Outside and down the street was a world-famous store called Safrique. It carried every imaginable item needed for a safari—from gasoline lanterns to canvas bathtubs to bush clothes. After a shower and an hour's nap, I walked to the store (downtown Johannesburg still was safe in those days) and bought Jean khaki culottes with a matching blouse straight out of the film *The Snows of Kilimanjaro.*

I flew on to Bulawayo the next morning and, while I waited in its airport for my flight to Victoria Falls, sat with Cuban soldiers injured in the war then under way in Angola. Parked outside was a Soviet military aircraft that was as large as a Boeing 747.

Fanie and Joyce Pretorius met my flight and drove me to the historic Victoria Falls Hotel, a stuffy colonial institution where each staff member wore a white jacket and a red fez. We had lunch outside under a huge tree and watched monkeys scamper through the branches above us. When Fanie and Joyce left me, I walked to the falls on a trail that led through a rain forest and past a statue of Dr. David Livingstone, the explorer said to be the first European to see the falls. There were only a few people on the path that runs along the canyon, and I walked slowly, enjoying every inch of the short hike. Incredibly, there was a place where I was able to stand overlooking the falls and hold a rainbow in my hands. It was an unbelievable experience.

That evening, after dinner, I bought a ticket for *The African Spectacular,* a show staged by a dozen male performers wearing tribal dress. I will never forget how one of the men was able to place an unattached sixteen-foot pole on its end and then climb all the way to the top and stand on it. There was nothing to keep the pole from falling except the man's incredible sense of balance.

Fanie and Joyce joined me for breakfast, then drove me to the other local tourist attractions: the "Big Tree" (a huge baobab said to be Africa's largest) and a crocodile farm with literally hundreds of crocs, including a monster that had to be five feet wide and twenty feet long! We then made a quick stop at my hosts' home and were on the road to my first African hunting adventure in their new Range Rover.

* * *

A wooden sign with carved letters proclaiming we had entered a concession called Westwood Wildlife Safaris Pvt. Ltd. of Victoria Falls, Zimbabwe, marked the entrance to their camp. The posts that supported it were topped with the sun-bleached skull of a Cape buffalo. A baobab tree almost as large as the one in Vic Falls stood just past the junction. A waterbuck bull walked slowly across the road as we made the turn toward the neat, tin-roofed and stuccoed, ranch-style house about fifty yards above a shallow ripple across the Zambezi River.

Flowers, trees, and Bermuda grass were being cultivated around the house. In the bed of a Toyota Land Cruiser that had arrived a few minutes before us was an African lion killed that morning by Marie Greco, an executive for a newspaper chain based in Charlottesville, Virginia. Although she had never hunted before this trip, she said she had always dreamed of going on safari and shooting a lion. She had come halfway around the world by herself to make her dream come true. Her trophy was a young male with a scant mane. Unlike those in East Africa, even Zimbabwe's oldest lions are rarely found with thick manes, Pretorius said. The big male we saw roaring at the start of those old MGM movies obviously did not have its hair pulled and snagged in Zimbabwe's thornbush country. (MGM now is using a young male with a mane much like the one on Greco's lion.)

While his men took my baggage to my room, Pretorius took me to his skinning shed, where we checked out the skulls and skins of recently killed Cape buffalo, kudu, bushbuck, eland, and sable. Weathered skulls of various antelope species were nailed to the posts around the high fence that surrounded his compound.

A man named Harry, a computer programmer for Federal Express in Louisiana, was packing his luggage for his return to the United States the next day. He had spent two weeks at Westwood and killed a Cape buffalo, a southern greater kudu, a Livingstone eland, and a Chobe bushbuck, and all would make Safari Club International's record book. He and I shared a bedroom that night, and when we were settled in our beds, as the generator went off, Harry said I would have a wonderful time hunting there.

He warned me not to leave the fenced area without a rifle because lion tracks had been seen just outside the front entrance. I also shouldn't go near the river behind the buildings, he said, because of its crocodiles. I followed his advice. I had read somewhere that as many as fifty humans were eaten by crocs along the Zambezi every year. That's nearly one a week, if those reports were true.

* * *

Westwood was formerly my outfitter's ranch, but it had been "nationalized" even before Rhodesia became Zimbabwe, and Pretorius was leasing it from the government as his hunting concession. He collected trophy fees from the hunters for the government when an animal was killed or wounded, and these fees helped support the country's national parks and wildlife department. Wildlife management policies didn't change much under the new government, I was told. Assistants who had served under white Rhodesians in the government wildlife agency were simply promoted to their former supervisors' positions, and the agency's best programs were continued. Those programs must have been working because there was wild game—I saw all of the African Big Five during my week at Westwood—in a country that had been engaged in a bloody revolution just a couple of years before I arrived.

* * *

At an abandoned and deteriorating tobacco plantation near the Westwood camp, it was almost impossible to tell that someone had farmed the land around it only a few years previously. There were no shell holes in the walls that were still standing, but when I let my imagination run free, I could picture a Rhodesian family defending the grand home their grandparents had built. They would be armed with sporting rifles and shotguns, fighting Russian-, Chinese-, and Cuban-trained men carrying rocket launchers, hand grenades, and full-automatic Soviet or Chinese rifles.

I was told the plantation had been taken over by the government and was being allowed to revert to nature to benefit wildlife. Only its well was being maintained. Pretorius stopped by infrequently to pump more water into a small water hole used by the animals. We talked mostly about hunting and Africa's game animals, but Pretorius did say the new government restricted the amount of money leaving the country, and this limited the hunting equipment he could import, as well as how much he could spend for advertising outside the country to attract foreign customers such as I.

The signs of war were subtle at Westwood, but they were there. In addition to the eight-foot-tall fence topped with barbed wire that surrounded the hunting camp, there was an armored personnel carrier, minus its wheels, sitting on blocks. My outfitter had used the mini-tank only to drive into Vic Falls to buy groceries during the "stickiest" part of the conflict, he said. The fence was put up during the war but was never needed because no one had bothered the Pretorius farm. The fence hadn't been taken down because it protected the lawn from wild animals, he said.

Except for one man, our trackers, skinners, and camp staff resembled each other and spoke the same language. Because this part of Zimbabwe was Matabele territory, I assumed they were members of that tribe. The exception was a Bushman—a short, thin, wild-looking fellow with bushy hair, missing teeth, and light brown skin. He, like the others, was always seen in brown overalls, but he did not wear the shoulder-length, knitted head covering that every other member of the black staff wore. He was the head skinner, and I never saw him without a knife in his hand, even when he entered the compound to get instructions from Pretorius. It was apparent that the other men either distrusted or were afraid of him, but it also was apparent that Pretorius liked the man.

As far as I could tell, none of the blacks spoke more than a few words of English, even though it was one of the official languages of the new Zimbabwe. Back in the States, I had heard rumors that there were government spies in every safari camp, but my white hosts laughed at this when I mentioned it. While I was there, Zimbabwe President Canaan Banana (it was illegal to joke about his name) announced that his country was a Marxist nation and would be appointing its own politburo and joining an association of socialist states.

I knew about the age-old struggle between the country's two major tribes, but I found no evidence of politics in the bush. The whites who remained in the country, such as my professional hunter Rob Martin and Pretorius, were as apolitical as anyone I've ever encountered. They could not have survived in their country if they were not.

The trackers and skinners all took cigarettes when I offered them, but they did not smoke them when I was around. Instead, they rolled some type of rough leaf into scraps of newspaper and smoked that. According to Martin, the leaves were from *dakka*, a type of marijuana that grew wild locally.

Near the end of my hunt, my professional hunter's young wife, Liz Martin, and their baby arrived from Bulawayo in a Volkswagen "bug" for a visit. She had used a road the U.S. State Department had deemed unsafe for travel because terrorists had attacked vehicles on it.

"There's no problem if you travel by day," she said. "The bad spot is only just outside Bulawayo."

Even so, Mrs. Martin kept a 9mm semiautomatic pistol next to her baby's car seat.

* * *

I had told Martin and Pretorius that I wanted to hunt antelope before taking on a Cape buffalo. Both smiled and said we would hunt buffalo whenever we found fresh tracks. Buffalo herds moved in and out of the national parks, they both said, and days sometimes passed with none entering the hunting concession.

On our way to an area where we planned to hunt a greater kudu the first morning, I spotted several large black shapes in high grass on the left side of the road. A second glance showed shiny black, curved horns that could only be worn by an African buffalo. The trackers riding in the back of the truck must have seen them but hadn't pointed them out to Martin. When I did, he only nodded. The left side of the road was closed to hunting, he said. I breathed easier. I had read enough horror stories to know that stalking Cape buffaloes in Peter Capstick's long grass can be unhealthy. Just about the time I settled back in my seat, the trackers began banging on the roof of Martin's Toyota. They were pointing and jabbering as Martin and I got out to look at the tracks and dung in the dirt road. A huge herd of buffaloes had left the park during the night and probably had not gone far.

"Get your .458," Martin said. "Load it with solids."

Three days after leaving Tucson, I was hunting one of Africa's five most dangerous animals.

At the Tucson Rod and Gun Club, I had shot a couple of dozen rounds through the heavy rifle to adjust its scope and make certain that its iron sights also were shooting at the same point of aim, just in case something happened to the scope. I also had fired three rounds off the hood (in Africa, they're called bonnets) of Martin's Toyota, and one round offhand. I don't know what spooked me more—the thought of going after my first dangerous game or the terrible recoil from that rifle. It's been said that women can take a rifle's kick better than large men because their bodies bend and flex with recoil. I don't know if that's true, but I do know that it hurt me each time I fired that .458. I had to keep reminding myself not to allow my right thumb to cross the stock. When I forgot, the thumb slammed my nose when the barrel rose up.

Martin and I completed loading our rifles at about the same time. While I stuffed my pockets with cigar-size cartridges, he strapped a belt containing at least forty rounds around his waist. Buffaloes are hard to kill, he said, before the three of us began following the tracks.

The tracker Cabbage was in the lead as we moved quickly and quietly upwind into a forest filled with buffaloes. There were at least a hundred of them—glossy black, fat creatures with meat hooks on their heads, barely visible at twenty-five yards in thornbush so thick we could see only a few animals at a time. The tracks and droppings on the ground and the cattlelike smells made it seem like a barnyard, but there also were the sounds of oxpeckers swarming the feeding herd and picking ticks off the backs of the beasts.

When Martin found a suitable bull, he silently grabbed my arm and pulled me into position to see the animal he'd selected. Cabbage then moved in and held up two sticks that had been tied together to form a fork to steady my rifle. The wind was blowing into our faces, and we were talking in the quietest of whispers. The herd did not know we were lurking in the brush just a few yards away. All thoughts of waiting and taking lesser game to gain confidence in my shooting skills before going after a buffalo were gone. I shot standing up, into the shoulder of the bull Martin had chosen, taking careful aim because I had been warned of the hazards of sloppy shooting on these animals. The 500-grain, solid-jacketed bullet did not do what it was supposed to do, however. It broke bones in the left shoulder, ripped through a lung, and exited behind the shoulder on the other side. But it failed to anchor that large and tough bull, and the buffalo ran off.

I could not believe anything could remain on its feet after being hit through the shoulder at close range with a bullet of that caliber. The .458 was designed by Winchester to be the ultimate rifle for dangerous African game and replace the so-called elephant guns of the past, including such time-tested calibers as the .470, .500, and .600. Nonetheless, a well-placed shot into the shoulder of a buffalo from my .458 did not put it down. I looked at Martin and saw disgust written on his face.

"What do we do now?" I whispered.

"We go after it," he said.

What happened during the next forty-five minutes was even more surprising than having a buffalo run away after being hit in the shoulder and lungs with a 500-grain bullet. We moved up and found the wounded bull, and I shot it again. We did this five times, and four more heavy bullets went into that same shoulder. Another plowed into the bull's rump in a botched attempt to break its spine. All five shots had exactly the same result: nothing. Martin, Cabbage, and I kept stalking and whispering. How could any animal take such punishment and continue on with only a slightly visible limp?

Each time we moved up on my wounded bull, Martin whispered that I should stay near a tree. None that I could see was large enough to be climbed, and most were covered with thorns. The brush was so thick that I doubted there would be time to find a suitable tree if bad things started happening fast. Eventually, the injured bull had had enough of us and turned around to charge. Martin and I fired our rifles together, and the buffalo went crashing down just a few steps from us.

Martin apologized for shooting, but I dismissed it. Professional hunters apparently believe they have failed their client if they find themselves forced to shoot. Me? I was glad he had shot. I didn't want any fun and games with that buffalo.

It was only after the bull was down that I realized that Cabbage had been at my side, unarmed, and that Martin was slightly in front and to the left of me. He had held off shooting until the bull let it be known that it was ready to fight back. Meanwhile, both Martin and Cabbage had kept themselves in a position to deflect the buffalo's charge away from me in the event that it tried to injure their client.

When I realized this, I also suddenly knew how we had managed to follow and find one wounded individual among two hundred buffaloes in those thickets. Martin's strategy was to press the herd, making it run away and leave the cripple behind.

Both men apparently knew from past experiences that a wounded buffalo eventually would want to even the score with the men who had injured it, and they were ready when the time came. I didn't fully realize how potentially dangerous a situation we were in until the buffalo was dead. At Martin's request, I excitedly fired an insurance shot into the buffalo's spine behind its head at point-blank range while holding the .458 away from my shoulder with just my right hand. All the recoil from that big rifle was transmitted to my three fingers behind the trigger guard. They ached for days. I was lucky nothing was broken.

I expected Martin and his crew would have to cut my buffalo into pieces to load it into his Toyota, but he and his men had done this chore many times. Instead of cutting it up, they dug a trench near its head so that when they backed the Toyota up to it, the tailgate was close to ground level. They then hooked the horns to a winch and slid the animal into the truck's bed. The entire process probably took no more than forty-five minutes.

Later that night, Martinus Nuade, Marie Greco's professional hunter, told of being attacked by a wounded buffalo a few years earlier. He found himself helplessly hung on the horn as the animal did its best to shake, scrape, and stomp him to death. The client kept calm and moved up and shot the buffalo in the neck, killing it instantly.

"Lucky for me, that was one time the customer didn't run," the hunter said.

He was lucky in at least two other ways. Had the horn gone inside his ribs, instead of on top of them, it might have ripped out his lungs and heart. Instead, he healed quickly after being rushed to the hospital at Bulawayo, where he sold used cars when he wasn't guiding foreign hunters.

He also was lucky that the client didn't get excited and shoot him. It has happened.

Kudus, Sables and Six-ton Rattlesnakes

Chapter 14

Camp life at Westwood quickly settled into a routine: up at 6 A.M., eat breakfast, and drive out to hunt. We would see dozens of animals, shoot one (maybe), return at lunch, go back out at 3 P.M., and return to camp at sundown. I then would shower with river water that had been heated outside in a wood-fired water tank and piped by gravity to the two bathrooms. After bathing, we'd eat, enjoy sundowner cocktails long after sundown, and go to bed at 9 P.M., when the generator was shut down.

The first night I did what all first-timers do: I asked the three professional hunters in our group which of Africa's so-called Big Five animals was the most dangerous. Rob Martin said it was the leopard because of its speed and the fact that it doesn't hesitate to attack a human when it is injured. Martin Nuade voted for the buffalo, because it sometimes attacks humans without provocation, and nothing will deter it when it decides to come for someone. Pretorius won the discussion hands down by merely pointing to his left leg and shoulder. He still was recovering from a lion-mauling a year earlier.

It happened while he and a tracker were following a lion a client had shot badly, he said.

"I saw him ahead of us, waiting for us," he said. "What I didn't know was that he was behind a log in the grass. All I could see was the top of his head. I had my double rifle, and when I shot, I hit the log. He was on me instantly. He grabbed my shoulder and started dragging me off. I was trying to kick him in the goodies, and when I did, he dropped me and grabbed me by my knee."

The tracker also was carrying a rifle, and when he ran up to shoot the lion at close range, Pretorius suddenly found himself staring into its bore. It looked much larger than it actually was, he said.

"My God, man," Pretorius yelled at the tracker. "Squat down and shoot it in the head from the side."

The shot killed the lion instantly, and now Pretorius found himself under a very dead 450-pound lion.

"I couldn't move until they pulled him off me," he said. "And when they stood me up, I couldn't use my arm or my leg. I had to hop around. I called my wife, Joyce, on the radio, and she got an airplane to come out to our house to take me to the hospital in Bulawayo."

Before he left for the medical treatment that would keep him hospitalized for more than two months, Pretorius hopped over to the back of his Land Rover and pounded on the dead lion's chest.

"I told him I won that match," he said.

✷ ✷ ✷

I trusted Rob Martin and his tracker, Cabbage, and I followed their instructions without questioning them. Their knowledge of Africa's wildlife and their hunting skills were like nothing I have ever seen in North America. I was impressed when, on my second day's hunt at Westwood, Martin and Cabbage were able to track a southern greater kudu for four hours after I nicked its left rump with a bullet from my .30-06. The bull was running for the brush across a "pan" (we call them meadows or *cienega*s in Arizona) when I shot. We could hear the bullet hit the animal at two hundred yards, but the trail of tiny drops of blood stopped soon after we entered the thickets. Martin and Cabbage stayed with the track long after it was apparent that the kudu wasn't badly injured.

"See that," Martin suddenly said, after the first hour of silent tracking. "Another kudu has joined your bull and is walking with him."

I couldn't see what he meant. There were all types of tracks—large and small—in the red sand.

Every time I suspected that these two men had lost the trail or were pulling a cruel joke on this American, I'd see a drop of dried blood on a leaf near my feet. How could they sort the trail of one kudu bull out of a mass of prints left by hundreds of animals? I'd hunted big game all my life and considered myself as good a tracker as any American hunter. But the hunters on my continent are in the minor leagues compared to those two men.

We had followed the kudu's tracks for at least two hours when Cabbage and Martin stopped and began to whisper to each other. I stepped up to them.

"What's happening?" I asked, as quietly as I could.

"Your kudu is just ahead of us," Martin said.

"Did you see it?"

"No, but—"

Before Martin could complete what he intended to say, a kudu bull stepped into an opening about eighty yards in front of us. I was raising my rifle slowly when Cabbage turned and signaled with his open palm for me to wait. I did, and a few seconds later another bull stepped into the opening.

"Shoot it!" Martin said, and when I did, the kudu dropped in its tracks. My second African animal was a good bull with thick horns that measured slightly more than fifty-two inches around the curls. I had been told a big bull kudu was about the size of a bull elk, but its body was considerably smaller. I've shot cow elk that were larger.

Its short coat was a dull gray, and it had long hair on its throat and belly and along the spine from the back of its head to its shoulders. It also had light-colored vertical stripes on its sides. It was a beautiful trophy, but I also was interested in learning what kudu fillets tasted like. For lunch and dinner in camp, we ate the choicest parts of the previous day's kills, and we'd not yet eaten kudu.

I found I liked it, along with eland, buffalo, impala, and warthog. There was absolutely no hint of the "wild" taste that is found in the meat of some North American big-game animals. One of our meals included the backstraps of eland, warthog, and zebra, served with locally grown potatoes and squash and homemade bread. The zebra meat was good, even though its fat was a bright yellow.[1]

This was Marie Greco's first hunting trip, and she still was not certain that hunting was a proper activity for her. Her friend and employer had given her a .375 H&H Magnum rifle and trained her to shoot it so that she could hunt her lion. He had done a good job, starting with a .22 rimfire and working past a .243 Winchester until she could handle the heavy rifle's recoil. Her professional hunter told me she had killed all her animals with one shot each, except for an eland, which required three shots.

Mrs. Greco still was trying to understand her motives, even after killing a half-dozen animals. Her professional hunter liked to tease her about eating what she had killed. She had trouble with the zebra.

* * *

Pretorius was surprised that we were seeing buffalo every time we went out. The hunter I met when I arrived had encountered only one herd during his two weeks at Westwood. I must have seen no fewer than six hundred buffalo during the week I was there, including the big herd that had at least a hundred animals in it. I'd been told that the *dagga* boys, the largest and oldest bulls, were usually found alone. That may be, but the few lone animals Martin and I came upon had broken their horns.

* * *

I learned to despise elephants. We saw them everywhere while I was at Westwood, and every single day at least one of them would make a mock charge at us. There was no way I could remain calm when one

---

[1]As did many Americans, I ate a lot of horse meat as a boy during World War II, when beef and pork were rationed, but it was so long ago I couldn't remember whether horse meat and zebra meat had a similar taste. I was surprised to learn that in Africa all game meat is called venison, and all antelope, both male and female, are called buck. Until my first visit to Africa I had thought that these words referred only to deer. "Rams" and "ewes" are used to distinguish the sex of smaller antelope. "Bull" and "cow" describe the larger animals.

of those huge beasts threw up its trunk, waved its gigantic ears, and ran trumpeting at us. These were not the docile, easily trained Asian elephants everyone has seen at a circus or zoo. If an adult male African elephant's head is three feet wide and each ear is four feet wide, it means that when it charges, it is eleven feet wide from the outside edge of one ear to the outside edge of the other ear! It stands ten to twelve feet high at the shoulder. There is nothing that walks on this earth that is larger or better equipped to kill a man.

Nobody had to tell me that if an elephant decided I was dead meat, there was nothing I could do to stop it from killing me, other than killing it first. I couldn't climb a tree. Elephants routinely knock down hundred-year-old trees while feeding. I couldn't outrun an elephant, and I certainly couldn't scare one away by bluffing if it was intent on doing harm. The best way I can describe suddenly coming upon an elephant is to say it is like bumping into a six-ton rattlesnake. Their grayish skin reflects no sunlight at all. If they were feeding quietly, we often didn't know they were around until we saw them just a few yards away. I know, you are thinking animals as large as an elephant can't hide. In truth, elephants can be hard to see, even in a minimum of cover, and even for someone who has lived among them all his life.

A case in point occurred the first afternoon I was at Westwood. Pretorius had taken me out on a short drive to introduce me to his area. He and I were talking when we drove past a lone tree near the edge of a pan. For some reason I looked back and caught a glimpse of something white that was moving, at least seven or eight feet up in the tree. It took a second or two for my brain to register that I had spotted an elephant's tusk. I tapped Pretorius on the shoulder and pointed to the animal after he had stopped his Land Rover. While we watched it, I could tell he was contemplating whether to allow me to shoot it. After seeing many hundreds of elephants since then, I now believe that bull's tusks would weigh between fifty and sixty pounds, a fair trophy by today's standards.

It wasn't until I was packing to return to Johannesburg that Pretorius told me he could have arranged for me to sell the elephant's hide for slightly more than the trophy fee. I wish he had suggested it while we were watching that bull. Today, the cost of shooting an elephant such as that one has skyrocketed, and it is my understanding that it no longer is legal to sell elephant ivory and hides, even inside Zimbabwe.

Once, while we were in the Toyota, Martin, Cabbage, and I found ourselves caught in the middle of a herd of elephants. A dozen or so were crossing the two-track road in front of us, and another dozen or so were behind us when we stopped the vehicle. Martin warned me to be quiet as I stood up on the seat with my camera. We were in what he called a "dicey" situation, because we couldn't drive away if they should decide to come after us.

Suddenly, one of the cows behind us spotted the Toyota, threw up its ears, waved its trunk, and, unprovoked, launched a screaming charge. For an agonizing moment or two, the Land Rover's starter motor dragged, and it seemed as if the engine would never start. When it did, there was a narrow gap in the herd on what was left of the road in front of us, and Martin drove us through it. The charging cow stayed behind us for a couple of hundred yards before returning to its companions. Martin laughed loudly about the experience for five minutes afterward. I had managed to snap a couple of photos of the charge, but they were out of focus and showed camera movement. That cow had scared me silly, but it was only playing, Martin said. I said he had my permission to tell the entire world that this greenhorn outdoor writer from the United States of America was a coward when it came to elephant. I refused to play with anything capable of tossing his Toyota around like a soccer ball or pulling down a tree and beating us to death with it.

At sundown that same day, Martin and I were afoot a few miles from that spot, returning to his vehicle, when five or six elephants that we couldn't see began trumpeting all at once. It was an interesting experience, but I didn't like walking toward the sounds. Martin said he never had heard an entire herd trumpeting together continuously, as these were doing. We stopped for a moment to listen to them. From a low hill we could see trees swaying several hundred yards away as elephants leaned and pushed on them. Their continuous trumpeting was broken only by the sounds of falling trees. We never saw that herd that evening because, to my relief, we stayed well away from it. However, the next day, when we walked through where it had been, the forest looked like a battleground. (I know, that's an overused description, but it is apt.) Huge trees were down and stripped. Brush was flattened, and the ground was turned over where small trees had been pulled up. Martin said there might have been fewer than a dozen elephants there during the night.

Later, I asked Pretorius where I should shoot an elephant if we were forced to shoot in self-defense. I expected him to describe exactly where an elephant's brain is found—something like, "Draw an imaginary line through the ear holes and tell yourself there's a loaf of bread exactly in the middle of that line, and shoot it."

Instead, he said: "You shoot him in the elephant and keep shooting him in the elephant."

It wasn't until several years later that something I read made me realize he was not being facetious. Unlike Cape buffalo, a charging elephant reportedly can be turned by shooting the animal anywhere in the head. The shot does not need to be fatal to get an elephant to turn away, or so the author said.

Before I left Zimbabwe, I promised myself that if I returned, I would shoot an elephant and sell its tusks and skin to take revenge for the rude way elephants treated me on my first trip to Africa. These were no gentle giants. The elephants at Westwood were aggressive monsters, and it took only a few encounters before I found myself fearing them. Despite my vow, although I returned to Africa many times and encountered many more elephants over the next two decades, I have never hunted an elephant. The fee for a trophy bull jumped from $2,500 to $6,000 to $10,000, and at this writing has leveled off at $25,000 to $30,000. Trophy hunters also must book three-week safaris at $1,000 to $1,500 or more a day.

Judging from what I saw, no matter what we were hearing and seeing on television in the United States, the elephants of southern Africa were not and are not in danger of extinction. That may have been true of the elephants in Kenya, Zaire, Angola, and elsewhere in Africa, where poaching teams employed by corrupt government officials were commercially hunting ivory. It was not true in the five African countries where I hunted other game from 1983 to 2007. I saw hundreds of elephants along the Zambezi and many dozens more in South Africa's Transvaal Province, Botswana's Tuli Block, and Zambia's Mumbwa hunting concession.

Kruger Park had so many elephants in 1983 that officials planned to shoot more than seven thousand of them to protect the park's vegetation. Elephants were being restocked on game farms and parks throughout southern Africa. The biggest threat to elephants wasn't poaching; it was a lack of enough land for them to roam in. Elephants need a lot of it.

* * *

It must have been my second or third day at Westwood when Pretorius, Martin, and I drove up on three white rhinos. It was my first sighting of these huge beasts in the wild, and we stopped long enough for me to photograph them. They had been born in South Africa's Omfolozi Reserve and brought to Zimbabwe and released in this concession. He hoped they would do well, Pretorius said, because he enjoyed seeing them. I had read about South Africa's successful efforts to restore white rhino populations, but I didn't know they had a large enough stock to send them to other countries. Sadly, the rhinos I photographed at Westwood were killed by poachers two years after I left the country.

* * *

Most hunters of Africa's so-called plains game place the greater kudu at the top of their lists of desired trophies. On my first trip to Africa, I didn't care if I ever shot a kudu. What I really wanted was a sable antelope.

Sables are Africa's most glamorous antelope, yet they are lesser known. They have ribbed horns that curl up to four feet back toward their spines. Females and young males are a brownish color, but the slick coats on the males turn glossy black as they get older. Their paunches and facial markings are pure white. They are plump and rounded animals that resemble quarter horses when they run. To me, they are Africa's most beautiful antelope.

Before my five days at Westwood were over, I was to see many sable bulls, but only two were considered shootable by my guides. The first of these was standing in the dark shadow of a mopane tree, making the jet-black animal difficult to see, even at a hundred yards. Pretorius and Martin took their time, checked out its horns carefully with their binoculars, and pronounced they could find me a better one. The decision whether to shoot this bull was mine, though, they said. They estimated its horns were thirty-nine to forty inches long, which made them only a representative trophy. I kept telling myself this was a motionless target at a ridiculously close range, and I didn't care if this one's horns were two or three inches shorter than what they said I might take if I waited. I had been shooting badly and might never have a better opportunity to collect a decent sable, I thought.

After a minute or two, I decided to take their advice. They were the professionals, and I knew absolutely nothing about hunting sable antelope or what I should expect to see at Westwood. I would not leave without dry-firing my rifle twice with the cross hairs on the sable's shoulder, though.

"That beautiful bull doesn't know it is dead," I told my companions, when it eventually got tired of watching us and walked regally into the bush.

Later that same day, we were eating a lunch of cold boiled chicken, hot tea, and cookies (they're called biscuits in English-speaking African countries) from Martin's "chop box" when Pretorius pointed across the clearing. A dark-colored animal was moving from left to right through the trees.

"It's a good bull," Pretorius said. "Go get it!"

I grabbed my .30-06 and tried to keep up with Martin as he trotted to an anthill at the edge of another corner of the pan. I was out of breath when we reached it in time to see the sable bull drop its head to drink from a puddle of water no larger than a kitchen table's top, about two hundred yards from us. At its feet were a couple of baboons, several vervet monkeys, and a covey of quail-like birds called francolin. My first shot—fired too quickly—was a miss, and its blast sent every creature in sight into panic. My second shot also missed, but my third shot struck behind the bull's shoulder, and it collapsed a very long way from our anthill.

I had taken my first sable antelope, and what a beautiful animal it was. I ran my hand over its curving horns, allowing my fingers to bump along all the ridges. I cannot adequately describe how I felt after making that antelope mine. It is one of my most cherished memories of Zimbabwe. I would shoot another sable antelope eleven years later, across the Zambezi near Kafue National Park in Zambia, but nothing could compare with taking my first bull sable.

It would have been a wonderful way to end my Zimbabwe safari, but I still had one more day left before I had to return to South Africa. I spent the early morning with Martin, walking the riverine thickets along the Zambezi, hunting for a Chobe bushbuck. We found only one male, but it saw us first, whirled, and was out of sight in an instant. It was the first of three bushbuck hunts I would make before finally taking my first ram in 1994 in Zambia. The hunting of these small, spiral-horned antelope is as challenging as hunting white-tailed deer.

My last afternoon in Zimbabwe was spent on the river, fishing for tigerfish, a fish that reminded me of something that might result if a striped bass, a saltwater bonita, and a piranha were crossed. For a freshwater fish they are amazingly strong fighters, and they have teeth that would make a tiger proud.

On the way to the river, the black men standing in the bed of our Land Rover pounded on the cab and asked us to stop. Across the wide river, on the Zambian side, an African woman was bathing. I knew that nudity still was not unusual in this part of Africa, so I asked Pretorius why they were so interested in watching her.

"They want to see a croc grab her," he said.

It didn't happen, at least during the ten minutes we watched her from our side of the river.

Pretorius had a fine, Zimbabwe-made, fiberglass runabout boat that we fished from, powered by a large Yamaha motor. There was no boat ramp. He merely backed his boat into the river and floated it off his trailer. Before doing so, he got out to inspect the spot, then called me to come quietly to him with my camera. A huge crocodile was hiding in the reeds, and only showed itself when Pretorius tossed a rock at it.

After it swam off, Pretorius, an apprentice professional hunter, and I got on board and began trolling up and down the river, dragging silver spoons along the edges of the reed beds. I caught one small tigerfish right away, and the apprentice caught another, and that was it for the day. After looking at the teeth of our catch, I understood why Pretorius insisted that I tie what he called a trace (steel leader) to my line. Regular monofilament, even the heavy stuff on his Penn saltwater reels, would be cut in an instant.

I was sad when my plane lifted off the runway at the Victoria Falls Airport the next morning. I didn't know it then, but I would return to Zimbabwe three more times and see Victoria Falls once more—this time from the Zambia side.

A Tour of the "Old" South Africa

Chapter 15

When I returned to Johannesburg after a week in Zimbabwe, the desk clerk at the Carlton Hotel was surprised to learn I had encountered no problems up north. When I told of seeing Victoria Falls, he sighed, saying, "We used to go up there on holiday, but no more."

I met several people who said they or their family members had lived in Rhodesia before moving to South Africa. They remembered the country fondly, but none had returned since the government changed to black rule in 1980, and none planned to do so, even though the shooting war had ended.

The front pages of the South African newspaper I read in my hotel room that first night had stories about crime in the United States, new utility rates for Johannesburg, a new sales tax, and runaway inflation. Financial-page stories were about the strong U.S. dollar and what it might mean for South African businesses. There was an environmental column saying South Africa was leading a worldwide anti-whaling campaign. A feature story on the front page of one of the sections speculated whether President Ronald Reagan dyed his hair. Another was an exposé about black prostitutes working the truck stops and harassing *bakkie* (pickup truck) and lorry drivers in northern Cape Province.

The "help wanted" ads sought people who could speak both Afrikaans and English. In most of the ads, the perks of the position included use of company cars. There also were ads for department stores, groceries, and computers, plus photos of weddings and car crashes, stock market and weather reports, movie times, and everything else that goes into a newspaper.

I was surprised to read an editorial that called for government reform and elimination of apartheid. Then I remembered that this newspaper's audience spoke English, and Afrikaners controlled the government. If I could have read the Afrikaans newspapers, the editorials might have been much different.

South Africa was an affluent, modern, and apparently self-sufficient nation in the early 1980s. The people I met were well informed of global news and were well aware that the rest of the world condemned their government's racist policies.

* * *

The history of White South Africa bears a certain resemblance to American history. White South Africans fought the English, trekked north across an unknown continent, and encountered hostile natives. They imported slaves and cheap labor from Madagascar and Indonesia, built farms, planted tobacco, raised cattle, and chased riches. Unlike Americans, some South Africans claim their ancestors had settled their land before the "natives" arrived, which to them meant that if anyone should leave South Africa, it should be the tribes that moved in after European settlers led by Jan van Riebeeck of the Dutch East India Company got there in 1652.

As did America's pioneers, white South Africans built railroads and kept rushing to frontiers. And, as their country prospered, it also began attracting hordes of immigrants from around the world. In addition to Dutch and English descendants, I met South Africans whose ancestors had come from France, Scotland, Scandinavia, India, Spain, and Paraguay. And, as in our recent invasion of illegal immigrants from Cuba, Mexico, and Central America, blacks fleeing oppressive governments and famines in neighboring countries were flooding South Africa in 1983. They came by the thousands, walking hundreds of miles from their homes in search of jobs in the promised land of South Africa.

Unfortunately, South Africa in 1983 was like the United States I had known as a boy, when, even in little Yuma, Arizona, certain public bathrooms and drinking fountains were for whites only, and there were signs in every restaurant saying, "We Reserve the Right to Refuse Service to Anyone," meaning "coloreds" would not be served. Yuma's African-American population was not large enough for an all-black high school, but there was one facility for black children of grammar- and elementary-school age.

Apartheid in the United States as I was growing up was called "separate but equal." In my country, change began with a Supreme Court ruling in 1954—the year I graduated from high school and started college—that said segregation in schools was unconstitutional. In South Africa, apartheid continued until 1994, when the country's first election open to all citizens was held.

✳ ✳ ✳

There was little traffic on the roads we drove in South Africa on my first trip there. Even so, the highway along the Indian Ocean north from Durban had overpasses and overhead signs. It resembled many freeways in America, minus the cars. It was apparent that South Africans in 1983 did not travel as much as we did. With gasoline costing the equivalent of about five U.S. dollars per gallon in South Africa and about ninety-five cents per gallon in the States, the reason was obvious.

I remember being driven back to Kimberley after a day of hunting gemsbok and springbok at the DeBeers Mining Company's Rooipoort Estate. I was with the South African Tourist Board's representative in Kimberley, and he was dumbfounded that we had met about twenty vehicles in thirty miles of nighttime driving.

"In any case, I wonder where they're all going," Sol said.

Sol was a short, round, and likeable Boer and spoke with a heavy Afrikaans accent. He kept throwing "in any case" into his conversation and had an uncommon interest in geology and rocks and minerals.

He loved showing visitors the Big Hole and the diamond museum in Kimberley. Looking down into the huge pit where many hundreds of people had dug for diamonds, he said: "In any case, can't you just picture all those people in there at one time?"

Sol pointed out the differences in the raw and cut diamonds on exhibit in the museum, then proudly took me around the displays of nineteenth-century shops and restored machinery. He also helped me select a diamond I bought for Jean, then suggested that the saleswoman give me a receipt for about half the purchase price. This would keep me from paying duty when I returned to the United States, he said. As it turned out, cheating the U.S. government wasn't necessary. The purchases I brought back with me did not exceed the duty-free limit. I did pay the full duty on the zebra rugs, bowls, jewelry, and elephant-hair bracelets shipped to Tucson by Johannesburg's Bushcraft Trading Company, however.

The day before I was to hunt gemsbok on the DeBeers' Rooipoort Estate, Sol drove me out to see what he called the "glacial paintings." This portion of the Kalahari Desert reminded me of home, especially when we stopped to photograph a windmill and a corral. That picture could have been taken near Casa Grande, Arizona. The fencing looked different, though. When I walked up to it, I saw that the wire had no barbs. According to Sol, Africa's farmers and ranchers believe barbed wire is cruel to animals. Barbs are used only to keep humans out.

Along the way to the glacial paintings, we stopped to watch pairs of ostrich perform their mating dances above the Vaal River. The males would squat and rub their penises on the dirt, spread their wings, then get up and chase the females. By the time one caught up to a female, it apparently had lost its erection and would have to repeat the ritual. It certainly was an enthusiastic process, but it can't be very productive. Although I watched more than a few ostrich pairs dance, I never saw a coupling.

I didn't realize that the Southern Hemisphere had experienced an ice age until I stood on rocks scratched flat and smooth by glaciers near Kimberley. The paintings weren't paintings. Instead, they were drawings of animals that were chipped in the rock by prehistoric African peoples, using techniques and designs that resembled those of Arizona's earliest inhabitants. Sol also showed me mounds containing hundreds of ancient stone tools that diamond hunters had thrown out of shallow pits while searching for diamonds. The primitive stone tools looked exactly like those I have seen throughout the southwest. Every rock fitted my hand, if I held it properly.

"See how this one fits and how sharp this edge is?" Sol would say. "In any case, it surely must have been used for skinning animals."

Sol said he would like to have a tumbler and rock saw someday to cut and polish the rocks he had collected since he was transferred to Kimberley a few years earlier. Gem and mineral equipment and supplies were expensive in South Africa because not many people there enjoyed rocks as he did, he said. I promised myself I would send him rockhounding catalogs and magazines when I returned home, and I did.

* * *

Ted Sweetnam, whom Holt Bodinson had arranged to guide me on a gemsbok hunt a few miles from Kimberley, was an attorney on the DeBeers Mining Company's legal staff. He met me at the Southern Sun's Kimberley Hotel about three hours before sunup, apologizing because the two professional hunters at the estate were busy preparing for a live-animal capture that day.

"I think we can get you a buck, however," he said.

There were elands, zebras, duikers, and reedbucks in the headlights as we drove into the Rooipoort Estate through a high fence and its eight-foot-tall gate. Sweetnam told us that this entire area was a diamond field that had never been "worked." I took this as an unspoken command forbidding my picking up anything on the ground. Possession of an unregistered raw diamond was against South African law, Sol had told me.

When we found a break in the fence along the highway, Sweetnam told us that poaching of wildlife by Kimberley's white residents was a continuing problem. Someone had cut the wire and driven through to pick up the hindquarters of an eland shot from the road during the night. The rest of that large antelope had been left to rot on the sand.

We sighted-in our rifles at twenty-five meters[1] at the Rooipoort Box, a nineteenth-century hunting lodge still used to entertain DeBeers executives and clients. Sweetnam had a .308 bolt-action rifle made in South Africa by the Musgrave Arms Company, and he kept apologizing about the firearm. He said South Africans believe the best moderately priced sporting rifles are made in the United States by Winchester, Ruger, and Remington, and the best expensive firearms come from England. Local hunters preferred imported firearms because quality control in South Africa's manufacturing left a lot to be desired, he said.

I couldn't understand why Sweetnam wasn't happy with his rifle. It was based on a Mauser-style action, a design proven in a world war and copied in some form by every bolt-action rifle maker since 1898. The rifle's stock and metalwork showed good workmanship, and it was equipped with a high-quality, Japanese-made, four-power scope. Sweetnam fired two shots that left holes in the paper exactly in the center of the target. Angus Anthony, one of the estate's professional hunters, said Sweetnam's rifle was among the "last good rifles" the company made.

We spent an hour or two sneaking through thornbush, trying to get close to a gemsbok that Sweetnam said would qualify for Rowland Ward's record book, but the animal eluded us. We moved to another area, where I shot a running gemsbok twice at about one hundred and fifty yards, but both shots struck the animal too far back. It went down within a few feet after being hit but got up and moved off while we were out of sight,

---

[1]Most high-powered rifles sighted to hit the center of a bull's-eye at twenty-five meters will place a bullet about two and one-half inches high at one hundred yards, and will be spot on at two hundred and seventy-five to three hundred yards.

climbing to get to it. Unfortunately, the black tracker was not Cabbage, and Sweetnam was not Rob Martin. We found a small puddle of blood where the animal fell, but that was all we could find. There simply were too many gemsbok tracks on that hill for any of us to determine which way mine had gone, so Sweetnam went one way, I went the other, and the tracker went someplace else. Sweetnam found the wounded animal and shot it three more times before it went down for good.

It was frustrating to be a half-mile away while someone else finished off my animal, but as I left the hill and walked toward where I'd heard the shots, I suddenly realized this was the first time I had been alone in the field in Africa. During the hour or so I had walked around by myself, I had come upon a dozen or so other gemsbok, several red hartebeest, two duiker, an eland, and about thirty springbok. It was an incredible experience to be alone with a rifle on my shoulder in Africa.

I made up for my poor shooting on the gemsbok by hitting a running springbok on our way back to camp. The forty-pound animal was in mid-leap when my first bullet struck, and it tumbled end over end. Sweetnam and the two blacks with us were surprised (but not as much as I was) that I had hit the swift little animal. I then missed four shots at a running black-backed jackal and one shot at a baboon. I was glad I missed the baboon, even though Sweetnam wanted it killed. (I have no desire to shoot a primate, and that was the only baboon I shot at in all my trips to Africa.) We did not shoot one of the six bat-eared fox we drove up on later. Sweetnam said they are insect eaters, making them "good" animals.

My limited experience on my first trip to Africa had impressed me with the need to know more about its game animals. I'd seen many photos of kudu, sable, gemsbok, and springbok before going to Africa. Books had told me their approximate weights, but I had never seen them on the hoof until I hunted them. It made guessing the range difficult when it came time to shoot. It wasn't until I walked up to my sable and gemsbok that I realized that these animals were much larger than I'd expected them to be. At a distance they seem to be only slightly larger than a mule deer, while they actually are closer to the size of burro. The kudu is much larger than a big deer and smaller than an elk, and a springbok (which reminds me of North America's pronghorn) is smaller than our little Coues whitetail.

At a *braai* (barbecue) that afternoon, where eight of us ate my springbok, accompanied by South African red wine and roasted vegetables, Sweetnam kept talking about the "incredible" and "spectacular" shot that had killed it. I was invited back to Rooipoort to show slides of North American scenery and wildlife and talk about America's hunting to a group of high-school boys that DeBeers hosts in a "winter" school. (I returned to Kimberley twice over the next two decades but never when the school was in session.)

I was on a plane heading for Johannesburg and would board another for Durban the next day. When we said our good-byes at the airport, Sol urged me to come back and be his houseguest, in any case.

✳ ✳ ✳

There were Kentucky Fried Chicken outlets and billboards for Coca-Cola and Lion beer in Durban, a large and modern South African seaport on the Indian Ocean in Natal Province. The Royal Hotel, where I stayed, was decorated in East Indian motifs and had a tapestry that must have been one hundred feet long in its marble-covered lobby. By far, this was the poshest hotel I'd seen anywhere, including the Beverly Hills Hotel, Madrid's Palace, and the Scottsdale Radisson, but its daily rate for a single room in 1983 amounted to only about U.S.$60.

I'd spent the morning in Pietermaritzburg, trying to chase down an official in charge of South Africa's black rhino restoration efforts; then I'd eaten lunch at a quaint roadside inn overlooking the Valley of the Thousand Hills before the SATOUR driver left me at the Royal. When I finally checked into my room, I was so tired I went straight to bed and slept for hours. It was about midnight when I woke, and when I couldn't fall asleep again, I decided to walk around the block. The smell of the Indian Ocean in the night air hit me the instant I stepped outside. I was surprised to see dozens of young black men lounging on cars parked in the street at the side of the hotel. I told myself that in downtown Durban of mid-1983 I probably was safer than I'd be in downtown Tucson after dark. Nonetheless, I quickly ducked back into the hotel. They probably were hotel workers waiting for someone to pick them up after working the late shift.

The traffic on the streets below my room was heavy, even at dawn. I walked to the beach, took my shoes off, and hit the water at the first glow of daylight. The water was colder than I had expected it to be.

I had breakfast that morning in the hotel's coffee shop with Tudor Howard-Davies, who then was the editor of *Man Magnum* magazine, southern Africa's oldest and largest hunting and firearms magazine. Howard-Davies said his staff consisted of just four people and he relied heavily on freelancers, including a few American outdoor writers. (I later learned that he was listed as a field editor on *Field & Stream*'s masthead and was a member of the Outdoor Writers Association of America.) Before taking up writing, he had been a professional hunter in South Africa and Zimbabwe. He was overworked and had few opportunities to go hunting, he said, but he was just back from the Ciskei homelands, where he had shot a black wildebeest. He envied my hunt in Zimbabwe. He would like to hunt Cape buffalo and see wild elephant herds again, he said. The only hunting he now had time for was on South African game farms.

He wasn't happy about the prices some of the farmers were charging. Nonetheless, the editorial policies of his magazine promoted paying farmers to raise game. Unless hunters paid the farmers, there would be nothing left to hunt, he said.

When I asked about South Africa's censorship, he said the RSA Board of Censors did not have to approve his copy, nor had he ever received warnings that his material was objectionable. Despite what he said, I knew the board distributed lists of banned books and sometimes arrested people for possessing them. That morning, one of the Johannesburg newspapers published the names of books recently added or deleted from the list. One of the "bad" books was

The Covenant, James Michener's recently published epic novel about southern Africa's history and racial problems. There also was a brief news item elsewhere in the paper that told of a twenty-four-year-old woman arrested at an airport terminal and quoted her as saying she had been out of the country and didn't know the book she was reading was banned.

Howard-Davies said his problem, as editor of South Africa's leading shooting and hunting magazine, was with the lack of quality control on things such as the components produced by South African companies for reloading sporting ammunition in 1983. By the time he could compile, test, and publish reloading data for his readers, the formulas had been changed, he said.

Almost eighteen months to the day after meeting him in Africa, I received a call at my office in Tucson. Howard-Davies said he was working late (it was 11 P.M. in Durban) and had decided to call me. He and I discussed stories we'd each proposed for the other's magazine; then he told me the real reason he'd called.

"The short-term situation isn't bad," he said. "So far, there has been no violence in Durban. I don't see any problems here for a long time. But I see no hope in the long run for South Africa, and I have two teenage sons. I'd appreciate it if you would let me know if you hear of any open positions in America for someone like me." [2]

This was not the only call or letter I would receive from people I'd met in southern Africa in 1983. All of the callers and writers were seeking a way to leave their countries before the expected revolution erupted.

In 1988 Howard-Davies moved to Canada to work as a hunt-booking agent for Canada North Expeditions in Toronto. When I talked with him in early 1989, his new job had taken him to all of Canada's major hunting fields, as well as Scotland and England. He

---

[2]The day after Tudor called me in June of 1985, rioting broke out near until-then peaceful Durban. Blacks broke into the village where Mahatma Gandhi had lived, attacking the "Asians" and "coloureds" who lived there and torching Gandhi's former home. It was the first of many outbreaks of violence in that area.

even visited Australia and New Zealand to set up red deer and Asian buffalo hunts. While he lived in Canada, he and I became good friends, and we bumped into each other at conventions frequently. Then, in early 1992, he suddenly moved with his family back to South Africa. He died of cancer in Cape Town that July.

* * *

I was told most of the shops in Durban were owned and operated by dark-skinned East Indians wearing turbans. The South Africans called these people "Asians." Children of racially mixed marriages were called "coloureds." "Asians" were descendants of workers the early Dutch farmers had brought to Africa from anywhere on that continent, but especially India. I saw neighborhoods in Durban that looked as if they could have been picked up and moved intact from Delhi. Not far from the city were the restored town and buildings Gandhi had built when he lived in South Africa, but I never got there. My schedule was too tight, and the next day I would be leaving South Africa from Richard's Bay, twenty-four hours and two hundred miles away.

I was inside only one Asian-run shop on my first trip to Africa, and that was a small tobacco store on Durban's main downtown street. My driver stopped to let me go inside for cigarettes, suggesting that because I smoked non-filters I should ask for the Gunston brand. I did and found that they tasted much like Lucky Strikes. The shop reminded me of Chinese markets that were family owned and managed in small Arizona towns before chains opened the convenience stores that put family markets out of business. There were strange smells and unfamiliar items hanging from every available nook.

In addition to the cigarettes, I bought two rands' worth of "venison" biltong to eat on the drive to Zululand. I'd tried biltong, the African equivalent of jerky, while visiting Kruger Park earlier that week and liked it. It could have been made from any type of meat, from elephant to duiker, my driver said. About the only types of game meat that aren't soaked in a solution of spices, dried for biltong, and readily eaten are lion and zebra, I was told.

* * *

At one of the bush lodges my SATOUR guides took me, I was treated to a "game walk," where a dozen other tourists and I walked for an hour along the edge of a small river and photographed various animals. The black man who led us was carrying a .375 H&H Magnum that looked as if it had been on the losing side in both world wars. It was for emergency use only, he said, just in case something might want to come after us. He smiled when I asked if the rifle was loaded, then dug into his pocket and produced a single, very shiny cartridge. It was the only ammunition he had been given, and he carried it in his pocket so that he could polish it whenever he had a spare minute.

It made me feel extremely uncomfortable when he led us down what obviously was a well-used hippo path to the river. The reeds were thick, and there was no way any of us could have gotten out of the way if a hippo decided it wanted to leave or return to the river. Hippo are considered one of the most dangerous animals in Africa, but it made me feel better to know an attack, if there were to be one, would come so swiftly that the guy wouldn't have time to load his rifle. I didn't want him shooting that thing within a hundred miles of me.

The hippo were at home in their little pool, and I was able to photograph them from a mere ten yards away with a normal lens on my camera and return to the lodge without incident.

"For As Long As It Takes"

Chapter 16

The drive north from Durban to Richard's Bay followed the Indian Ocean coastline through cultivated forests of pine and wattle trees and hillside plantations of sugar cane and sisal. Large, picturesque residences were scattered among the green fields. Much of the countryside resembled Southern California's seacoast, but the terrain and scenery changed immediately when we crossed a river and entered Zululand.

One side of the river was a beautiful rural area, with vast fields, open spaces, and abundant ground cover and trees. The other side was a hodgepodge of grass shacks scattered here and there on land that had little growing on it. It bothered me when the SATOUR driver said there were few wild animals left outside the game parks on either side of the river. I knew that every inch of this land had been intensely developed nearly a century earlier, but this was Africa, and I wanted to think that leopard still stalked bushbuck, impala, and nyala just off the highway.

Although that was no longer possible, I knew that the South African government was committed to restoring and preserving wildlife. Its huge Kruger National Park was known around the world, and there were many other parks, plus private wildlife reserves and many hundreds of hunting areas, that had been restocked with game. Even so, after hunting along the Zambezi River and seeing Zimbabwe's free-roaming wild animals, the smaller parks and game farms I visited in South Africa reminded me of American "Safariland" joints and game ranches. The animals I saw on my SATOUR-sponsored tour of South Africa—even lion, cheetah, and elephant—seemed to be bored. They had posed for so many pictures that they now ignored humans. I shot seventy-two photos of a cheetah from the back of a Land Rover as we followed the animal for a half-hour at one of the places SATOUR took me. In only one of all those slides was the animal looking at the camera. It apparently knew it could not escape our vehicles and could only ignore us. When it grew tired of having us follow, it simply plopped down and stared at everything except us.

At the same park where I photographed the cheetah, I rode in one of four Land Rovers that surrounded a pride of six lionesses and a dark-maned lion as we followed the pride's nighttime hunt. The lights from the vehicles confused a herd of impala and allowed one of the cats to pull down a ram thirty yards from at least two dozen tourists. Blood soon covered the faces of the animals as they ripped the impala into pieces and began gorging themselves. The sounds of the kill and the smell of warm guts eventually attracted hyenas, whose eyes glowed in the dark at the edges of our lights. Exciting? Yes. But something was wrong if we could be in open vehicles and ignored by these meat-eating animals. Our drivers said similar kills were witnessed three or four nights a week.

David Varty, owner of Londolozi Lodge, which is located on the border of Kruger Park, proudly told me his place was an experiment in habitat and wildlife management. He was trying to show other South African landowners the benefits of restocking their farms with native game and restoring native vegetation. Unless they believed wildlife had a value, they wouldn't keep it around, he said. He and other landowners in his region had sold their livestock and were removing their fences, creating a large, privately owned wildlife area along the park's boundaries. They also were removing "invader" plant species and stimulating native vegetation by burning and bulldozing. Varty said he would like to see his experiment spread throughout all of southern Africa.

When I was there, only part of his place was set aside for camera safaris. The remainder was being hunted. Fees from both operations meant the land did not have to support cattle or crops, Varty said.

Even in 1983, there already were many game farms in South Africa, and some of their animals were going to zoos and other game farms all over the world. While I was there, for example, a TV news announcer told of ten white rhinos and a dozen baby elephants being shipped to America. Newspaper stories I read back home said that Texas ranches stocked with African animals were helping to preserve endangered species. In South Africa, however, every wildlife biologist I met was involved in culling animals to keep growing herds from eliminating their food supplies.

I took a game drive at Zululand Safari Lodge, north of Durban, and shared a Land Rover with a man and his wife from Scottsdale, which is just 120 miles from my home in Tucson. We photographed one white rhino, one ostrich, two nyalas, three blue wildebeests, a couple of giraffes, and several small bands of impalas and zebras during our short drive before breakfast. We also foolishly (I thought) left the vehicle and walked unarmed within a few yards of the white rhino cow. The guide allowed us to get close before he announced that we should leave immediately because he could not locate her calf.

On our way back to the truck, a half-grown ostrich trotted up to us and began begging for attention from our guide. He stroked its neck and allowed the giant bird to take his hand into its mouth. I was struck by how big and heavy an ostrich's feet seemed to be in proportion to its body. The guide said the feet are the bird's best weapons, and we should avoid them at all costs. The bird had been a camp pet when it was younger, he said, and now that it was nearly grown, it was getting harder to get it to stay away from humans. Ostriches have no teeth, he said, so there was no danger of it biting us. Would I like to touch it? When I did, the bird grabbed my right thumb and tried to pull it off. My attraction to ostriches ended then and there.

Another Land Rover passed us as we returned to the lodge. The occupants also had been hunting, but they were using rifles instead of cameras. We could see the carcass and spiraling horns of a kudu in the back of their truck. The woman from Scottsdale was angry that someone had killed an animal. I didn't tell her I had shot a kudu in

Zimbabwe just one week earlier or that the wildlife we were seeing would not be there for us to enjoy unless people like me and the two Americans in that truck were willing to pay to hunt it. The trophy fee on that kudu in 1983 probably was about $500, and that was in addition to the daily fees of $100 to $150 each man was paying to hunt. The lodge could charge at most only about $80 a day per person for a photo safari in 1983.[1]

Camera safaris were a barely profitable sideline, and even if prices were raised to change that situation, animals still would need to be killed or removed to keep their numbers in balance with their food supplies. The only alternative would be to remove all fences everywhere and allow game to roam freely across many hundreds of miles. That was not likely to happen in my lifetime, I was told.

* * *

Zululand (now KwaZulu-Natal) was not one of South Africa's independent black homelands that American journalists liked to scoff at in the 1980s. Its status was more like the Indian reservations of Arizona and New Mexico. There was a tribal government, but the people lived on a reserve under the jurisdiction and protection of the government in Pretoria. The Zulus are South Africa's largest tribe, and their leaders resisted the homeland arrangement. I thought Zululand was the most colorful and interesting place I visited in South Africa.

There were Zulu women and children walking at the edges of the highways throughout Zululand. They all wore brightly colored skirts and blouses, making the road's crowded edges look like a patchwork quilt. Nearly every Zulu woman carried something on her head— bundles of grass for thatching, wattle logs, a stack of salvaged cardboard, or a huge basket. One woman had a small refrigerator precariously

---

[1]In 2007 Namibian outfitter Jan Oelofse said the annual revenue from the fifty hunting safaris on his properties in Namibia exceeds that from the seven thousand tourists who visit his Mount Etjo Safari Lodge every year.

balanced on her head, but I couldn't understand how she would use it. I saw no electric lines going to any of the grass-thatched huts visible from the highway.

My driver stopped so that I could buy a rhino carving made of wattle from one of the many young Zulu kids who stood along the road and waved their hand-carved products at passing motorists. The price was three rand, about $2.40 at the 1983 rate of exchange, but all I had was a ten-rand note and he had no change. He didn't speak English, but he certainly knew what I meant when I told him with a wave of my hand to keep the change. He beamed from ear to ear and ran off into the bush. He still may be talking about the crazy foreigner who paid him more than three times what he had asked for a carving.

The rondavels and huts along the road reminded me of the Navajo and Apache wickiups and hogans in Arizona and New Mexico, except that the Zulus lived closer together. There were other things in Zululand that year that reminded me of the reservations in our southwest: the many roadside vending stands where beads, grass mats, carvings, and baskets were sold; the scarcity of adult men among the hordes of people we saw walking; the miles upon miles of huts and the apparent absence of grocery stores and small businesses to serve them. Unfortunately, nobody learns anything about Native Americans—or Zulus—from watching them through the window of a fast-moving automobile.

I asked my driver how the Zulus earned their living and was told that a few of the men worked on farms, but the majority worked elsewhere—at the Johannesburg gold mines three hundred and fifty miles away, perhaps. There were schools run by the tribal government. Pretoria and Cape Town did not determine the curriculum.

"Are there Soviet-trained terrorists moving into the homelands and places like Zululand, as there were in the old Rhodesian tribal villages?" I asked.

The driver said there probably were, but they were of no concern.

"How much longer can a comparatively few whites control South Africa?" I asked.

The answer was an angry one, but it meant, "For as long as it takes."

This was in June of 1983. Over the next few months, bloody riots broke out in every corner of the country. Some of the most violent acts would occur in Durban and Port Elizabeth, only a few hours' drive from this spot in Zululand. Some of the people we saw along the road undoubtedly would have been participants. Eighteen months after my visit, thousands of Zulus would stand on their side of the river and chant threats and insults to Pondo tribal members in the Transkei homeland. This would take place almost weekly, and a few Pondos or Zulus would eventually become so angered by the other tribe's insults that they'd cross the river and be clubbed, stabbed, or kicked to death.

In one four-week period in early 1986, more than a hundred black South Africans were killed by members of other tribes. Just minutes before writing my notes on this that year, I read a news report of a similar incident in Zululand. Instead of saying "tribal," the reporter for the *Washington Post* said "ethnic group." For some reason, the American media refused to acknowledge that Africa's historic tribal rivalries had never ended.

There was a Zulu teenager, wearing a short black skirt and nothing else, sitting on a low wall outside the office at Zululand Safari Lodge. She paid no attention to me as I passed her and went inside to register. A co-worker in Tucson had a photo of herself posing with a group of topless Zulu women as a souvenir of her visit to Zululand, and I wanted a similar photo, so I asked the office manager if it still were possible to photograph people in their "traditional" dress. He said it would take about an hour to arrange it, but it could be done. Thinking I would be driven to a village somewhere, I went to the rondavel that was my room for the night, unpacked what I thought I would need that afternoon, and loaded my camera.

I had slept in a similar round hut in Skukusa, a village inside Kruger National Park. These grass-thatched structures with conical roofs are efficient and probably cheap to build. I was especially impressed with the ingeniously designed support systems for their roofs, although it took some time to become accustomed to the sweet odor from the grass in the thatching. I have never seen the inside of a Zulu's hut, but I am certain the Zulus' huts are not as well constructed as those made for tourists. Theirs certainly did not have the flush toilets, running water, and electric heating and air-conditioning that I had in all the huts I have used.

I had finished unpacking when the telephone rang. The manager said he had arranged for me to take my photos. The owners had re-created a Zulu village just beyond the veranda of their lodge, and six black women (two of them wearing beaded vests, the others nude above the waist) and the manager were waiting there for me to photograph them. I took several photos of the women and handed my camera to the manager so he could photograph me standing among them. When we were finished, I gave him some rands to pay my models. Everyone who sees the prints made from those slides remarks how awkward and embarrassed I seem in the pictures. When this happens, I tell them the rest of the story.

There were six waitresses wearing starched white cotton uniforms in the lodge's main dining room that evening. I recognized several of the women, but I couldn't remember where I had seen them. The meal was almost over before I realized that they had posed earlier for my photographs. I found it strange that seeing them fully dressed made me feel more embarrassed than when they had been topless.

* * *

The officials who ran South Africa's national parks were like government officials everywhere. Everyone I talked with said there was too little money for his or her important tasks. Even so, it was apparent that they loved what they were doing.

The two top executives at the Transvaal Nature Department in Pretoria said they had few opportunities to get out of the office and were eager to take me on an excursion to a park nearby, which they planned to open soon. The two executives and I spent the day there, watching and photographing zebras, blesboks, black wildebeests, and elands, not far from one of Africa's largest and most modern cities.

We ate lunch at a cafeteria on the preserve, and I had my first and last African hamburger. The hard, cooked meat was chopped and not ground, and served open-faced on a hard roll with a red-colored cheese sauce poured over everything. The best thing I can say about it is that it was perfectly awful.

My hosts said that when the preserve opened to the public, it would be on a permit-only basis. They believed that too many visitors would ruin the park and create too many problems in managing people. So, as do their counterparts at government-owned parks around the world, instead of designing facilities to handle the people the place would attract, they opted to keep all but a few people out. They did this, they said, so that visitors would have a "quality" experience. This type of thinking is common throughout the United States, but I didn't expect to encounter it in Africa.

Meanwhile, while the roads and buildings were being completed, the officials were using the park as a retreat for bureaucrats. A half-dozen white families and a black staff of who knows how many people were living there and operating the facilities, such as the cafeteria and a large museum. I was interested in the museum's diorama. It depicted the highveld outside and had not yet been completed when I was taken behind the glass to inspect it. The painting was incredibly realistic and had been well executed by an American landscape artist, but the mounted animals were examples of what taxidermy shouldn't be. A stuffed cheetah chasing a stuffed duiker deserved to be called "stuffed" instead of "mounted," the word skilled taxidermists use to describe their art.

The American had taken two years to do the painting, which he had estimated would take only one year, the officials said, and all the money they had budgeted for the diorama had been spent on the painting. They planned to replace the animal exhibits later. (When I returned in 1996, museum-quality mounted specimens had replaced the stuffed animals.)

There apparently was considerable controversy over what should be done with the preserve's re-created Boer farm. Some did not want it fenced because they wanted the park animals to eat whatever crops could be grown there. Others wanted to protect the crops so that sales of produce could offset part of the park's operating expenses. I offered my opinion that the Boers would either have had a fence or would have been waiting with rifles for the animals. The problem, the officials said, was that there was no money for fencing materials.

One of the officials had visited the United States and was impressed by Arizona's Grand Canyon, but he couldn't believe that he had not seen the entire canyon from the South Rim's viewing areas. This man, although he complained a lot about his agency's lack of money, believed that South Africa's method of using general tax funds was better than having hunting and fishing licenses pay for wildlife conservation, as is done in most states in America. His comments about using only tax money to run his agency were so profound that I wrote them down as soon as I returned to my hotel room.

"The way we do it, I—as a nature department employee—am not beholden to shooters and anglers. I wouldn't want to have some shooter make me explain or defend our programs," he said.

To be polite, I remained quiet. But I wanted to point out that the Transvaal Nature Department was forced to supplement its income by selling live wildlife to private game parks or by selling horns, bones, meat, and hides from the animals the government shooters culled each year. Because they were not "beholden" to shooters, they did not use sport hunting as a management tool. Revenue from hunting licenses went to other programs, and not to the nature departments. When animal populations exploded, which they frequently did, cullers with refrigerated trucks—and not sport hunters—were called in.

Although the nature department people claimed wholesale shooting by professional marksmen was more efficient and humane than declaring a "wide-open" hunting season, hearing about it reminded me of the market hunting done on North American bison herds in the nineteenth century. And that reminded me of the bison I'd killed in Arizona as a young man, and how bureaucrats way back then felt they should manage the wildlife they were responsible for.

I was shocked to realize that I had not met anyone in Africa who felt that the hunting heritage should be protected for "ordinary" (make that read "nonwealthy") citizens on that continent, the promised land for the rest of the world's big-game hunters. Instead, most people, even the nature-department employees who hunted, felt hunting meant killing meat to dry and make into biltong. Trophy hunters were from "overseas" and were always rich, they believed. When herds had to be reduced, the best way to handle it, everyone told me, was to call in professional cullers. The surplus animals were shot from helicopters or Land Rovers and Toyotas. The meat was processed in refrigerated vans and then sold in Africa or Europe.

* * *

One of the places I enjoyed most on my SATOUR tour was Kruger National Park, but it wasn't because of the number of animals my tour guide showed me—I'd seen more game while hunting in Zimbabwe and on the Rooipoort Estate. It was because of the park's director, a pleasant fellow named Bruce Bryden. He was an avid hunter, and in that respect he was unique among national-park employees I've met. He was interested in seeing and handling my rifles, and before my visit was over, I got to see many behind-the-scenes things few tourists know about. For example, he took me to a group of corrals where dozens of baby elephants were being held. There must have been four or five corrals, and the baby elephants in each corral were all of the same size. They were orphans that had been captured in the park's culling operations, Bryden said. Babies smaller or larger than a certain size were killed, along with the rest of their herds, but these were old enough to survive without their parents and young enough to be handled.

Bryden said the culling was done by shooting the animals with tranquilizing darts from a helicopter, and then men on the ground would kill each drugged animal with a bullet to the brain. The specially designed darts were shot from a Japanese-made, over-under 20-gauge shotgun exactly like one I had bought two years earlier in Tucson.

I was so fascinated with the mount of a freak Cape buffalo in Bryden's office that I exposed most of a roll of film on it. Instead of growing out and down, then curling up, its horns grew almost straight down. Despite all the shots I took, my photos were not as good as I'd hoped they'd be.

Before I left Kruger, Bryden took me to a storage room stacked from floor to ceiling with elephant tusks seized from poachers and collected by rangers during the culls. This was before ivory sales were banned, and all of the tusks (except for one pair) were scheduled to be sold at auction to buyers from around the world. The proceeds would be used to help pay for the park's operations, he said.

The tusks that would not be sold were from one of the park's so-called Magnificent Seven elephants, a bull called Mafunyani. Its carcass was found just a few weeks before I arrived, and the tusks—they were so long they had dragged on the ground and dulled their tips—were collected for display at a small museum being built at Skukusa, the park's headquarters. Bryden was kind enough to have them taken outside so that I could photograph them before I left.

✳ ✳ ✳

The man in charge of Hluhluwe and Omfolozi, the Natal Province's flagship rhino preserves in Zululand, was shouting into a radio, solving emergencies in the bush with loud commands from his little office, when my SATOUR guide drove me there. He had no idea how many rhinos resided in the two preserves, but he hoped to find out when the government finally approved the rental of a helicopter. Meanwhile, his most important task was keeping poachers from killing his charges. His staff had discovered a few months earlier that several of the Omfolozi preserve's game guards were selling rhino horns from animals they had killed within the preserve. Those guards now were in jail.

"We have a room full of horn here," he said. "Do you want to see it? We collect it from every animal that dies and from those that we seize from the poachers. If we sell it, we might be able to flood the market, lower the price, and keep more rhinos from being killed. But the minute we do, we can expect someone to criticize us. What should we do?"

I didn't get to see the room because I had to catch a plane at Richard's Bay, two hours away on a dirt road. But I had seen a similar vault at Kruger.

* * *

It was no secret that many whites in southern Africa in 1983 considered South Africa to be the last chance for a non-socialist government on the continent of Africa. Many of them had fled Ethiopia, Mozambique, Angola, Sudan, Tanganyika, Central African Republic, the Congo, Rhodesia, Somalia, Libya, Chad, and other formerly colonial countries. They believed they had no place to go if South Africa moved to majority (black) control. Those I met in South Africa that year said I should look at the history of other African countries, where governments were failing because the new leaders were corrupt and could not or would not provide enough food and jobs for their citizens.

They talked about atrocities we never heard about in the United States—hundreds of political prisoners in African jails with nothing to drink for days except their own urine; the wholesale slaughter of blacks by blacks from opposition tribes in every new black country on the continent; the herding of thousands of people into areas where no food or medicine was allowed in. Uganda and Angola were mentioned frequently, and not just because of the well-documented killings by Idi Amin's troops in Uganda. The death count in those two countries had reached well over two million people during the previous decade, and these were blacks slaughtered by other blacks, the expatriates emphasized. They also told about newly independent governments purposely causing entire villages to starve to death. Most of the stories were difficult to believe, except that I was hearing them too often.

According to these white Africans, the history of "reform" in Africa usually progressed this way: First, there were strikes and acts of dissent and terrorism designed to make the world notice the inequalities of colonial rule. Next came protest marches in Brussels; Lisbon; Paris; London; Washington, D.C.; or wherever, to capture the attention of the press "at home." This was followed by riots in villages, with blacks killing other blacks. There were killings of whites by blacks, and blacks by whites, but mostly it would be blacks against blacks, responding to age-old tribal rivalries. Responding to complaints from other countries about human rights issues, an embarrassed England or Belgium or France or Portugal would throw up its hands and turn the country over to home rule. The next step would be a much-publicized election in which a president or a prime minister would be selected. The world then would cheer the switch to majority rule and promptly forget about that corner of the globe.

The country's name would change to Tanzania, Zambia, Zimbabwe, or Zaire. (In the early 1980s, Zania was the name selected for the Republic of South Africa by a group that advocated violent overthrow of the Pretoria government.) Meanwhile, there would be rumors of widespread graft and corruption among the new leadership. There would be leaks that members of the tribe in power were reducing the opposition by killing members of other tribes. In each country, bloodbaths and power struggles were accompanied by the failure of the country's economy, followed by famine that reduced the opposition tribes even more. Tribal rivalries, the expatriate whites told me, always continued despite changes in political systems. Blacks have been killing blacks in Africa for centuries; I shouldn't expect that to change soon, they said.

There was a phrase I heard the whites use a lot in South Africa in 1983. It went something like this: "No matter how cruel they say we are to blacks, what we have done is nothing compared to what blacks are doing to blacks here and everywhere else in Africa."

I met several white southern Africans who had fled to South Africa after losing guerrilla wars in their native countries. When they fought in Rhodesia, Uganda, or Angola, they'd gone off to war for a few months and then returned to run their farms for a year or two. They had expected that the West's major powers would rescue their struggling governments. They were bitter that Great Britain and the United States had ignored their pleas for assistance and placed sanctions on shipments to their crippled and dying nations. They could not understand how the free world could stand by and not come to their aid while Russia and China were supplying their country's terrorists with all the tools of modern warfare. A war, if it came to that in South Africa, certainly wouldn't be fought part time, they vowed. Too many of them had learned bitter lessons in the countries they had fled.

* * *

At Jan Smuts and other airports in South Africa, I saw many injured young white soldiers. Were they back from the frontiers of Mozambique and Namibia? Had they been wounded in raids across the borders into Zaire or Angola? I didn't ask, but I noticed that South Africans seemed to treat their soldiers—wounded or not—with respect, just as I remember we treated our vets back from World War II and Korea, and not in the shameful way our Vietnam vets were treated.

* * *

South African television? I twice watched *The Gods Must be Crazy*, the South African-made movie that eventually became a cult film in the United States. It was the only locally produced movie I saw on television during the time I was in that country in 1983. However, there were many American reruns on the English-speaking station. (There were three networks: one in English, another in Afrikaans, another in a tribal language.) A U.S.-made program called *Dallas* was popular, and when I told people that the series South Africans watched on Wednesday evenings was two years behind what was being shown in the States, they all wanted to know what would happen to their favorite characters. They were disappointed when I told them some had married or died and others had been replaced. Invariably, their first question, when the discussion turned to TV, was, "Who really shot J.R.?"

Those television shows must be the reason many South Africans attempted to imitate Americans. Sol's teenage son treated me as a celebrity in Kimberley and said he would go to America someday. He wanted to know if it was difficult to drive on the "wrong side of the road

251

back home in America" and how many servants my wife and I employed. Many young people in Durban wore T-shirts with slogans on them. I saw one that said "I Love New York." Some wore punk-style haircuts and outlandish clothing, apparently trying to imitate the American musicians they had seen on the tube.

My drivers all were young urbanites. They read books and magazines published by American conservation groups, and they quoted Sierra Club slogans such as "Leave only footprints and take only photographs." To them, *safari* meant a weekend at a game lodge in the Transvaal or Zululand or driving through Kruger National Park, photographing semi-tame animals from a Land Rover. I doubt that any had ever seen wildlife outside a park or a game farm. They could not believe that wild meat-eating animals ever attacked humans without provocation. They didn't know that wildlife management meant that Kruger National Park's rangers needed to kill thousands of elephants to keep the animals from turning that great park into a desert, or that part of the responsibilities of the game guides at game farms was to drive around at night with small-caliber rifles, "culling" hundreds of impalas every year. They were as ignorant of the realities of the wild land around them as are the urban children in the United States who believe meat is created in a plastic wrap through some sort of immaculate conception.

This was the Africa I had dreamed about all my life. It was hard to believe that sentimentalists had reached it before me. Urbanites living on a continent with more carnivores than in the rest of the world combined believed predators killed only the old and weak, that wild animals tiptoed around talking with each other, that animals couldn't overpopulate. I couldn't convince them that while we debated our sides of the animal-rights issue, healthy but unlucky prey animals were being eaten alive or that animals were starving somewhere in Africa.

Does it take only a generation in a city to lose touch with what happens in the real world?

Collecting Specimens for the SCI Museum

Chapter 17

After only one trip to Africa and another to Spain, I naively considered myself a seasoned international traveler. My second trip to Africa, in September 1986, lacked the excitement of anticipating the unknown that I'd experienced a few years earlier. As soon as the South African Airways jet left Heathrow Airport, I changed into a comfortable jogging suit and settled in for the eleven-hour flight south from London. I fell asleep during the movie and didn't wake up until we were over the tropical marshes of the Ivory Coast. I was asleep again soon after learning that passengers could not leave the plane while we took on more fuel in Abidjan.

On my first trip to Johannesburg, I'd spent most of the flight from Isle lo Sol, where we'd taken on fuel after flying southeast from New York, watching for my first glimpse of the shores of Africa. This time, I waited until the steward said we were about an hour from landing before shaving and changing into khaki slacks, an oxford shirt, and a blazer. As a representative of Safari Club International on a trip to collect specimens for the International Wildlife Foundation's museum, I wanted to be properly dressed.

Alex Jacome, who had taken the same flight, joined me when we stepped off the plane. I'd flown on a coach ticket, but one of his daughters was an American Airlines flight attendant, so he had flown first class.

Jan Smuts International Airport hadn't changed in three years, nor could I see any difference in the security measures. I had heard stories from other hunters, who said everyone walking into the terminal had to be searched and that it was no longer possible to drive up to the terminal's front doors, but this apparently wasn't true. We spent less than five minutes getting the permits we needed to possess our rifles, shotguns, and pistols in South Africa, and then Alex and I checked our guns and baggage onto our flight to Kimberley.

We hired a taxi to take us into Johannesburg, and the black taxi driver suggested that we drive through Soweto, as a cab driver had done on my first trip. We declined the invitation, partly because we had only eight hours on this layover and partly because I didn't want to be anywhere near the site of possible violence. There was nothing to fear that day, but the next week black youths rioted and damaged several homes in Soweto. The newscasters said the rioters were protesting the deaths of workers in a fire at a mine.

The driver took us to the Carlton Centre, where I'd stayed on my first trip to Johannesburg. Alex and I quickly walked through the mall, ate a great lunch at the Carlton Hotel's coffee shop, and signed the register at the Rowland Ward shop run by two widows of East African professional hunters. About half of the diners in the coffee shop were black. Both of us were surprised to see couples of mixed races, some of them holding hands, in the mall. Two years earlier, under a law banning marriages between races, these couples would have been arrested and brought before a magistrate. The law was dropped in early 1986, but world media had given it little publicity. It seemed to us that this change might have been one of the most significant reforms ever made in South Africa.

We used a shuttle for the trip from the hotel back to Jan Smuts. The driver was accompanied by a woman, and neither was interested in talking with us, so Alex and I watched the streets and freeways zip past us on the long drive to the airport. Many of the houses had red tile roofs and wrought-iron window coverings and gates, making the streets seem a lot like those in Mexico. We arrived at the airport about an hour before takeoff and passed the time watching people move through the terminal. Most were well dressed and seemingly affluent. A large percentage of them were East Indians wearing turbans.

* * *

Alex and I were waiting for our bags to be unloaded at Kimberley Airport when a smiling Ted Sweetnam strode in with his hand outstretched. I'd spent only a day with him during my visit in 1983, but we'd struck up a friendship.[1]

It was about 7 P.M., and Alex and I hadn't eaten since noon. Sweetnam joined us for the meal of cold cuts he'd reserved for us at the Kimberley Club, a prestigious private club in downtown Kimberley. Even though it was late and we were the only guests in the dining room, Sweetnam made certain we followed protocol by choosing a table that wasn't assigned to a member. The place was tehr-dib-bly British, don't you know?

The club was built in the nineteenth century, and its walls were covered with walnut panels heavy with the patina of age. The carpeting was rich but worn, even threadbare, in places. Photographs of English military officers, heroes of the British-Boer conflicts, were hanging everywhere. An antique machine gun greeted visitors at the front door, and huge brass shells from artillery were on the landing above the stairs. Polished silver and brass decorated the varnished bar in the lounge. Outside, a three-foot-long arrow made of lead was inset in the concrete sidewalk exactly where Cecil Rhodes had scratched an arrow pointing north in the dirt, saying that this was the direction to look for him if he did not return from his expedition into what was to become the two Rhodesias. The Kimberley Club facility and its furniture obviously were expensive, but they showed signs of a century of use, and there was a musty smell to them. It was easy to see why the South African government had declared the place a national historic site.

Sweetnam now was vice president in charge of the DeBeers Consolidated Mining Company's legal affairs in Kimberley, and he announced that Alex and I would be the guests of his company during our week at the club. This required that we be made temporary members

---

[1]Ted and I had written and called each other several times in planning for this trip, and he'd helped me obtain the collecting permits I needed. I later was his sponsor for a spot on a team that competed at the Lander One Shot Antelope Hunt in Wyoming.

so we could buy drinks by signing chits and take our meals in the club's dining room. DeBeers paid 15 rand (less than U.S.$7 then) per day for each of our rooms. We paid only for our meals and box lunches, beverages, phone calls, and laundry. After eight days there, our tab was just 385 rand, or about $175. I knew of no place else, even in South Africa, where two people could eat, make two international phone calls, and have their clothes laundered for $22 per day!

The rooms were large but poorly planned. The bathroom in mine, for example, looked as if it had been added as an afterthought, and probably was. There was no closet, and a small armoire barely held the clothes from one of my two suitcases. The wallpaper and the furniture looked as if they needed replacing. My suite was called the Cecil John Rhodes Room, apparently because Cecil Rhodes had slept there. We were told some of the rooms at the club had been used by English royalty, but I never learned who had occupied them and when.

I woke long before daylight and rambled around the club. There were no television sets in the sleeping rooms, but I turned on the set in the reading room and sat back in a worn but comfortable leather chair. The announcer on the early morning show from Cape Town alternated between Afrikaans and English, and it quickly became apparent that he was simultaneously broadcasting on radio because the pictures on the screen frequently had nothing to do with what was being talked about. I kept watching for news of anti-apartheid violence, but there was none.

Outside, the town was coming alive with the first signs of daylight. Dozens of Africans on bicycles and on foot were on the street below when the waiter found me looking out the large window in the reading room and delivered my morning coffee and newspaper. The paper carried two or three very small stories on the inside pages about scattered incidents of unrest, but, unlike the newspapers at home, I found nothing that said South Africa was in the early stages of a racial revolution.

Alex was still asleep when I cautiously stepped outside the club's front doors and walked out on the sidewalk. After all I had read and seen in American media, I did not know whether it was safe for a white man to walk the streets of South Africa alone. But no one gave me a second glance. I walked three blocks up to the main street, then around that block and back to the club. I hadn't seen Kimberley's business district during my 1983 visit and was surprised to see that it was clean and well kept. There were no empty stores, and all the buildings had recently been painted. There was no litter on the streets or any graffiti.

Alex was up when I returned, and we were the first to have breakfast in the dining room. The waiter seated us at a table near the door and served us an "English" breakfast—two fried eggs, toast, three strips of bacon, a slice of ham, and a large Boer sausage—within minutes after taking the order. The table was formal, with sterling silver tableware, crystal glasses, fine china dinnerware, and monogrammed white linens. I had to ask for water. As on my first trip, coffee was not served until after we had eaten.

We spent that first day in Kimberley preparing for the next day's collecting trip and touring the town. At Sweetnam's office in the quaint old DeBeers building (also a national historic site), we met Angus Anthony, the manager and professional hunter at one of the DeBeers ranches on which we would hunt, and Andrew Sweetnam, Ted's teenage son, who would guide us.

Sweetnam sold us hunting licenses and then took us to the Northern Cape Province's nature department offices to introduce us to Henny Erasmus, the chief of research for the region. Next, we rented a small *bakkie* and drove to a taxidermy shop to arrange for the care of the specimens we intended to collect.

It was uncomfortable operating the controls from the right side of the little truck, but it was nothing compared to the feeling of panic that hit me when I first pulled out into the traffic on the left side of the road.

Lunch was at the Kimberley Hotel, where I had stayed on my last trip, and dinner was at the Mohawk Spur, one of a chain of South African cafés featuring motifs supposedly borrowed from the American southwest. The cowboy steaks were large, but they were covered with a bad-tasting "monkey-gland" sauce and barbecued on a gas grill that reeked of the sauce. The menu had a line drawing of what was supposed to be a Plains Indian with a feathered headdress, and the walls had murals of Indian life. The problem was, the Indians looked more like black Africans.

Andrew Sweetnam was on holiday from high school and had volunteered to guide us during our week in the Kimberley area. He and his father arrived at the Kimberley Club about seven the next morning to tell us that Rooipoort had been leased to a family of Americans for a hunting safari that week. Angus Anthony, who was conducting the safari, had asked only that we stay along the Vaal River, where we wouldn't interfere with his clients' hunting.

Few things looked the same as I remembered from my first visit to Rooipoort, and I had to dredge up all my memories of my one day there to find out why. Then it struck me: There was no grass then. This time the countryside was covered with two-foot-tall yellow grass. It made everything look more like scenes of East Africa we've all seen, with spectacular rolling plains and scattered thorn trees. Before, the countryside reminded me of the most arid regions of southern Arizona and New Mexico, a rock- and sand-covered desert. The high entry gate leading into Rooipoort hadn't changed, and as we drove in, we again saw elands, warthogs, and duikers from the road.

We picked up a tracker at the Rooipoort Box and then headed for the Vaal River, stopping only to photograph our first giraffe of the trip. There's something about giraffe. I can see all types of African wildlife, including elephants and rhinos, but until I see a wild giraffe, it never seems that I actually am in Africa.

Just as we were approaching the river, four sable antelope broke out of the thornbush and paused on the side of a rocky hill before going over the top. I'd seen lots of sables, but that was in Zimbabwe's mopane habitat. Seeing these beautiful antelope in this semi-desert didn't seem quite right. Young Sweetnam explained that his father had gotten the DeBeers company to buy thirteen sable antelope from an animal dealer and set them free on Rooipoort the year before. This was the first sighting since the release, he said. He was encouraged that one of the animals was a calf, proof that sables were reproducing on Rooipoort. There also were plans to reintroduce buffalo, but they would have to come from herds that were proven free of bovine diseases, Andrew said.

We parked at an opening in the brush along the river. An old *braai* pit and faint evidence of past tented camps could be seen in the sand among hundreds of kudu tracks. This spot was a favorite for evening barbecues traditionally held for visitors to the Rooipoort Box. Baboons were barking from a little hill nearby, and birds were calling from the trees and along the river.

Alex, Andrew, and I loaded our two shotguns and the .22 rimfire Mauser rifle the DeBeers company had loaned us. Three goliath herons were resting on the banks above the river, and there were dozens of ducks, cormorants, and egrets along the water. The plan was for Andrew and me to cross the water and try to get close enough to kill one of the herons with the .22. Alex would stay on the other side of the river, just in case the birds flew toward him.

It worked almost exactly as planned. Sweetnam missed with the little rifle, but the heron flew toward Jacome's shotgun. He waited until the bird was directly overhead before firing. The bird staggered, then folded and crash-dived with a loud thud when a second round of No. 4 shot hit it. That goliath heron, a magnificent eight-foot-tall bird with a nine-foot wingspan and a beak almost two feet long, was the first of seventy-eight museum specimens that Alex and I would collect in the next sixteen days. Few of them would come so easily, however.

Jacome and I spent eight days in Kimberley, six of them afield on the three ranches that DeBeers owns there. Ted had arranged for Henny Erasmus and Sandy Cox, owner of Secretarius Safaris, to go out with us on the days Andrew couldn't go.[2]

On our first day with the two men, Sandy announced that we "needed" to shoot a couple of springboks for a *braai* the local Kiwanis

---

[2] I was shocked when Sandy's twin sons died in an awful accident a few years later. One twin was driving to Kimberley while his brother was driving to the family farm from Durban. Neither knew the other was on the road when their vehicles collided at night, killing both of them. I was told young Andrew Sweetnam also was killed several years after we'd hunted with him, but I never learned the circumstances.

Club was holding that weekend. Henny, Sandy, and I were in the cab of the Toyota, and Alex and two trackers were riding in back. We hadn't driven far when Henny spotted a springbok staring at us. Henny and I grabbed our binoculars to get a better look.

"It's a ewe, Alex," I said, and almost before the words were out of my mouth, Alex shot and killed the animal. He apparently had been watching it through his riflescope.

"Why did you shoot that ewe?"

"You said 'you,'" he said.

Unlike back home, there was no stigma against shooting females, but we had been asked to shoot only two springbok. I'd taken a fine male on my first trip, so I asked Alex to shoot the second one for the *braai,* which he later did.

Jacome and I spent three of our nights in Kimberley driving around with Henny Erasmus. We were collecting, not hunting, and there was no attempt to make the effort sporting. We shot genet, jackal, springhare, rabbit, wildcat, and porcupine from the back of the nature department's Ford pickup truck. Spotlighting from a vehicle was illegal in South Africa, just as it is in North America, unless you happened to have collecting permits or were a nature department employee. With Erasmus along, we qualified on both counts.

I found the "work" enjoyable. The outdoor world was confined to the depth of field provided by the one-million-candlepower Q-beam spotlight we'd brought from Tucson, but that world was filled with strange creatures that one never sees in daylight, such as springhares that resembled giant Arizona kangaroo rats. We saw them by the hundreds each night we hunted.

My permits allowed us to shoot two each of just about everything that moved, and we did.

Erasmus and the three men he brought along one night seemed to thrive on the thrill of racing after animals in the dark, and they didn't seem too optimistic when I said I could lure black-backed jackal to a gun with a predator call. To collect jackal, their strategy had always been to drive around until they found them in their headlights, then chase them down and shoot the running animals from moving Land Rovers with shotguns.

I was able to bring jackals to us each time we stopped and called. However, the Afrikaners would not take calling seriously and would talk or move about. This was enough to keep the coyotelike animals from coming close enough for precision shooting. We'd see their eyes and their slinking shapes, but they usually stayed too far out for us to risk a shot. Only one jackal was dumb enough to approach close enough for us to shoot it. Erasmus stepped out of the truck, leaned over the bonnet, and shot it with his .222 Remington (he called it a "two-two-two"). The bullet raked the animal, and it ran off into the night.

Erasmus jumped back into the truck, and we raced off-road as fast as he could drive for about a quarter-mile. He slammed on the brakes when we encountered a fence. This did not stop the three Afrikaners. The two in the back were out of the truck almost before it skidded to a stop. They then threw themselves on the wire and laid the fence down, and Erasmus roared across it. Unfortunately for one of the men, the truck's rear bumper caught a wire and stretched it like a rubber band as we drove over it. When the wire finally slid off the bumper, it acted like a slingshot and flipped the man backward. He and his companion seemed none the worse for the incident, though, and they climbed back into the truck, laughing loudly, as we drove after the jackal again. It was fortunate for him that most African fences are built with wire without barbs. When we finally caught up to the jackal, Erasmus jumped out like a rodeo bulldogger and caught it by the neck, held it up, and swiftly choked it to death. Alex and I watched with wide-open eyes. The man seemed to have no fear of the creature or its teeth or, more important, of contracting rabies.

The bullet had torn the jackal from brisket to rear leg, and its skin was not suitable for mounting. But all the other animals and birds we shot went to a taxidermist in Kimberley, a Portuguese man named Pareida, who prepared them for shipping to Pretoria and on to the United States. The stomachs of all the specimens, including the bullet-torn jackal, were saved for use in Erasmus's study of the effects of the insecticides that were being used in the area. He said it was too soon to tell what he might find. However, it was apparent that a local campaign to combat a plague of locusts had already reduced the area's bird life.

We spent a day with Erasmus on a farm where workers were spraying liquids into aardvark holes. Erasmus showed us swarms of half-inch-long locusts that were pouring out of the holes by the thousands. These little insects would quickly grow into three-inch-long creatures and gobble up crops and grass. A couple of wet years had launched their incubation, he said. The treatment used to fight locusts, however, also was killing hundreds, maybe thousands, of birds. There already was evidence that this was happening, even though we never saw a dead or dying bird. The only pasture where we could find a black korhaan, Namaqua dove, plover, guinea fowl, francolin, or any other bird, for that matter, was one where crews had not sprayed every hole in sight.

We took one day off from collecting and went hunting for ourselves. Alex and I both shot black wildebeest, and I shot a blesbok and a trophy steenbok with the longest horns I've ever seen on those little antelope. It happened this way.

Sandy Cox and I were sitting in a truck watching Alex and Henny moving across the canyon from us. We had seen a greater kudu bull cross the opposite ridge an hour earlier, and Alex and Henny went looking for it for Alex. When I turned my head, I spotted movement in the grass about thirty yards to the left of our truck.

"How big does a steenbok need to be to be shootable?" I asked.

"Anything with horns longer than its ears is a good one," he said.

I didn't say another word. The blast of my .30-06 surprised Sandy.

"What did you shoot?"

"A very good steenbok, I think."

When Sandy and I reached the place where the little antelope lay, he took off his hat and walked around and around the animal, saying, "Oh my Jesus, oh my Jesus. It's bigger than Paul's."

My friend Paul Casey, whom I'd met through Safari Club International, was spending a lot of time in Kimberley and eventually bought a farm there. According to Sandy, Paul had taken the largest steenbok ever seen in that province—until I shot mine. Alex brought me back to earth when he returned.

"What'd you shoot that jack rabbit for?" he asked.

Before we leave Rooipoort, I need to tell the reader about our meals on that huge estate. The Kimberley Club's kitchen sent us afield most days with cold lobster and chicken, a green salad, bread, and wine, packed in wicker baskets with condiments, a linen tablecloth and napkins, genuine sterling silver tableware, and crystal glasses for four persons. The two days we hunted with Sandy, though, we were treated to a South African *braai*, complete with grilled vegetables and venison *boerwors*.

We usually were back in town in time for dinner each evening, but there was one day we weren't. Sandy, Henny, Alex, and I, along with two trackers, had traveled to a far corner of Rooipoort and were heading back when we realized we were hungry and at least two hours from town. Alex had shot a springbok that day, and Sandy had saved its heart and liver in an ice chest. While the trackers built a small fire in the middle of the two-track trail, Sandy proceeded to cut out the antelope's tongue and plop it into the fire with the heart and liver. He didn't wait for the fire to burn down to coals, and he didn't place the meat on a grill. A couple of minutes later, he dragged the meat out and scraped off the dirt and charred wood, cut it into strips, and passed it around. I don't eat liver, but that heart and tongue were the best I've ever tasted.

The next day Sandy and two of his friends accompanied us, and this time he brought along an ice chest of food, including *boerwors* and chops, and we experienced a great Afrikaner *braai* in the middle of the bush.

From Kimberley, Alex flew to Namibia to hunt a kudu and collect several types of hornbills that eventually were used with a pair of caracals in a small diorama at the SCI museum. I traveled to Durban and on to Zululand to finish collecting the birds on my permits, including two oxpeckers for the museum's water-hole diorama. I found more evidence of unintentional chemical warfare against bird life when I reached

Durban, however. I'd seen oxpeckers by the hundreds around Cape buffaloes, kudus, and sables in Zimbabwe—the birds eat ticks from the backs of big game and livestock—and expected no problems. I planned to collect a pair by shooting them with an air rifle off the backs of cattle in a livestock-processing area.

I never saw an oxpecker in Natal, however. Biologists there said it was because of a successful campaign to dip all domestic livestock in that province. The dip may have poisoned many oxpeckers, but what it did more than anything else was remove a major source of food for the birds. As a result, in just two years the oxpecker had become an endangered species in that province.

* * *

After landing in Durban, I again spent the night at the Royal Hotel. I had breakfast with Tudor Howard-Davies and then rented a car to drive up the Indian Ocean coastline to Trevor Shaw's Zulu-Nyala Safaris, a game farm near Omfolozi and Richard's Bay. (Shaw, a Johannesburg diamond dealer and an international director of Safari Club International, said I would be the first person he'd allowed to shoot birds on his place.) I'd driven on the left side of the road for the past week in Kimberley, but Alex had been my navigator. I was on my own on this part of the trip.

I wasn't comfortable driving on the highway that led north out of Durban, especially when turning into exits and on-ramps. I had to keep reminding myself which lane I needed to turn into. After the traffic thinned, though, I began enjoying the scenery. My route followed the Indian Ocean for a while, then moved inland through forests of cultivated wattle and pine. As I'd seen on my first trip to Zululand, there were hundreds of women in colorful dresses along the sides of the road, some of them trying to sell baskets and rugs they'd made from local grasses. The air was filled with the sight and smell of the white smoke from the fields the farmers were burning.

I stopped for lunch at the same roadside inn where my SATOUR guide had taken me two years earlier, and again enjoyed eating kingklip, a delicious fish found in the Southern Hemisphere. By the time I turned off the pavement, I was bragging to myself about my driving skills.

Shaw's instructions called for me to travel ten miles or so on graded roads before turning onto his property. Without white lines to follow, I soon was driving on the wrong side of the road without realizing it. When I saw a vehicle coming toward me, I first got as far right as possible; then, realizing what I'd done, I darted back to the left side. The driver of the other car must have thought I was crazy or playing "chicken" with him.

I eventually pulled up to Shaw's gate, got out, opened it, and returned to the car to drive through. Even after all the driving of vehicles with controls on the right side, I was shocked when I forgot and opened the left door—and didn't see the steering wheel!

Zulu-Nyala's office was a mile or so down the road. I drove past warthogs and impalas—including a ram with horns longer than any southern impala I've seen on the hoof before or since—before stopping at a tin-roofed ranch house. I was greeted by three young professional hunters who worked for Shaw and had seen my name in *Safari* magazine, which they read from cover to cover every two months. I felt like a minor celebrity.

They had been expecting me, and after spending an hour or so talking about a dozen subjects, one of them gave me the keys to a four-wheel-drive Toyota and asked me to follow him to the rondavel where I'd be staying. An American family was hunting on the property while I was there, but he said I probably wouldn't see them if I did my collecting on the far side of the ranch near the rondavel. A tall black man wearing brown coveralls and a black watch cap was waiting at the rondavel when we drove up. "Sam" was the only name I was given for the man who would be helping me during my stay. He did not speak English, but we managed to communicate with our hands.

In Zulu, my young guide told Sam that he should be at my rondavel thirty minutes before daylight each morning. My meals would be served at the ranch house, he told me.

I was awake and dressed when Sam politely tapped on my door the next morning. I grabbed my shotgun and a box of shotshells and headed for the Toyota. Sam was sitting on the passenger side. He expected me to drive while he pointed out which trails I should take. I shot several types of African ducks and a pair of Egyptian geese along a narrow but apparently deep river that cut through a corner of Shaw's place. I had seen spur-winged geese from a distance in Zimbabwe and along the Vaal River at Rooipoort, but I hadn't seen those huge birds in trees until that morning. Their feet not only are webbed for swimming, as are the feet of other ducks and geese, but they also are able to grip small tree limbs.

There must have been thirty or forty of them in a tree a quarter-mile from the river when I spotted them. I drove as close as I thought I could without spooking them, then got out and walked directly to the flock, only to have them fly off before I could shoot. I chased that flock and others all over that part of Shaw's, and they stayed just out of shotgun range. I was able to collect several other birds I had permits for, though.

I must have seen at least twenty nyala bulls that day. The males of these antelope look nothing at all like the females. The gray-colored males are about the size of a large mule deer and have yellow legs; tall, lyre-shaped horns with white tips; stripes on their sides; and shaggy hair hanging from their bellies. They are extremely handsome animals. The females are much smaller, and, although they also have stripes, their sides are a bright red color. Sam and I saw them everywhere we went.

A pair of spur-winged geese fell to my gun the next morning when they flew over me. One hit the ground with a loud thud; the other splashed water four or five feet into the air when it fell into a marsh. Sam was reluctant to wade after it. It took a minute or two of hand signals until he got me to realize there were crocodiles in that shallow water, and he wanted me to cover him with my shotgun while he went after my bird. Before wading to the goose, he took off his overalls and boots. It was then I realized just how poor the man was. His T-shirt and undershorts, although clean, were more holes than fabric. Before I left Zululand, I gave Sam all my underwear and shirts—clean and dirty—saving only what I needed to get home.

I was asleep that evening when another man tapped on my door. Outside was a Toyota Land Cruiser with its headlights on and its engine running. Though I'd never seen this black man before, I had no choice but to follow him when he gestured and said a single word: "Come." He drove, while I asked myself what I was doing riding around in the middle of the night in Zululand with a Zulu I didn't know and couldn't communicate with.

We passed the ranch house I'd left just an hour earlier and drove another ten minutes or so to a group of rondavels I'd never seen. A big fire was burning inside a *boma,* and sitting around it was a family of Americans. The youngest was about twelve years old. The father introduced himself and said he had hired Zulu dancers to entertain them and thought I might enjoy watching the show. The man who'd brought me there served me something from a tray of finger food. I politely turned down my host's invitation for a drink and asked for a Coke without ice instead.

I've forgotten who my host was, but he and his family were pleasant and immediately made me feel comfortable. Nearly everyone had taken all the animals he wanted, except for the father, who had not seen a Natal red duiker, a miniature antelope found only in that corner of the world. I'd seen the same little animal two days in a row in a certain place, I said, and gave his professional hunters directions to it. The man thanked me, and said the next day was the last day he'd hunt on this trip. He was taking his family to see Kruger Park after that.

A truck bearing Sam and what must have been all the black men on Shaw's place, except my driver, soon arrived with seven or eight bare-breasted young women. The women danced around the fire, then formed a line and, with loud shrieks, began kicking and stomping in unison. It was quite a show, and it went on for at least forty-five minutes. Sam was among the grinning guys who drove the girls home.

The next afternoon Sam and I found a dead nyala female on the edge of the road we drove daily. The tracks showed it had been killed by a leopard and dragged to that spot not long before we drove up. Sam wanted to put the carcass in the back of the Toyota and take it to where he lived, but I refused. The thing smelled like last week's road kill, but I'm sure he intended to eat it.

That evening at dinner in the ranch house, we were joined by two men I hadn't seen before. One was a professional hunter; the other was his American client. They'd leased Shaw's place for a day so the client could collect a nyala.

C. J. McElroy had arranged for me to spend one day hunting for myself at Zulu-Nyala. My professional hunter (whose name I've forgotten) was a surly fellow who could have passed for American country-western singer Kenny Rogers. He lived in Durban and hadn't been home in several weeks, and he missed his girlfriend, I learned. He was unhappy about being asked to spend a day guiding me.

I shot one of the larger warthogs that hung around the ranch house, and then he took me back to where I'd been seeing nyala. He suddenly stopped when we reached a nearly dry water hole. A nyala bull had died from exhaustion there during the night, buried up to its belly in the mud. I waited while the PH carefully worked his way across the mud to the animal and cut off its head. Shaw would want its horns, he said.

He and I, along with a Zulu tracker, drove a short distance, parked the truck, and began walking. A few minutes later, the black man showed us the tracks of a nyala bull, and we began following them. We were in single file, the Zulu in front, the PH next, and I bringing up the rear. I cannot describe adequately how tired I soon became. It was one of the many times I wished I were not so tall. Following a nyala's tracks is best done by midgets and Pygmies. This bull had no need to stick to trails because it could easily walk under the acacia trees. Me? I had to squat and bend halfway over to get under them. After thirty minutes of this torture, the Zulu suddenly stopped and pointed by lifting just a finger. The PH grabbed me and pulled me in front of him.

"Shoot," he whispered.

"Shoot what?"

"Shoot that bull."

"I don't see it."

We were in a dark thicket of brush and short palms, and I couldn't see anything.

"It's right there in front of you. Just three meters away. Shoot it!"

I raised my rifle, hoping that I'd be able to see the animal in my scope. I was able to find a horizontal line and what I thought were light-colored stripes. I held the cross hairs a couple of inches below the line, hoping for a spine shot, and fired. But the nyala was standing to the right of the palm frond I'd shot, and it whirled at my shot and was gone.

The PH was not speaking to me as we headed back to the ranch house for lunch. We were almost there when two nyala bulls ran across the road. We caught up to them in less than five minutes, and I shot the larger of the two as it darted around a bush. Even this did not change my PH's mood. He still was scowling when I tipped him before he left for Durban later that afternoon. I suppose he wanted more money, but what I gave him was a good tip for a day's work in South Africa then.

I enjoyed spending the evening with the visiting PH. He was friendly, and he laughed and smiled a lot, which was a welcome change after spending the day with an angry man. Somehow our conversation got around to using varmint calls and the leopard-killed nyala cow Sam and I had seen. It wasn't long before the PH and I returned to where we'd left the carcass. It was gone, but whether Sam or the leopard moved it I'll never know. I'd had luck attracting jackals at night in Kimberley by calling from the back of our *bakkie* with a powerful spotlight pointed straight up. It cast a circle of light around the truck, and even before a jackal stepped into that circle, we could see its glowing eyes. At any rate, there I was, blowing a varmint call during a very dark night in Zululand. The leopard didn't show up, and it's probably a good thing. Leopard weren't on my license, and we hadn't taken a rifle with us.

We were heading back to the ranch house when we heard on the truck's radio that the U.S. Congress had overridden President Reagan's veto and voted to approve sanctions against South Africa. My newfound friend couldn't understand how this could happen.

"Don't they know that Communists are behind all the unrest in this country?" he asked.

My collecting over, I joined Alex in Cape Town the next day. It was the first time either of us had been there, so we rented a van and hired a driver to show us the city. Before the day was over, we had seen most of its best-known sights and taken a cable car to the top of Table Mountain. I knew that Himalayan tahr had been introduced to that mountain, but I saw none on the trip up and down.

That evening Alex and I had the driver take us to a restaurant called On the Rocks to celebrate my fiftieth birthday. Its name was apt. It had been built on the boulders overlooking the Cape, and we watched the ships pass offshore until it was too dark to see. Dinner was served in six or seven courses. The main course was a fish caught just minutes before by one of the dozen or so black youngsters who were fishing below the restaurant with handlines. As soon as one caught a fish, he ran to the kitchen to sell it. A waiter then brought it—still flopping—on a tray, with great stateliness, to our table for us to inspect.

I was overcome with sadness the next day when I looked out the window as our plane left Johannesburg to return Jacome and me to New York. I was certain it would be the last time I would see Africa.

I Find the "Real" Africa

Chapter 18

I took a variety of antelope on my trips to Africa over the next two decades. Except for the warthog and impala I shot each trip, and a second sable antelope, I did not take more than one specimen of the same race, however. The most memorable of all those trips was to Zambia with C. J. McElroy.

After being forced out of his post at Safari Club International, Mac formed a booking agency he called McElroy's Global Adventures to sell safaris with a likable and capable outfitter and professional hunter named Henri van Aswegen. As a favor to Mac, I wrote and designed a series of full-page ads that ran every month on the back page of SCI's *Safari Times* newspaper, featuring the budget-priced Cape buffalo hunts he was offering in Zambia. When Mac asked me to accompany him when he checked out van Aswegen's concession, he didn't have to ask twice.

* * *

I'd purposely scheduled a four-hour layover in New York to allow plenty of time between my domestic and international flights. After waiting until what seemed the very last moment to board the South African Airways 747 jetliner, I'd given up on Mac and Darlene Rogers arriving before takeoff, and I was having my ticket checked at the gate when they ran up. Their connecting fight had been delayed, and they'd landed in New York with only thirty minutes to get from the domestic terminal to the SAA gate at the international terminal. What I expected to happen did: Their luggage still was on a cart somewhere at John F. Kennedy International Airport when we landed in Johannesburg nineteen and a half hours later.

It was April 1994, and we had booked our flights knowing that the first elections open to every adult South African would be held the same day we left Tucson. We had no idea what we might encounter when we landed in Johannesburg, so we reserved rooms overnight at a hotel across the street from Jan Smuts International Airport, figuring it might take a while for widespread riots—if they were to break out, as some people were predicting—to reach us. We needn't have worried. Nelson Mandela won the election, as expected, and there was no violence. All of the country's various factions respected him, making him the perfect choice to lead what would be called the New South Africa.

We returned to Jan Smuts after breakfast the next morning and boarded a plane for my first trip into central Africa. When we landed in Lusaka, Zambia's capital, I was immediately struck by the difference between Johannesburg's modern airport facilities and Lusaka's, which reminded me of something from poverty-stricken rural Mexico before a middle class developed in that country. The Lusaka International Airport looked as if it had been built in the 1960s. It was clean enough, but it certainly needed some paint and a lot more care than it had been getting.

I was especially surprised to see how lax the airport's security was. In every other airport where I'd entered a country, new arrivals got their luggage and then passed through Customs before being met by someone. In Lusaka, Henri van Aswegen was waiting for us where the baggage was dropped. He had the Zambian firearms permits I needed for my 7mm Remington Magnum and the .416 Weatherby Magnum I'd borrowed from the Weatherby Company in California. After he helped me get my two bags and rifle case and Mac's and Darlene's carryons through Customs in what must have been record time, he told someone at the SAA counter we'd be spending that night at the Pomodzi Hotel. He also left a map showing the location of his camp, just in case Mac's and Darlene's luggage arrived after we left the city the next day.

Henri's fiancée, Riana, had parked their four-door Toyota pickup truck a few steps from the terminal's main doors. After introductions, we loaded my baggage into the back of the truck and set off for our hotel. While Mac and Henri talked, I took stock of Zambia's capital from the window.

My first impression didn't change after seeing more of the city. The people were dirt poor, and the infrastructure was deteriorating. I saw several streets with ditches that had been dug for sewer repairs several years earlier, and no one had bothered to cover them up. I knew this because one of them had a small tree growing out of the ditch!

I had been told the Pomodzi was one of the two best hotels in Lusaka in 1994, but, like the city and its airport, it had seen better days since colonialism had ended in Northern Rhodesia thirty years earlier. There was hardly enough space in my little room to turn around, and, although I will eat just about anything, the restaurant's food was not good. It was served buffet style and may have sat in the warming trays for several days. There was a casino on site, but I didn't bother to go there. Instead, I chose to unwind by watching television before taking a shower and going to bed. I had to laugh at the commercials on the television's only station. Most of them were for "beer gardens" and showed black Zambians enjoying themselves. One commercial actually showed a young man passed out with his head on a table!

The man at the front desk had warned us not to leave the hotel's compound on foot.

"It's not safe," he said. "Crime is terrible here."

That fact became apparent the next day, when we visited downtown Lusaka. Shoppers had to get past armed guards to enter most of the city's stores. I wasn't stopped when I stepped inside a bank to change a few dollars to *kwacha*s, the Zambian currency.[1] I suppose the armed guards outside and inside figured I didn't fit the profile of a bank robber.

---

[1] I learned later that *kwacha* means *dawn* in the Bantu language. It derives from the slogan after Zambia's independence in 1968, "New Dawn of Freedom."

I'd read that Zambia had one of the world's highest rates of unemployment. Indeed, there were hundreds of young men with nothing to do, leaning against parked vehicles and buildings and sitting on the curbs—the only places left where they could sit. Every low building had concertina wire on its roof, and sharp pieces of broken glass set in mortar covered the tops of the walls, fences, and every conceivable place where someone with nothing to do might sit.

We made three stops before leaving Lusaka that day. One was at a video store, where Henri left Mac, Darlene, Riana, and me in the Toyota while he went inside to speak with the store owner, a former policeman who also was president of the Zambian Professional Hunters Association. He and Henri had a personality conflict, and, without our knowing it, Henri's problems rubbed off on us when Mac and I failed to pay the man the courtesy call he felt he deserved. That unintended slight to his perceived self-importance—and the fact that Henri was a South African trying to do business the man felt should be open only to Zambians—resulted in his hostility to me when I returned to Zambia and finally met him two years later.

Our second stop was to meet the Zambian minister of tourism and wildlife and pick up my hunting licenses. Outside the government building that housed his office there were vehicles bearing signs for agencies of the United Nations and five different international wildlife conservation organizations. Inside we found walls that were cracked and dirty and an elevator that didn't work. Two flights up, we entered a small space that reminded me of a waiting room in my dentist's office, except that it needed new furniture and carpeting and lots of patching and painting.

Henri and his financial backer, a South African certified public accountant who had accompanied us, let a secretary know we'd arrived for our appointment with the minister. Three or four people who apparently had been waiting in the reception area for some time seemed surprised when we were ushered into the minister's office before them.

The minister, a large man with glossy black skin, stood up behind his desk when we entered. He seemed totally out of place in that dreary office. His beautifully tailored dark suit had not a single wrinkle, and he was wearing a red-and-blue-striped silk tie, highly polished shoes, and an expensive watch. The cuffs on his white shirt had large cuff links that probably were gold. After our introductions, he talked about spending the previous weekend in Paris and how much he enjoyed his monthly trips to Europe. He knew McElroy was the founder of the world's most influential international hunting organization, and, knowing I was the editor of a magazine that could publicize his country's hunting opportunities, he seemed genuinely pleased to see me. Before we left, he had "ministerial permits" issued, which allowed me to take a zebra, a warthog, several types of antelope, and a lion.

Our final stop in Lusaka was to buy groceries on our way out of the city that afternoon. Outside the store was a sign indicating the distances to various African cities, such as Cairo and Nairobi. I doubt anyone seeing that sign would ever attempt to drive to those places. The store was surprisingly well stocked. Darlene wanted to be certain that we had enough bottled water, so Henri added a couple more cases to those he had ordered. I've forgotten what else he bought, but I do remember him paying for the supplies with a stack of colorful *kwacha*s. At the exchange rate of one U.S. dollar to 3,000 *kwacha*s, it was a very tall stack.

It took more than four hours for our two vehicles to drive the one hundred and twenty miles or so to the entrance of Kafue National Park. There were potholes up to a foot deep every few yards for almost the entire length of the highway. Henri and every other driver chose to avoid the tarmac and drove along the edge of the road, however. Every few miles we'd pass settlements of small thatched or mud-plastered shacks, their inhabitants standing at the edge of the road, trying to sell travelers something. Many had images of animals they had carved out of some kind of soft wood, but I also saw a young man proudly holding one small dried fish that resembled the tilapia that were introduced to Arizona in the 1960s. One woman offered for sale a cardboard box that once had held a kitchen stove. In Zululand, people also set up booths or stood along the roads selling things, but the Zulus seemed more prosperous than these people, and so did the Matabeles I saw at Victoria Falls.

What I'd seen in South Africa and Zimbabwe was interesting, but Zambia was everything I'd imagined the so-called Dark Continent would be. I finally had reached the "real" Africa.

I saw several large baobab trees along the main road, but there were virtually no small trees of any kind in sight. All had been cut down for firewood, I suppose.

When we reached the tsetse fly-checking station at the entrance to Kafue National Park, the road suddenly improved. (Tsetse-fly control consisted of a man taking a freshly cut branch and flicking its leaves over our two vehicles.) Before we continued on, Henri drove a short distance to a small concrete block building that served as the park's headquarters and introduced us three Americans to the young black man responsible for the huge park. Henri had brought a fifty-five-gallon drum of gasoline with him, saying whoever had developed the park's budget hadn't included the price of gasoline for its antipoaching efforts. What Henri didn't know until then was that the park's only vehicle was wrecked, and there was no money to repair or replace it. The obvious prosperity of the Zambian Tourism and Wildlife Agency's top man apparently had not trickled down to his national parks or his men in the field.

We drove twenty miles or so on pavement before turning onto a wide, graded road that was the border for one of the hunting concessions that Henri had leased from the government. The only animal I saw as we drove through the park was a common reedbuck that darted into the brush before our vehicle reached it. It was a different story after we entered our hunting area. A band of impalas stood at the side of the road and stared at us. Branches and large limbs, torn off trees by elephants, littered the road. Henri stopped soon after we turned onto the two-track road that led to his camp.

"Riana and I saw a big lion right there when we drove out yesterday," he said, pointing to a tree where a chunk of meat was hanging.

When I asked about it, he said he'd shot a buffalo to feed his men and left one of its rear legs for bait, just in case the lion decided to return.

The road to Henri's camp took us across a small dam that backed up perhaps two or three acres of water. When I looked at the stream below the dam, I saw an oribi staring at us. These small antelope are considered rare, even endangered, in South Africa, but Henri said they were plentiful in that area.

The camp impressed me more than the luxurious lodges I'd hunted from in South Africa. Those came complete with manicured lawns, gardens, and swimming pools. Henri's camp consisted of three "chalets," a hut for dining and cooking, and a ramada for his vehicles on the banks of the pond. Nearby were huts for his staff and a skinning shed. A low fence made of thatched grass surrounded everything. Inside the compound, the earth was swept clean. There wasn't a leaf in sight.

I was interested in the way native materials were used in the camp's construction. A few nails and bolts may have been used somewhere, but I saw none. Thin logs were tied together with strips of bark and covered with grass thatching to make the walls, roofs, shutters, and doors. The windows had no glass, but thatched shutters could be opened and closed. Each chalet had a toilet, wash basin, and shower, with water from the pond piped from barrels placed atop a nearby termite mound. While we were in camp, a fire burned constantly under the hot-water barrel. The barrels were well above the level of the pond, which meant they had to be filled with buckets.

After stowing my gear in the chalet assigned to me, I walked over to the dining hut and found Henri, Riana, Mac, Darlene, and the accountant already there. Hanging on wires at one end of the structure were strips of meat cut from Henri's buffalo. They'd been marinated and hung to dry for biltong.

Our lunch consisted of buffalo backstraps, boiled potatoes, vegetables, and bread. I was shocked to hear how Henri had killed the animal we were eating. He had lost the front sight on his .458 Winchester Magnum, so he got as close as he could to the animal and merely sighted down the barrel to shoot it. I couldn't believe that anyone would hunt one of Africa's dangerous Big Five with a rifle without sights!

When Henri said he planned to carve a sight out of a warthog's ivory tusk and drive it into the barrel's dovetail slot, I suggested that he use the handle of a toothbrush instead because it would be more durable and easier to shape, and that's what he did. I didn't suggest that he shoot the rifle to see if the sight needed adjustment. If he had to shoot to back me up, it would be at close range, where long-distance accuracy isn't important; but I vowed not to let us get into a situation where my bad shooting would require him to shoot something that wanted to stomp, gore, or bite us.

We spent a half-hour checking the sights on my rifles that afternoon. I kept the muzzle brake on the .416 Weatherby while shooting it, but Henri wanted me to remove it when we hunted. I couldn't blame him. The rearward blast from the muzzle brake of a Weatherby rifle at close quarters could leave one's ears ringing for weeks or, more likely, permanently damage them.

After I was convinced my rifles still were shooting where they should, we set off to have a look around Henri's concession. Henri and I and a tracker he called "Victah" stood in the back of his Toyota while Mac and Darlene rode inside the cab. One of Henri's men, a man he called "Toolbox," was driving. An hour later, we found several places where buffaloes had crossed the two-track road. By then, we also had seen perhaps a dozen oribis and duikers, as well as a Lichtenstein hartebeest bull with a small herd of females. The bull was young, and I didn't have permits for buffalo, oribi, or duiker on this trip, so we drove on.

Henri had spent the week before we arrived burning tall grass to create open areas, and we left tracks on the blackened areas as we drove along. Popping up all over the burned places were new green sprouts of grass that already were attracting antelope and warthogs. We really weren't hunting yet, but if we had seen a good specimen of one of the animals on my license, we would have tried to take it.

I was enjoying the drive and being in Africa again when Henri suddenly pounded on the truck's cab and told Toolbox to stop. He had seen the tracks left by lions in front of the truck, which I had missed. When we all left the truck to inspect the round pug marks, I again was in awe at how large lion tracks were. I'd seen them in Zimbabwe, but it had been many years earlier. The largest of the lions here had feet almost as large as small dinner plates.

"There were three, just here," said Victah, staring at the ground while bending over and grasping both hands behind his back. Then he stood straight and grinned widely.

He didn't talk much, and when he did, he spoke softly.

Henri agreed that three lions had been on the road not long before us, and pointed to the prints the animals had left behind.

"That's a young male," he said. "And here's a female. This one is a big male."

I looked over at Mac and saw him taking long steps where the older male had rolled and stretched.

". . . two, three, four," I heard him say.

I had a hard time believing that a lion could stretch twelve feet from its nose to the tip of its tail, but I couldn't argue. The evidence in the soft, red African sand was clear. Henri joined Victah in grinning.

"That's a big lion, and we're going to get him," he said.

AFTER A MISS, MY BEST-EVER TROPHY

CHAPTER 19

After Henri and I found fresh lion sign, the first thing on our agenda was to collect meat for bait, and the first animals on my license that we encountered were zebras. I had not shot a zebra on earlier trips to Africa because I had done the math and found a tanned zebra hide cost hundreds of dollars less than the cost of a trophy fee, tanning, and shipping. There were no trophy fees attached to my ministerial permits, and we needed bait. Darlene also had announced she wanted a zebra rug, and I was Mac's guest, so Henri and I began a stalk.

Before seeing my first zebra in the wild, I suffered the same delusion as everyone else who has never hunted them: I thought zebras were merely donkeys wearing striped pajamas and would be easy to hunt. Although I didn't hunt them, I saw enough zebras on various trips to realize they are suspicious of anything (especially humans) that approaches them. That striped coat they wear is an effective camouflage because it breaks up their outline.

This herd was feeding in one of the burned areas when we rounded a corner and suddenly came upon it. Every animal jerked up its head, took a quick look at the truck, and ran off. Henri and I jumped out and started trotting toward where we had last seen the zebras. We found the animals a few hundred yards away, watching their backtrail.

"Shoot the one on the left," Henri said.

I didn't have time to find a rest for my rifle, so I shot offhand and missed two shots at the animal he'd selected. It was running flat out when my third shot connected. The zebra continued, seemingly unhurt, for another thirty or forty yards before collapsing. Darlene had her rug, and we now had our bait.

Mac and Darlene arrived in the truck as we were approaching the downed animal. I was surprised to see that she was crying. It was the first time she'd seen an animal die, Mac said.

The bullet from my 7mm Remington Magnum had struck the side of the zebra and angled into its lungs without exiting, so there would be only one small hole in its skin. It was a beautiful animal with dark stripes and would make a gorgeous rug. The problem is, even without a trophy fee, it would cost close to $1,000 to have its hide tanned and shipped to Tucson. I'd bought two already-tanned zebra rugs for $500 each on earlier trips.

Mac and I wanted to help Henri, Victah, and Toolbox load the animal into the Toyota, but I'm afraid we weren't much help. The three men had done this chore many times and quickly got the whole zebra into the truck, mostly by themselves. We were back in camp a half-hour later. While Mac, Darlene, Henri, and I rested, the trackers delivered the zebra to the skinning crew. Two hours later, we again were in the truck, this time with a naked zebra carcass in the back, heading for where we'd seen the lion tracks.

Henri wanted a bait site with enough cover to hide us on the down side of the prevailing wind. What he found was a termite mound perhaps a dozen feet high. Unlike the tall, thin, conelike mounds in South Africa and Botswana, the termites in Zambia move literally tons of dirt and create huge piles. This one was at least sixty feet in diameter and twelve feet high, and was so old that it was covered with trees and brush.

Toolbox backed the truck up to a skinny tree, which Victah quickly climbed. He ran a rope over a branch while Toolbox used the rope's other end to tie all four of the zebra's legs together. With Henri's help, they hoisted the carcass as high as they could and then tied it securely to the branch with wire, leaving the zebra's legs sticking straight up, far above the ground. I'm six feet four, and I had to stretch to touch the zebra's spine.

"Don't worry," Mac said. "They can reach it."

He meant the lion. He obviously had read my mind.

Before we left, the men took the zebra's entrails and dragged them around the area and up and down the road before leaving them below the carcass. They then cut leafy branches, which they used to hide the carcass from vultures and other meat-eating birds. Next, they erected a screen of tall grass to create a blind in front of the termite mound. They had me stand and aim my rifle at a spot below the carcass so they could know where to leave a shooting hole in the screen. They then erected the shooting sticks, which they would leave overnight in the blind, and had me mount my rifle on them to check the hole they'd made. Their final task was to create a path back to where Henri would park his truck when we returned to check the bait the next morning.

I had to admire how carefully they worked. They not only cut brush, but they also swept the ground of every leaf and twig. The sun was setting when I saw them draping pieces of toilet paper along the path, and I was about to ask Henri what they were doing when it occurred to me that it would be dark when we returned, and the scraps of white paper would help us follow the trail.

I had a hard time falling asleep that night, and it wasn't just because I was excited about my first lion hunt. My chalet was built just six or seven feet from Mac's and Darlene's, and with only two thin walls of grass separating us, I could hear Mac snoring as if he were in a bed next to me. I was awake when Victah knocked quietly on my thatched door, long before daylight. I quickly dressed and was walking to the dining hut when I saw something large move across the path from my chalet. I still have no idea what it might have been, but I suspect it was a hyena.

It still was dark when we arrived at where Henri planned to park. I don't remember whether Toolbox was with us. I do remember Mac and Darlene staying behind in the Toyota while Henri, Victah, Henri's stepson, and I prepared to walk the quarter-mile to where the zebra was hanging. I was loading the .416 Weatherby when we heard the first roar. The lions had found the bait!

282

Henri already had loaded his .458 with its toothbrush sight. He whispered that I should follow him closely, while Victah walked behind me and Henri's stepson followed with a video camera. I was surprised to see that the black man was carrying only a homemade ax with a short handle. (Henri would later tell me that axes in the hands of men like Victah are the most effective weapons when lion are close enough to hurt us. I was so impressed with that axe that I bought it from Victah and brought it home in my luggage.)

I can tell you I felt uneasy walking in the dark, following pieces of toilet paper, toward the sound of lions roaring. It still was dark when we reached the blind, but our eyes had adjusted enough to see that the lions had knocked down the shooting sticks the men had left behind overnight. The lions had been in our blind while we were gone!

I could hear the lion feeding a few yards in front of us, but I could see nothing as Victah slowly and quietly set the sticks up again. I don't know how long we stood there in the dark with the lions just spitting distance away, but eventually we could see dull shapes. When one of those shapes moved over to the bait tree, stood up, and ripped a chunk of zebra off the carcass, there was barely enough light to see that it was a lioness. It walked silently toward us and plopped down on the other side of our screen of grass, almost at our feet, and started eating noisily.

Almost immediately, I spotted another moving shape. As soon as I realized it was a lion with a mane, I brought up my rifle, moving just a fraction of an inch at a time, until I could place it noiselessly on the shooting sticks. When I brought my cheek to the stock and peered through the 4X Weatherby scope, I was shocked to see—nothing! Riflescopes are supposed to "gather" light and enable us to shoot minutes before we can see clearly without them. Not with that scope, though. (Ed Weatherby would later tell me he was not happy with the quality of the Japanese-made scope on the rifle I'd borrowed, and his company was now buying scopes from a different maker.)

I searched frantically until I eventually found a gray lump I was certain could only be the lion. The more I stared, the more I was convinced that's what it was. I could make out its head and its mane. I held the cross hairs at the front of the shape, waiting for enough light to shoot. As I waited, I was certain I saw the shape move.

For some reason it was at that moment I remembered reading that lions that fed all night would leave the bait before first light. I now had no doubt it was the lion, and it was standing there, not moving, just a few feet from the bait tree. I took careful aim at what seemed to be the center of its shoulder and squeezed the trigger. Flame flashed out of my rifle's barrel and lit up the scene for a millisecond as the recoil lifted it and pounded the stock against my face and shoulder. It was a bush and not the lion I'd hit, however.

I was crushed. I never saw the lioness or the lion leave. They didn't wait around to give me a second shot. I looked at Henri and Victah and could see they were disgusted. I was worried that I might have wounded the lion, the worst possible thing a client can do with dangerous game. We were searching for blood when Mac and Darlene arrived with the Toyota. They had heard the shot, and they drove up expecting to see Henri and me standing over a dead lion. I have missed animals before—anyone who hunts eventually will miss an easy shot—but I have never felt more awful. How could anyone miss an adult African lion fewer than twenty yards away? No one said much as we drove back to camp for a late breakfast, except that Henri and Mac tried to console me. I was certain I would never have another opportunity to shoot a lion.

We were eating lunch when Henri said there was a chance the lion might return that same evening. *Sure, Henri, and the Easter Bunny and Santa Claus are real, too.*

But that's what it did. We were standing in the blind as the sun hit the horizon when the lioness suddenly appeared and walked up to where it had dropped its meat that morning, plopped down, and began to finish its meal. A couple of minutes later, I saw the male lion walk up the two-track road toward us. I couldn't believe it. There still was ample light to see it clearly. Its mouth was open, and it appeared to be panting like a huge Saint Bernard with a mane as it plodded along.

When it stopped broadside to us, no more than five yards from where we were standing, I already had my rifle up and had the cross hairs aligned on its shoulder. Henri fired a fraction of a second after I did, and the lion roared, jumped up like a huge house cat, and fell down facing the direction it had come with two holes in its shoulder. It didn't kick. I have no idea where the lioness went, but it was no longer there.

I still was a smoker, and the first thing I did was light a cigarette. Henri looked at me and frowned that I would approach a five-hundred-pound, meat-eating cat so casually. I had no doubt that it was dead, but Henri was taking no chances. He had his rifle up, ready to shoot, as we walked up to it.

"Shoot him in the spine," he said, as he motioned me to approach the animal from behind, and I did.

Unlike I had done with my buffalo, I remembered to pull the rifle tightly into my shoulder and grip it with both hands.

"Shoot him again," Henri said, and I did.

At the time I felt foolish pumping bullets into a dead animal, but I realize now that Henri wanted to make certain that lion would not harm us.

It's a cliché to say that Mac and Darlene arrived in a cloud of dust, but that is exactly what happened. I still don't know who was happiest because Mac was grinning as he congratulated Henri and me at least three times. I wouldn't have been surprised to see him clap his hands in joy. Both Mac and Henri told me this was the largest lion they had ever seen. I don't know whether they said this for my benefit, but I do know it was much larger than I ever dreamed a lion could be. I'd seen lions in zoos and in circuses, of course, but none was anywhere near the size of the one I'd just shot. It seemed even larger when we loaded it into the Toyota. It was all Henri, Toolbox, Victah, Mac, and I could do to get it in the truck. Unlike antelope and elk, there was nothing to grab onto.

While we were photographing and loading the lion, Victah had made me keep my rifle close at hand. He obviously was worried that the lioness might return.

The trip back to camp was exciting. All the way back to camp, the men chanted a song whose refrain was, "*Shumbah, poro! Shumbah, poro!*" (the lion is dead). The road took us past a training camp for game scouts, and it seemed everyone there turned out to cheer for us. The camp staff obviously had heard us coming because they were dancing in the road outside the camp when we arrived. They also were singing, "*Shumbah, poro!*" and took turns pounding the lion's chest, after we parked and dragged the carcass onto the tailgate so they could see it better.

McElroy had always made it a point to say at every appropriate opportunity that he did not drink alcohol because an abusive alcoholic stepfather had caused him to leave home while he still was a youngster, but he made an exception that night when he asked Henri for a beer to celebrate my lion. I was so excited I don't remember us eating dinner that night.

We slept late the next morning, but when I got up, the first thing I did was walk to the skinning shed to see the lion again. It was more like a cage than a shed—heavy poles that supported a small room for meat had been sunk in the ground, each almost touching another, around a hard-surfaced floor. It looked like a jail, and was sturdy enough to keep out hyenas and lions. On the floor were the skins of my lion and zebra, and the lion's flattened skin was larger than the zebra's. I had a hard time leaving it, or believing that I had shot that lion.

The rest of the three weeks of that hunt were leisurely. We'd go out at dawn, return around 10 A.M., have brunch and sleep to about 3 P.M., and go out again. I shot another sable, a Lichtenstein hartebeest, and a warthog before we left the concession to look for a puku and have a picnic on the banks of the Kafue River.

We spotted a male puku almost as soon as we reached the river, and I wanted to shoot it.

"It's only a small one," Henri said.

I had no way of judging the size of the straw-colored antelope. Its horns were lyre-shaped but smaller than those on impalas. Reluctantly, I put my rifle back onto the rack in the back of the truck.

Henri's partner, the accountant, was following us in his Volkswagen *combi*, the South African word for van. I'd never seen a four-wheel-drive VW before, and I was amazed at how well it did in deep sand and steep places.

Several things of note are worth mentioning about that day. For one, I saw my first roan antelope on the trip to the river. There were five or six of them, and instead of running away when they heard our vehicles, they were staring at us from about seventy-five yards away. I could have shot any one of those floppy-eared, short-horned antelope, but they were not on my license, so we continued on. We stopped at another camp only so Henri could tell the professional hunter that the minister of tourism and wildlife had given him permission to take me into his concession to collect a puku.

The picnic along the river was an enjoyable respite from all the driving we had been doing. Tall, thick, gnarly trees shaded the riverbank. Heads of hippos rose out of the water repeatedly in front of us, and they opened their mouths and yawned. They seemed to prefer just one spot on the river, and they still were there when we packed up to go after my puku.

We found it feeding in a clearing among perhaps thirty or forty impala, and I shot it. That lone male ended my hunt. We had only a Crawshay defassa waterbuck license to fill, and Mac wanted it. For some reason he hadn't collected that particular animal yet.

After loading the puku, we were returning to our camp when Henri spotted a waterbuck bull with a harem of six cows moving off a ridge about a half-mile away. Henri stopped the truck, Mac loaded my 7mm Remington Magnum, and the two of them and the trackers began a stalk. I stayed with the truck, hoping to see all the action. It was not to be, though. The waterbuck moved out of sight, and the hunters soon were hidden by brush.

A few minutes later, I heard a shot, then another, and another. When the shooting stopped, I started the truck and drove over to where everyone was standing over the dead bull. After congratulating Mac, I checked his animal. He had hit it three times through the shoulder, and when I asked how far the shots were, Henri pointed to a spot a long way off. Henri and I agreed that it was more than three hundred yards, and

Mac had hit the waterbuck with three of his four shots. He may have been in his eighties, but he still could shoot.

Interestingly, while we were admiring Mac's trophy, a shy black couple dressed in rags suddenly appeared, seemingly out of nowhere. They were fishermen, Henri said. They said nothing, even to our trackers, but just stood there watching us from a dozen steps away. They apparently wanted meat, but, with a long trip back to camp, we were not ready to open up the waterbuck or my puku and expose the meat to the dust. I gave each of them a couple of cigarettes, and they thanked me the African way, by bowing with their hands together.

Everywhere else I had hunted in Africa, even in Zimbabwe, the local people called me "Boss," although they pronounced it "baawhs." In Zambia, Mac and I were "bwanas." I felt as if I were in East Africa with Ruark or Hemingway whenever they said it.

The trip back to Lusaka would have been uneventful, except for the passenger who joined us when we returned to the tsetse-fly control point. The manager of Kafue National Park needed a ride to the city to meet with his superiors. He and his men hadn't been paid for six months, he said, and he also needed another vehicle. His men went out each day on bicycles to look for poachers and illegal woodcutters in the park, he said.

On the trip to Henri's camp nearly three weeks earlier, I had noticed something curious in the park I had not seen anywhere else I'd hunted. Two parallel tracks ran across almost every *dambo* (meadow) the road crossed. One track would be about fourteen or fifteen inches wide and the other no more than six inches wide. They ran about a foot apart for as far as we could see. I knew they were not animal trails, and when I asked Henri what they were, he said the trails were made by poachers walking alongside bicycles loaded with the bush meat they had poached. After hearing the manager's story about not being paid, I wondered if his game guards and their bicycles had made the tracks.

My new room in the Pomodzi was even smaller than the first. There was just enough room to squeeze around the bed to turn on and adjust the television set. The food at the buffet hadn't changed, though. It was as awful as ever. Nonetheless, I decided to spend the two days in Lusaka before flying back to Tucson. Mac and Darlene drove with Henri, Riana, and the accountant to Victoria Falls. I'd seen it from the Zimbabwe side in 1983, and I was looking forward to resting and being alone for a while. The three of us got back together in Johannesburg in time to catch our flight to New York.

* * *

I hunted with Henri again two years later, but Zambia was not the same. I could not get the permit I needed to take a leopard, so my friends Boris Baird and Fritz Selby and I spent two weeks collecting defassa waterbuck, oribi, grysbok, duiker, and other antelope I hadn't taken on my previous trip. After that, I returned to southern Africa about every other year, taking one or two animals on every trip. The most enjoyable of those trips was in 2005, when my granddaughter Natalie and I spent a month visiting friends in five African countries. I took her to Kruger National Park and Victoria Falls, and bought her a small diamond in Kimberley after Sandy Cox arranged an underground tour for us in the mine. The only hunting I did was to shoot a red hartebeest with Sandy. I hope Natalie will always remember that month as I do.

My last trip to Africa was in 2007, when I spent two weeks in Namibia on business and about ten days in South Africa visiting friends, among them Fiona Capstick, Adelino Serras Pires, Coenraad and Vicky Vermaak, and Henri and Riana van Aswegen. I also had the opportunity to interview Ian Player, Africa's best-known conservationist and brother of the famous golfer Gary Player, at his home in KwaZulu-Natal. Although this was not a hunting trip, Henri arranged for me to take a blue wildebeest and an impala for *braai* meat.

Africa is like the old ads for potato chips: Nobody can eat just one. I can never get enough of that continent.

My Mongolian Adventure Begins

Chapter 20

Beijing was not as strange a place as it might seem for launching an elk hunt in 1990. The world's second-largest city was where American hunters rested before flying on to Mongolia after eleven-hour flights across the Pacific. At least a half-dozen hunt-booking agencies in the United States, Canada, and Germany were promoting Mongolian elk hunts that included tourism in China. These packages were so reasonably priced they sold out a year in advance.

The combined cost of an elk hunt and round-trip airfare to Mongolia that year was less than $4,000 and included everything except tips, curios, and the excess baggage fee for shipping trophies home. That "everything" included a lot—hotels and food in China and Mongolia, sightseeing trips, services of guides and interpreters, gun permits and licenses, and the many things that often are extra when hunting everywhere else. The price was less than what a topnotch elk-hunting outfitter in Wyoming, Montana, Idaho, or Colorado charged at the time. It certainly was a heck of a lot less than the $14,000 that Arizona's White Mountain Apaches were charging to hunt trophy elk on their reservation just three or four air miles from my cabin that year. (The last I checked, the Apaches were charging $16,000, plus a $5,000 trophy fee.)

For me, the attraction wasn't the opportunity to hunt an elk. I already had shot good bulls in Arizona and New Mexico. I saw it as an opportunity to visit one of Asia's remotest wilderness areas and see a country that has changed little since the Great Khan and his hordes rode out of Mongolia to conquer the known world. I also wanted to shoot a Siberian roe deer.

If you're wondering what elk are doing in Mongolia, it's only because you haven't heard that North American herds originated in Asia. They reached our continent when Siberia and Alaska were connected during the ice ages by what we've come to call a land bridge. Other familiar North American animals made the journey, too, including moose, sheep, ptarmigan, caribou, and others.

The large animals we call elk are called *maral* by Asians, red deer by Europeans, and *Cervus elaphus* by scientists. They are the world's most abundant and widespread deer. There must be a million or more of them living in the forested regions inside a wide band that extends around the world from British Columbia to Arizona, from the former Soviet Union to southern China, and from Scandinavia to Spain. A very few endangered, indigenous red deer also still may be found in northernmost Africa, and elk or their red deer cousins have been introduced to New Zealand, Australia, and several countries in South America.

There are sixteen subspecies of *Cervus elaphus,* but the race we hunted in Mongolia was *sibiricus.* The Rocky Mountain elk (one of the three types still found on our continent) in Arizona are the *nelsoni* subspecies.

My friend Lynton McKenzie was one of the world's two best-known firearms engravers before his death from cancer a few years after this hunt. (The other engraver has the improbable name of Winston Churchill.) Lynton and I bought our hunts from San Antonio booking agent Burt Klineburger. On 2 November 1990 we flew from Tucson to San Francisco and joined Sergio de Cima and Fernando Letamendi of Mazatlan, Mexico; Pat Green and Bill Anthony of Dallas; and George Lenar from New Jersey. The seven of us flew nonstop on Air China to Shanghai, changed planes, and traveled on to Beijing.

Klineburger had arranged for us to be met in Beijing by a representative of a government agency called the China Women's Travel Service. She was a young woman named Dingh, and she was our tour guide and interpreter for the two days before our flight to Mongolia and the three days we'd be in Beijing after the hunt. Moving our firearms and baggage past Chinese Customs, military, and agricultural officials went smoothly, except for a brief period when we feared we might have to give up our rifles. Beijing's Customs officials thought we were part of the group of six or seven young American missionaries we had met on our flight from San Francisco. They also were heading to Mongolia, but not to hunt. They were taking Bibles and church pamphlets that had been translated into Mongolian.

The Chinese wanted to know where our "subversive" materials were hidden, and they wanted to see the missionaries' rifles. Dingh had to stay behind the Customs line while this was going on and couldn't help us, but things eventually got sorted out, and she led us to the military office where our rifles and ammunition were to be stored in a large safe. The officials had a list of serial numbers from our rifles that Klineburger had sent them earlier, and they checked each rifle against the list before giving Dingh a receipt. The missionaries stored their printed materials with our rifles, after it was decided there would be no danger to the People's Republic of China if their pamphlet-filled suitcases were locked up while they were in Beijing. Chinese Communists apparently didn't want Bibles distributed in their country, even those printed in a language few Chinese can read.

During the flight to Shanghai, I sat next to a Chinese expatriate who had obtained U.S. citizenship. He also was on a Christian mission, but he wasn't going to Mongolia. He talked about his plans to spend the next six months in China, where he hoped to join up with a group of students who had an illegal printing press. He gave me religious materials in Chinese and English, but I left the pamphlets on the plane. Meeting these determined people made me remember reading about the early Asian expeditions of hunter-explorers such as James Clark Powell and Kermit and Theodore Roosevelt. Each of these heralded adventurers wrote about bumping into missionaries on their treks across Asia. Even then, missionaries were at risk on that continent.

Our group was in a line, pushing carts loaded with baggage and gun cases and following Dingh as she walked briskly through Beijing International Airport, when one of my companions loudly announced that we should call ourselves "Dingh's Ducklings" and started quacking. The name stuck throughout the trip.

Outside the terminal, we loaded our baggage into a bus Dingh had waiting and climbed aboard for the long drive to the city. Although it was midnight and there was little traffic, the bus crept along the tree-lined rural road at an agonizing forty kilometers (twenty-four miles) per hour, the maximum speed limit there at the time.

It was after 1 A.M. when we reached our hotel and met the three others in our group—Pat Brooks of Oregon; his uncle, Paul Casey, from California; and Paul's son Mike, also from Oregon. They had completed an add-on tour of southeastern China to see, among other things, the site where the famed Terracotta Warriors were excavated.

We spent our first days in China visiting the Temple of Heaven, the Forbidden City, and Tiananmen Square. Everyone except Dingh had seen the movie *The Last Emperor,* which was filmed in the Forbidden City, and we all wondered how accurate the movie was. To me, the ancient and picturesque Imperial Palace inside Beijing was much more impressive than the Great Wall we would see later. Dreary Tiananmen Square was behind the Forbidden City and was dominated by a huge portrait of Mao Zedong, founder of the People's Republic of China. Red flags flying near a giant statue and bandstand gave the granite-paved park its only color. Hundreds of people, including military personnel wearing pajamalike uniforms, were walking about, taking photographs of each other, or just sitting on the ground in the world's largest public square. There were no chairs or benches. I looked for tank tracks or blood that might have been left after a well-publicized rebellion when more than two thousand pro-democracy protesters were killed in that square just one year earlier, but I found none. I found it ironic that its name in Chinese means Gate of Heavenly Peace.

Beijing's skyline was lined with modern, western-style hotels, government buildings, and row upon row of ugly concrete apartment buildings. Crowded between these recent structures were old and dirty shacks that were the same grayish brown as the city's thick air. We could smell the long-stemmed cabbages that were brought into town on trucks and bicycles the night we arrived. Cabbage was stacked on every street corner, and citizens were busy packing it to their apartment landings. Dingh said cabbage was her country's winter staple, and every family was issued a three-month supply when the crops were harvested. I saw no attempt to refrigerate it or protect it from freezing.

Cartoons of pandas, the official symbol of the recently concluded Asian Games, were everywhere, as were patriotic slogans in English and Chinese. I had expected the people of Beijing to be wearing blue Maoist coats and caps, but nearly everyone who wasn't in a military uniform wore western-style clothing. Many wore surgical masks, apparently to protect their lungs from the polluted air.

There were more bicycles in that city in 1990 than I could ever have imagined existed on this planet. Many were heavy-duty, three- and five-wheeled affairs, loaded with lumber, scrap steel, large boxes, even people. Some pulled overloaded trailers. Ordinary citizens apparently did not have automobiles then because Dingh said the few vehicles we saw on the crowded streets belonged to politicians, movie stars, or military leaders.[1] So much for the popular belief among environmentalists that eliminating automobiles is the solution to everything. Beijing, where seven million people were crowded into a relatively small valley, ran on bicycle wheels in 1990, and it was nothing to emulate.

The next day Dingh took us to the airport seven hours before our flight was scheduled to leave. We needed time to claim our rifles and be certain of getting seats for the weekly flight north to Mongolia. Air Mongolia often was oversold, and seats were not reserved, she said.

We were at the front of the crowd with our boarding passes in hand at the gate, but we were far from the first to board. Pushing, cutting into lines, and stepping on toes apparently was a way of life in China. The resemblance to being herded like cattle was so great that someone in our group began mooing like a Hereford cow. The humor apparently escaped the Chinese around us because they did not join in our laughter.

---

[1]Scenes on television and stories I've heard from friends who have visited China recently have astounded me. It is as if the country has leaped into the twenty-first century overnight. There now are highways with heavy automobile traffic and modern cities in places where there were only bicycles and villages when I was there just eighteen years earlier.

The Mongols and Chinese beat us to the plane by running across the tarmac. By the time I got on board, there was only one aisle seat left. Nobody had to tell me why no one wanted it. The back of the seat in front of it was broken, and the Russian sitting in that broken seat was stretched out, almost flat. I had precious little space in which to squeeze myself during the flight to Mongolia's capital. I was luckier than the three Asians who didn't get a seat and wound up standing at the rear of the plane all the way to Ulaanbaator.

Even if the seat in front of me had not been broken, I could not have sat in my seat properly with my long legs because there were only about twenty inches of space between each row in the Russian-made airliner. So I rode sitting sideways with both legs in the aisle. (It was not the only time I was to be reminded that Asia is no place to be tall.) I had to move my legs out of the way when the stewardess pushed a cart down the aisle, and to do so I had to push up the broken seat. Each time I did this, its occupant gave me a stern look, which I ignored.

The stewardess was serving food on plastic plates covered with clear plastic wrap. The presentation was nice, but there was no way I would do as the Asians did, which was to eat raw bacon and sliced cucumbers.

It was dark and minus fourteen degrees Fahrenheit when the airliner finally stopped on the icy runway outside Mongolia's capital. Unlike our experience in Beijing, getting through Customs in Ulaanbaator took just a few minutes. English-speaking representatives of Zhuulchin, the government's tourist agency, helped us fill out our papers and carried our baggage to a waiting bus. Nobody seemed concerned about our rifles and ammunition. Mongolia was known for its wild sheep, ibex, moose, elk, and roe deer hunting, and nearly all of the three hundred or so Western Europeans, South Americans, and North Americans who arrived in Ulaanbaator that year were hunters, our interpreter said.

Our three-room suites in the 1920s Ulaanbaator Hotel were once grand but had seen much better days. The furnishings were at least a half-century old. We had hot water for a shower, but a minute after I got the heat adjusted and stepped into the stall, the water suddenly turned cold. The toilet paper was only about two and a half inches wide and was as rough as crepe paper. Sheep and ibex hunters in Mongolia today are booked into newer hotels, but when we were there, the Ulaanbaator Hotel was the country's finest. Ordinary citizens were constantly coming up to the street-side windows to stare into the lobby at a lifestyle they could never afford. This would bring the concierge running to shoo them away.

Our group came together again for breakfast in a huge, nearly empty dining room with chrome-legged, red Formica-topped tables and chairs covered with 1950s-style bright red plastic. In the center of one wall was an American-made Wurlitzer jukebox, complete with flashing lights. Most of the recordings in the machine were American. It was here that I learned that cuisine was not one of Mongolia's strong points. I ordered eggs and wished I hadn't. The yolks were broken and fried hard. The edge of the egg white was crisp and brown and looked like lace. The white surrounding the hard yolk was barely cooked. How they could have done this is a mystery to me! The coffee tasted as if it had sat in the pot for a week. That was it for breakfast: two eggs and bad coffee. I was served nothing else—not toast nor potatoes nor any meat.

An Alaskan hunting guide and his wife, who had booked their elk hunt with another booking agent, joined us that morning, expanding our group to twelve. They had traveled from Beijing to Ulaanbaator by train, which I would have liked to do. From thirty thousand feet up, I got to see little of China, except for places around Beijing.

After breakfast, we were assigned interpreters, drivers, and guides. Lynton McKenzie and I were to share a camp with the Mexicans. The eight other hunters were assigned to two other camps a hundred miles or so from ours. We were scheduled to leave on our expeditions soon after breakfast, but "soon" apparently had a different meaning in Mongolia because we didn't leave until the next day. Our interpreters said it was because someone had to siphon (steal) gas from a school bus. The Soviet government was falling apart, and the Russians had stopped supplying food and gasoline to Mongolia, they said.

Although we were warned to stay inside the hotel while we waited, a parade with a small marching band drew McKenzie outside to a park in front of our hotel, where he photographed demonstrators pulling down what I think was a statue of Lenin.

The first group of hunters left town at 11:30 A.M. the next day; the second, at 12:30 P.M. Their three vehicles eventually met somewhere in the back country, and they traveled the last seventy-five miles in a caravan. It was 2 P.M. when we finally got going—two Mexicans, two Americans, two Mongol drivers, two Mongol guides, two Mongol interpreters, and a ton of baggage and assorted gear packed tightly into two small Russian-made four-wheel-drive military vehicles.

As we drove through the city of seven hundred thousand, I was impressed with Ulaanbaator's wide streets, the scale of its political buildings and statues, and the way the city dwellers dressed. Fur hats, high boots, and long wool sweaters were the norm for both men and women, making the people appear more prosperous than those in Beijing. There were many trucks, buses, automobiles, and taxicabs. We saw no bicycles and the air was clean.

I remember two things from the brief shopping trip our interpreter, McKenzie, and I had made in downtown Ulaanbaator earlier. The first was how the Mongols packed themselves into their buses. It was almost comical. Every window was completely covered with the faces and hands of people squashed against the glass. The other was the absolute lack of anything of value in the three shops we entered. I wanted to buy curios to take home, but there was none to be found. People were lined up at the door of one shop, and the interpreter led us around the line and shoved us through the doorway. Inside, a single ashtray made of green stone was displayed on otherwise empty shelves that covered the four walls of the little shop. There was nothing else, and I couldn't understand why the people were lining up to get inside.

Civilization ended abruptly when we left the city. The road simply vanished after about thirty miles. Twenty miles or so after that, we left the tracks we had been following in the snow and drove across country. Sometimes we could see the vehicle that accompanied us, but usually we could not. There were no towns, but we did pass two open-pit coal mines about twenty miles apart. Each had an ugly high-rise apartment building that apparently housed the miners. Our interpreters said the coal was used to generate electricity, which was transmitted to Ulaanbaator on wires strung on thin wooden poles that couldn't have been more than ten feet tall.

The few people we saw along the way wore costumes that hadn't changed since the time of Genghis Khan—long, heavy overcoats (they're called *del*) made of yak felt and tied at the waist with colorful sashes. Some of the men had heavy boots with curled and pointed toes. All wore strange-looking hats with earflaps. I saw no one wearing gloves, despite the cold weather. Instead, the sleeves of their coats were longer than their arms. When they needed to use their hands, they merely pulled their sleeves up.

In the foothills we would occasionally see "ranches" consisting of one or two yurts (they're *ger*s in Mongolian); herds of yaks, shaggy cows, and a hybrid of the two bovine species called *haing*s; and Mongol ponies. Mongols also raise two-humped camels as beasts of burden, but I saw none on this trip.

We drove across long, wide valleys and over low hills. Everything was snow-covered, and there were many frozen creeks and a wide, shallow river to ford. We stopped twice: once in the middle of nowhere to buy gasoline from a primitive pump outside a small steel building, and again for the Mongols to perform a ceremony in one of the passes we crossed. Atop a pile of rocks were sticks with strips of rags attached to them like small flags, giving the place the look of an American Indian religious site. Travelers were expected to leave small gifts and walk around the *ömoo* three times in a clockwise direction. Doing so brought good luck, the Mongols said, so we four North Americans marched around the rocks and donated something to their god, too. I left a single cigarette, as did our driver.

Ten hours later, it was dark and snowing, and we still hadn't reached camp, nor had we seen the headlights of our companion vehicle for at least an hour. Our driver, who spoke no English, apparently realized he was lost when we crossed the tracks our vehicle had made earlier. An hour later, we drove up to a high wall that surrounded a group of thirty to forty yurts. He went inside and began knocking on doors until he found a teenager who could guide us to our camp. Our vehicle now was so crowded that the boy had to sit on my lap. He wore the traditional heavy overcoat, which must have been handed down for at least three generations without ever being washed. Its horrible stench was almost as bad as the kid's body odor.

It was only an hour or so before sunup when we finally drove up to the five yurts that would be our home for the next week. Hot meals— foul-tasting noodles and pieces of some kind of meat about the same size, shape, color, and hardness as hockey pucks—were quickly prepared for us. We were handed cans of orange soda to drink. We were asleep when the other vehicle finally showed up.

After our hunt, we learned our eight friends, who had left Ulaanbaator earlier than we, were not so fortunate on the trip to their camp. One of their vehicles broke through the ice and got stuck while crossing a stream, and they temporarily abandoned the vehicle. Everyone piled into two already crowded vehicles and drove on in the storm. When they couldn't find their camps, they stopped and spent the night where they were—eight Americans and nine Mongols in two small, uninsulated vehicles. Paul Casey said it was so crowded that he spent the night outside, jogging in place to try to stay warm. At daybreak, they located landmarks and found their camp was only a couple of miles away in another valley.

I Pet a Yak, Sleep in a Yurt, Hunt a (Y)Elk

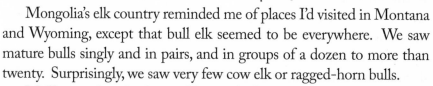

Chapter 21

Mongolia's elk country reminded me of places I'd visited in Montana and Wyoming, except that bull elk seemed to be everywhere. We saw mature bulls singly and in pairs, and in groups of a dozen to more than twenty. Surprisingly, we saw very few cow elk or ragged-horn bulls.

McKenzie shot the first and largest bull taken by our group of twelve hunters. We had spotted it on a slope high above us the first morning. It was so far away that we could tell only that it had antlers. I sat in the truck with the driver, who spoke no English, while the local guide, the interpreter, and McKenzie made the stalk. As his bull fed into the grove of trees where they were heading, I watched in my binocular and waited to hear a shot. When I heard nothing, I assumed the bull had gotten away. An hour or so later, however, I spotted the three men coming off the mountain with the bull's head, cape, and antlers on the shoulders of the young guide. McKenzie had shot a beautiful seven-by-seven bull with the single-shot .30-40 rifle he'd built especially for this hunt.

I later learned the two hunters from Dallas also shot their elk that first day and spent the rest of the week hunting grouse and wild boar. De Cima, Letamendi, and the Alaskan guide shot their elk the second day. The hunters from New Jersey, California, and Oregon all shot theirs by sundown of the fourth day. Every bull but one, a large five-by-five, had six points per side.

I could have shot a bull every day, but I was picky after seeing the antlers on McKenzie's elk. Believe it or not, I really didn't care if I shot an elk in Mongolia. There didn't seem to be a dime's worth of difference between the wapiti of Asia and the elk I'd killed in Arizona and New Mexico, and one trophy bull-elk mount should be enough for anyone. What I really wanted was a Siberian roe deer.

Before leaving Ulaanbaator, I'd obtained permission to collect a roebuck if I paid an additional trophy fee. Unfortunately for me, the Mongols in my camp were focused on elk, and I couldn't convince my interpreter that I'd take a roebuck over an elk. And although we saw roe deer every day while hunting for elk, we saw none with antlers. We must have seen several males, but the interpreter said all the roe deer in the area already had dropped their antlers. (The roebuck rut occurs in the summer, which means they shed their antlers weeks before elk and other deer do.)

I was having trouble getting around in the eight-thousand-foot altitude and extremely cold weather, and it didn't help that the two young Mongols trotted uphill ahead of me for hundreds of yards, then stopped to rest, and took off again when they were fully rested, without allowing me to catch my breath when I reached them. I've used that technique to purposely walk other people into the ground in Arizona, and I told them so when I called a meeting back at the truck.

I told the interpreter to tell the guide, "I'm paying you to get me a shot at an elk. If I get an elk, you'll get a tip. If I don't shoot an elk because I can't keep up with you, you'll get nothing."

They waited for me and allowed me to catch my breath during the next couple of stalks, and then they started leaving me behind again. Nine times during the first three days we used binoculars to find five to twenty bulls on snow-covered slopes eight hundred to one thousand feet above us. Nine times the Mongols and I climbed up and tried to intercept them. Eight times the Mongols spooked the elk before I got close enough to shoot. The ninth time, two bulls stared at us from about 150 yards away.

I inspected their antlers closely with my binocular and saw that although each had six points per side, the main beams on their narrow antlers were short. I would have shot one of them if I hadn't suddenly realized my roe-deer hunt would end the instant I touched the trigger.

I was the only hunter in camp who didn't have an elk, and the entire crew was eager to pack up and head back to Ulaanbaator. I could tell my guides weren't pleased when I backed away without disturbing the two small bulls.

By 8 A.M. the next day, I didn't have to smell their breath to know that my interpreter, local guide, and driver were sneaking gulps of vodka almost nonstop. They were singing and laughing as drunks do, and it was only two hours after sunup! When I looked at the interpreter who was sitting next to me on the rear seat, it was obvious that he was having trouble keeping his breakfast down. I pounded on the back of the guide in front of me, trying to get him to stop the truck and open the door so I could get out (the inside door handle on my side of the vehicle was missing). I was too late, though, and when the interpreter vomited on our seat, some of that vile stuff wound up on my leg. Although the Mongols tried to clean it up, the smell lingered in the vehicle the rest of my hunt. It was especially foul-smelling after dark, when the driver turned the heater up full force.

That same afternoon, we drove up on a red fox jumping from spot to spot, trying to catch mice in the snow.

"Do you want some target practice?" asked my interpreter, whose health had improved slightly.

More than the opportunity to shoot something, I wanted the fox's thick red pelt. I got out of the truck and killed the animal. What the Mongols hadn't told me was that I would have to pay a trophy fee for that fox before I could leave the country.

That afternoon, while following yet another bull elk, I was looking down from a ridge at a small dark object in a snowbank about three hundred yards below me. It was a roe deer! When I saw a flash of antlers in my binocular, I lay down in the snow, fired my 7mm Remington Magnum, and sent the little deer tumbling down the hillside. A minute or so later, my young guide ran up, screaming what I am sure was the equivalent of four-letter words in Mongolian. Soon after that, the interpreter arrived and wanted to know why I'd shot.

"You ran off the elk we've been following," he said, when I told him I'd killed a roebuck.

He was angry that I had taken what he considered a lesser game animal and delayed his return to Ulaanbaator one more day.

"I don't care," I said. "I got what I wanted."

"You better hope the antlers didn't fall off," he said in disgust.

"If they did, we'll spend the rest of the day digging in the snow looking for them," I said.

The deer probably weighed no more than ninety pounds, but I was as happy with it as McKenzie was with his first elk. The Siberian roe deer is larger than the European variety, with much larger antlers that typically grow at an angle from the head, unlike the common European roebuck, whose antlers are nearly parallel. The antlers on the one I'd shot (although I never entered it) were briefly the world record under the Safari Club International measuring system. Records mean little to me. This beautiful specimen was the seventeenth race of deer I'd taken.

My guide and interpreter were so angry that I had chased away what they claimed was the largest bull elk in Mongolia that they didn't allow me to take a field photo of my roebuck. They dragged my prized deer in the snow to the truck without stopping and literally threw it behind the seat and slammed the doors. After I climbed inside, we roared off in search of more elk. They didn't speak to me the rest of the day, except to chastise me after I missed what the interpreter claimed was an "easy" shot.

It had come while we were heading back to the yurts when we spotted an average-size bull in the middle of a vast valley. There wasn't a tree or a bush in sight when the driver stepped on the accelerator and raced across the Mongolian steppes after it, sending us flying around inside the cab with every bump we hit. Until you have been bounced and banged in a Russian military vehicle's little cab, you will never know just how many sharp corners it has. I was hurting when the driver slammed on the brakes and yanked open my door. The interpreter was screaming for me to get out and shoot the elk. Our wild ride had cut the distance a bit, but not much. The bull still was running flat out after being chased more than a mile, and it was at least three hundred yards off when I shot at it and missed. The interpreter ordered me to shoot again, but I refused, which made my crew even angrier with me.

Just before we reached our camp, I interrupted the silence to ask the interpreter to have my entire roebuck cooked that evening. The food they had been serving us not only tasted awful, but there was not enough of it. After another supper of hockey pucks, rancid noodles, and sliced pineapples canned in North Vietnam, I marched to the dining yurt with our four plates and demanded more meat.

"All gone," someone said.

"What do you mean?" I asked.

My deer must have yielded at least forty or fifty pounds of meat. I knew they preferred mutton and seldom ate wild game, but even if everyone in camp had eaten some of it, there should have been something left. You can imagine what I said when I was told they'd fed the deer to the camp's dogs.

Things still were quiet in our vehicle on the last day of my hunt. The only difference between this day and the others was I was determined to shoot the first mature bull elk we saw. For some reason, though, we saw no elk that morning in the places we'd been seeing them all week. At noon we stopped to eat lunch—a cold and greasy leg of mutton that had been wrapped in a dirty towel. The Mongols unwrapped the towel, ripped off chunks of meat with their teeth, and passed the leg to me. One taste left a coating of lard on the roof of my mouth, but I said nothing. Other hunters had warned me about the food served in Mongolian elk camps, so I'd brought several bags of trail mix and cans of Spam for moments just like these. Although I shared my food with the Mexicans and McKenzie, I never ate from my stash when my guides were near. I was rationing it, and if they'd seen my food, I would have had to give them some, too.

We found my bull at dusk that last day. Like the two bulls I had passed up earlier, it was standing at the edge of a grove of larch trees. But it was a long way off, and it was ready to bolt. There was no way to get closer, so I aimed over the bull's back to compensate for the distance, held my scope's vertical post as steady as I could in line with the front legs, and squeezed the trigger. The bull whirled and ran into the forest at the shot.

"You missed," the interpreter said.

I had time to say, "I don't think—" before the sound of the bullet hitting meat reached us. The elk already was out of sight. It hadn't gone far, however. We followed its blood and tracks in the snow and found the animal in a shallow depression about fifty yards from where I'd hit it. At first glance it looked like any other elk I've taken, but there were some minor differences. Its brow tines grew out of the burrs of its six-by-six antlers, for example. There usually is a small gap between the burr and the first tine on the elk of North America. Its coloring, especially its rump patch, also seemed to be more reddish than that of our elk.

My Mongolian adventure was nearly over.

I'd finished packing my gear the next morning and was showing my elk's antlers to the two Mexicans. A Mongol was squatting on the ground nearby, fleshing and salting my elk's cape, and when he heard us speaking Spanish, he surprised us by saying something in that language. He had learned Spanish while attending a university in Cuba, he said. I've forgotten what he had studied, but I was sure it would have qualified him for a better job than what he was doing. He must have sensed what I was thinking because he quickly told us that working in a hunting camp paid better than any other job he'd had. Education was part of the Communist Party's plans to bring the country into the twentieth century, and our interpreters and others in the camp had graduated from universities in Moscow, Beijing, and Havana.

Next came the ten-hour drive back across frozen streams and roadless steppes, and another night in the Ulaanbaator Hotel, where the capes and antlers of our animals were stored next to argali and ibex horns on the hotel's roof. The next morning, after another terrible breakfast, we visited an ancient Buddhist temple that had escaped destruction when religion was banned by the Soviets after the People's Republic of Mongolia was established in 1924. We also spent at least an hour in Mongolia's National Hunting Museum, where Lynton must have shot five rolls of film. At first I thought he was interested in the badly mounted specimens of the country's native game animals, and then I saw he was attracted by the unique designs painted all over the museum's walls and dioramas.

After lunch, we were taken on a tour of the city that included a stop to photograph a herd of elk outside one of the city's schools. We left Ulaanbaator that afternoon and flew south to Beijing, where we spent two nights in the elegant New World Hotel. We visited the Great Wall, the Ming Tombs, and a golf course, where someone in our group wanted to buy golf shirts with the club's logo. The course was well groomed, and the clubhouse and shop were as modern as anything I've seen in the United States, although I'm not a golfer and haven't seen that many courses. The Chinese like to say everyone is equal under Communism, but an ordinary Chinese citizen wouldn't have been able to get past the front gate of that country club.

Before leaving China, we were treated to dinner at what Dingh claimed was the restaurant where Peking duck (now called Beijing duck) originated. We ordered duck, of course. It was the best food I'd eaten since leaving home. I tried using chopsticks in honor of the occasion but eventually brought out the fork I carried and had used the entire trip. The next night, a group of Mongolian singers and dancers entertained us at dinner. After Beijing, the group was headed for the United States to perform on Johnny Carson's *Tonight Show*, Dingh said.

As we flew back to San Francisco after leaving Shanghai, I was surprised when nearly everyone on my side of the plane got up and looked out the windows across the aisle, and I joined them. We were over Japan's Mount Fuji, and its white peak was poking out of a flat sea of even whiter clouds below us.

It will be a long time before I forget the sight of my eleven companions going with me through the crowded Customs line in San Francisco with baggage, rifle cases, and the antlers of a dozen bull elk on our carts. Burt Klineburger had warned us that we would be charged excess baggage fees for our elk capes and antlers. To keep the cost down, we split the skulls and taped pieces of garden hose with duct tape

I Pet a Yak, Sleep in a Yurt, Hunt a (Y)Elk

on the antler tips, and then wrapped everything with more duct tape. The antlers and hides of a dozen elk made a heavy, nearly unmanageable package, but we were charged only $200, which we split twelve ways.

To get Customs officials to clear our trophies, they first had to be inspected by someone from the U.S. Fish and Wildlife Service. The young woman took one look at the bundle of antlers and hides taped together and immediately signed her name on several documents without inspecting it further. We were not the first American hunters to bring back Asian elk trophies, and she rushed through the paperwork until she came to my roe deer and had to find its scientific name in a guidebook. The entire wildlife inspection process may have taken less than a half-hour, including the time we waited for the young woman to show up. Outside the Customs barrier, someone was waiting to gather our trophies and ship them to Klineburger's Taxidermy in Seattle.

There have been many changes in the way Mongolia handles hunters from overseas since our trip there in 1990. The problems we experienced in traveling the long distances to and from Ulaanbaator were eliminated when helicopters shuttled hunters and supplies to the camps. A respected North American hunting outfitter also was hired to work with the Mongols for a season to improve the food and camp conditions and weed the alcoholics from the crews. Friends who hunted there later said all aspects of their hunts were handled professionally.

During our layover in Ulaanbaator after our hunt, our guides drove us up a winding road to a peak where we could overlook the city. Along the way, and from where we parked, we saw a great many elk. My interpreter said the mountain above the city had been closed to hunting for more than a hundred years, but his superiors planned to sell a few handgun and archery hunts there the next year. The special hunts were indeed held, but some of the clients were far from happy with the results.

I was shocked to see a proposed ad for *Safari* magazine that Eric Hubbell, our advertising director, brought to me a year after my hunt in Mongolia. It read, "Would I Go Back to Mongolia? Only If I Can Lead the Air Attack!" The handgunner who had written that ad was angry after finding bull elk without antlers during his hunt. Most of the canyons in that little mountain range had elk traps that the Mongols used to capture elk, sawing off their antlers for sale in the antler trade and releasing the live animals. Although all of the handgunners and archers went home with antlered bulls, they claimed they were disgusted after stalking bugling elk only to find many of the bulls had no antlers.

Nonetheless, I rejected their ad.

Despite all the things that went wrong during my only excursion into Asia, I remember that hunt as one of my most treasured experiences. I'd go back to Mongolia tomorrow if I were younger. For a while I contemplated booking an ibex hunt, but I kept putting it off until I was physically incapable of getting around in the rough, rocky terrain where those unique wild goats live. Such hunts are not for old men.

Many of us who had been there found it hard to believe when the Mongolian government suddenly closed elk hunting in the late 1990s. The reason given was that local citizens were killing too many elk for their antlers. Hunters from around the world still go there for ibex, sheep, moose, roebuck, and wild boar, but the elk that seemed so plentiful when I was there are fully protected now, presumably permanently.

Europe, the South Pacific, and South America

Chapter 22

It was fascinating to watch the Spaniard prepare to smoke. He began with a generous pinch of tobacco and a cigarette paper, then shaped the tobacco and rolled the cigarette with the fingers of just his left hand before sealing it with his wet tongue. Then, with his right hand, he hit a steel striker against a piece of flint held between the thumb and forefinger of his left hand, causing a spark to fall onto the combustible wadding in his palm. He encouraged the spark by blowing on it, and when a flame erupted, he lit his cigarette and pinched out the flame. After that, he inspected his work, rather proudly, I thought, and drew a long puff of smoke into his lungs. The process took about as long as it takes to tell about it.

I offered to give him cigarettes and even my extra butane lighter, but he only shook his head. He obviously enjoyed entertaining visiting hunters.

* * *

It would be tough to find a more colorful character than Crestancio, a gamekeeper at the El Castaño hunting estate in the Toledo Mountains south of Madrid. Above his baggy corduroy pants he wore a hand-knitted wool sweater and a green leather beret. His belt was a piece of rope, and his sandals had been made from an old tire. He looked as if he had stepped out of the pages of Ernest Hemingway's *For Whom the Bell Tolls*, and when I asked about his life, he claimed he had lived in that place all his life, never going farther than sixty kilometers (thirty-six miles) from where we stood. I didn't want to embarrass myself by asking his age, not after the trouble I'd had keeping up with him on the hills where we hunted Spanish stags. He had an old man's stoop and a weathered face and hands, but he could have been fifty or eighty. He spoke a little English, but mostly we communicated in my border Mexican and his rural Spanish.

At sundown, he took me to a place where large patches of earth had been dug up the previous night. I chose to sit with my back against a tree and settled in with my rifle in my lap. Crestancio sat nearby with a small flashlight. This seemed a strange way to hunt a wild boar, but I didn't question my guide.

An hour later, my legs were cramped and I was restless. It had grown increasingly colder as it grew darker, and I had only a light jacket. I was ready to tell my guide I'd had all the fun I needed that night when the first animals arrived and began rooting in the ground all around me for acorns. I couldn't see them, but I certainly could hear them. They were just a few feet from where I sat. I was wondering why Crestancio didn't switch on his flashlight when every animal in the little herd suddenly woofed and bolted. All was quiet for a while, and then I heard a single animal rustling leaves in front of me.

"*Listo, señor,*" Crestancio whispered.

A few seconds later, a large shape suddenly was visible about twenty yards away in the dim light from his flashlight. The flame from my rifle's muzzle temporarily blinded me after I found the shape in my scope and fired, but I could hear the boar kicking in one place as it died. My guide was on his feet, congratulating me for taking my first Spanish boar.

"*Siempre mujeres y niños a primero,*" (always females and babies first) he said, when I asked why he hadn't turned the light on earlier. "*Los machos mas tarde.*"

Sure enough, the last to arrive was an old male. It wasn't as large as I expected a European wild boar would be, but Crestancio said it was typical of the mature boar in Spain, and it had a good set of teeth. The animal looked nothing at all like the so-called Russian boar found in America. Coarse brown hair covered its entire body but was longest on its forehead and along the ridge of its backbone. Its long tail had not a hint of curl in it.

I was in Spain for a joint meeting of Safari Club International and the CIC (the European-based International Council for Game and Wildlife Conservation) that would lead to the World Hunting Congress being held a few months later in Las Vegas. Spain's King Juan Carlos, Nicolas Franco, world deer authority Kenneth Whitehead, and many of the best-known figures in European and North American hunting and wildlife-management circles attended the meetings. Afterward, a few SCI members and staff hunted red deer and boar on two estates several hours south of the capital.

Jean does not like airplanes, but the lure of visiting Spain was too much for her, and, aided by a tranquilizer our doctor had prescribed, she accompanied me on this trip. We visited the famed Prado Museum, the Royal Palace, and El Greco's home, and had lunch in the ancient city of Toledo. We also spent a couple of hours shopping at Spain's largest department store, El Corte de Inglés, and had drinks at a little-known place where some of Spain's best flamenco dancers performed. Most of our time in that country, however, was spent in meetings, in hotel rooms, and on Weatherby Award recipient Ricardo Medem's estate.

I shot my boar the third evening we were at El Castaño, and the next day I shot a six-by-six red stag. Although taxonomists say red deer and elk are the same species, *Cervus elaphus,* the red deer I shot at El Castaño, looked nothing at all like the elk I've taken in Arizona, New Mexico, and Mongolia. Its body was about the size of a large mule deer, but its head and neck seemed much larger in proportion to everything else. Though its antlers grew up and toward the rear, as do those on elk, the top three tines on each side formed "baskets" seldom seen on elk. It also lacked the mane found on bull elk in the winter. Its coat was grayish, much like the color of a mule deer in winter, and not red.

The greatest difference between red deer and elk is their rutting call, however. The rut (it's called "the roar" in Europe, for good reason) had ended a couple of weeks before I hunted at El Castaño, but not every stag had gotten the message. A stag was calling on the hillside above the lodge when I walked out in the dark to join Crestancio my first morning there, and it sounded like a Brahma bull bawling. If it had been a bull elk, it would have been bugling, squealing, and grunting.

The red deer on Medem's place also seemed warier than any other elk I've hunted, perhaps because it was late in the hunting season. Each time Crestancio and I crept over a ridge to check the country beyond it, every red deer out to six or seven hundred yards would immediately spot us and run off. After a few frustrating and unsuccessful stalks, I was wondering whether I'd made a mistake by turning down several small stags. Fortunately for me, we finally found an unlucky stag with fair antlers, and I shot it.

I'd known El Castaño's owner for a couple of years before this trip. He was a close friend of SCI founder C. J. McElroy and served on SCI's trophy records committee. He had raved about the thrills of a traditional Spanish *monteria* and promised to arrange one for our group while we were there.

A *monteria*, we learned, is a social event involving an organized drive with dogs and beaters. It apparently is an honor to be invited to participate. We were stationed along a firebreak and told to shoot every red deer or boar that crossed the opening between two flags. When all the shooters were in position, word was sent to a line of beaters waiting about a mile down the ridge, and suddenly there were people yelling and dogs yapping as they advanced toward us. The dogs were of assorted sizes, colors, and breeds, and not the English foxhounds I expected they would be.

When I heard something moving in the brush across the firebreak, at least five minutes before the dogs reached me, I raised my rifle, flicked off its safety, and got ready to shoot. I expected a deer or a boar to cross the opening at any second, but nothing happened. Whatever the animal was, it stopped out of my sight when it came to the firebreak.

It made not another sound for a long while. Then, when the dogs and beaters were only a couple of hundred yards away and I least expected it, a wild boar leaped across the opening and was gone before I could shoot.

Only two or three animals were taken on the *monteria* that day. I still don't understand the attraction such events hold for Spaniards.

Hunting on Two Islands

My first visit to the South Pacific began with trying for four days to catch a trout in the streams that feed Lake Taupo, New Zealand's largest lake.

"You should have been here last week," my host said. "The fishing was good before the rivers got muddy."

There were three of us fishing—my host, his son, and I—and I caught the only trout, a twelve-inch rainbow, during those four days. I didn't experience the red-hot fishing action shown in the angling magazines and videos about New Zealand, but I got a lot of practice casting weighted flies on a floating level line. I also visited author Zane Grey's fishing shack and fished where he had fished, and had a wonderful time in a beautiful place with friendly people. It would have been more fun if the fish had been hungry, though.

* * *

After my time at Lake Taupo was up, Paul Bamber, owner of Wanganui Safaris, drove me to his place above the Whanganui River. When we stopped along the way to visit a museum filled with artifacts from New Zealand's military history, I was once again reminded of the inadequacy of the American educational system. I had lived through World War II without realizing that New Zealand and Australia had helped defeat Germany in two world wars and Japan in World War II. Bamber seemed surprised at my interest in an exhibit that depicted the World War I Battle of Gallipoli, when Turkish soldiers slaughtered ANZAC (Australia and New Zealand Army Corps) in 1915. It was an important and bloody battle over control of the strategic strait Dardanelles, but I'd never heard of it until that moment. Like many

North Americans, I reached adulthood knowing little about the world beyond our continent. Brief hunts in Africa, Europe, and Asia expanded my knowledge a bit, but it wasn't enough. I promised myself that I would never again visit a place without knowing something about its history and traditions before I arrived, and it was a promise I've kept since that day.

When Paul stopped at the rural mailbox at the junction that led to his home a mile or two above us, I was surprised to see the latest issue of *Safari* magazine in his mail. After the problems I'd experienced entrusting the U.S. Postal Service to get the magazine to SCI's international members, I'd given a trial run to a new company that planned to specialize in drop shipping. The company had promised to shorten our delivery time by picking up the overseas copies at our printer's plant and sorting, bundling, and dropping them the next day at key post offices in fifteen or sixteen cities on six continents. We had decided we'd hire the company long-term if it could do this. Obviously, the company had won the contract. That issue had gone to press in Long Prairie, Minnesota, the day before I'd left Tucson, five days earlier! By regular mail, it was taking two to three weeks (and sometimes a lot more) to reach addresses in the South Pacific.

✳ ✳ ✳

Most of the photos I had seen of New Zealand showed the South Island's Southern Alps, and I was not prepared for the thick vegetation I saw on the North Island. It wasn't a rain forest, but it was overgrown with brush and almost impenetrable, especially along the wide river we followed on the way to Paul's lodge. I was relieved to see that the brush grew thinner as the dirt road climbed out of the canyon. By the time we reached the gate to his place, tall, thick grass covered the ridges and sun-facing slopes. His lodge was on one of the highest ridges, and from its porches I could see the Ruapehu Volcano in the distance and look down into a series of long canyons. Most of them were choked with brush and quite steep. It was a scenic setting, but the first thought that popped into my mind was that hunting there would not be easy.

Paul's wife, Maureen, greeted us and showed me to my room. Their outfitting company was a two-person operation, and she was the other half. The meals she served us included an outstanding leg of lamb with a kiwifruit dessert. I don't think I ever saw her when she wasn't smiling.

One of the first things I did after unpacking was to assemble the Ruger .257 Roberts rifle I'd brought. I'd had trouble in Spain with little cars and big gun cases, so I'd removed the stock and shipped the rifle's two parts in a short shotgun case with my bags to New Zealand. I was surprised to find its zero hadn't changed when I fired a couple of shots at a target I'd brought.

When Tudor Howard-Davies had arranged this trip, it was to be a hunt for only a Sika deer, and we began our search for it that first afternoon by walking down one of the long ridges, then climbing back to the lodge on another. It had rained during the night, and I soon was carrying at least fifteen pounds of sticky mud on my boots.

Although we saw no Sika deer that afternoon, we did roust three trophy-class red stags out of one of the side canyons. They ran to a ridge, then stood and looked down at us. These were descended from red deer imported from eastern Europe and were not the small subspecies I'd hunted in Spain. They were large animals with massive antlers. We watched them until they grew tired of staring at us and walked away.

A dozen or more feral goats were feeding in the next canyon, and Paul asked me to shoot as many as I could. Their numbers had grown out of control, and he wanted to remove most of them, he said. I shot two and then watched the rest of the herd run off.

We were climbing the hill, heading back to the lodge, when an animal that had to be the grandfather of all Sika stags ran out of a cut about two hundred yards below us and stopped.

"Don't shoot!" Paul yelled, when I threw my rifle to my shoulder. "It's a hybrid. Its father was a red deer."

With my binocular I could see that the deer was not a Sika stag or a red deer but had characteristics of both. Until then, I didn't know that the two species would cross. It apparently happens often when the two types of deer come together.

We were approaching a ridge the next morning when there was a loud whistle and the sound of the stamping of hoofs above us. We'd intruded on a Sika stag's territory, Paul said. We took a few steps, and when the stag trotted into the open, I sat down and shot it. It was much larger and had longer antlers than the little Japanese Sika deer introduced to Texas.

I was ready to put my rifle away after lunch when Paul asked if I wanted to shoot a red deer, quickly adding that there would be no charge. What a question! An hour later, we found the stag he wanted to cull, and I shot it, too. It was a beautiful animal that I would have mounted when I returned to Arizona, but the genes that had produced its six-by-seven antlers were not what Paul wanted in his herd.

I'd had a great two days of hunting, and I didn't know what to say when Paul announced he also had arranged hunts for chamois and tahr for me on the South Island. We said good-bye to Maureen the next morning and drove about forty-five miles to Palmerstown North, where we caught a flight to the South Island. My rifle was in its shotgun case with my checked baggage, but Paul had brought his .308 Winchester in a soft case and merely handed it to the pilot to keep on the flight. Imagine doing that anywhere in the world today!

To pass the time in Christchurch before our next flight, we visited a university museum that had a reconstructed skeleton of a giant stag from the Pleistocene Epoch on display. Its palmated antlers were at least ten feet wide. I'd seen photos of these long-extinct deer, but until I stood under the skeleton's antlers, I had no idea how large they were. The sign on the exhibit called them Irish elk, but they actually were the ancestors of today's fallow deer.

* * *

I've forgotten the name of the outfitter Paul arranged to take us hunting in the Southern Alps. He talked nonstop, and the stories he told about his hunting and mountain-climbing feats seemed far-fetched, but I didn't question them. He and his wife, a Maori woman, had a large, nearly new home on a hundred acres, where they raised red deer and sold meat, hides, and antlers. A river ran along the side of their land, and the Tasman Sea was across the road. Paul said his closest neighbor lived about five miles away. I was impressed with his property. When I asked how much a similar place might cost in U.S. dollars, he smiled and thought a minute before proudly saying, "I wouldn't take less than fifty thousand dollars for ours." I had expected him to say at least ten times that amount.

I'd never thought about how Himalayan tahr and chamois are hunted in New Zealand, and when a helicopter hovered over the house and landed outside after we'd finished breakfast, I suddenly remembered stories I'd heard about people shooting game from the air. I didn't want to do that, I told him.

"Don't worry, we'll go in on foot," he said, as he shouldered a bag packed with ropes and climbing gear.

The helicopters I'd ridden in on the Arizona Game and Fish Department's game surveys and fish-stocking trips were small, underpowered machines painted gray or army green. The large helicopter outside was brightly colored and looked as if it were new. It easily lifted into the air with power to spare with the pilot, the guide, Paul, and me aboard. I was glad to see that its passenger door hadn't been removed, and not just because it was cold outside. I had meant what I said about not shooting from the air.

Our flight took us over a long glacier, and when we reached a high saddle where a bank of white fog suddenly blocked our view, the pilot stopped our forward motion and hovered for a minute or two. I couldn't believe it when he slowly moved the helicopter into the stuff. He apparently knew what he was doing because we were safely through the cloud in a minute. I'd seen two chamois from my window on the way up but hadn't said anything. They were running uphill below us in a place so steep I couldn't believe any four-footed creature could move around on it, and the pilot was taking us to a place that seemed even steeper.

317

Almost as soon as the sky cleared, I spotted five or six shaggy animals feeding uphill with their heads down, far in front of us. The pilot obviously had seen them, too, and he banked our machine sharply to the right and gained altitude to keep from spooking them. When we were at least a half-mile away, we flew along the side of the mountain, high above the animals, before hovering above a cliff.

"Here's where we get out," the guide said.

He opened the door, tossed out his bag, and carefully stepped from the strut to an ice-covered rock. I handed him Paul's rifle, and he helped me out, too. (I was using the .308 because tahr have a reputation for being tough to put down. I'd brought my little .257 Roberts to New Zealand thinking I would shoot only a small deer.) As soon as I was out, the helicopter left and landed on a flat spot on another ridge. The guide and I suddenly were alone on one of the steepest slopes I've ever been on.

"Get ready," the guide said, after we had made our way to the edge of a crack on the mountain. "They'll be here soon."

He knew what he was talking about. The first animal to feed toward us was a female, and he whispered for me not to shoot. The next was much larger, and when the guide nodded his head, my shot broke both shoulders and killed the tahr where it stood. The guide slapped my back and was so excited I wouldn't have been surprised to see him dance a jig.

"That was an easy shot," I said.

"I know," he said. "But I don't need my ropes to get to him."

We returned to the guide's home, towing my tahr on the cable below the helicopter. Alone in my room that night, I asked myself if the way we had used the helicopter to hunt was unethical. There were no roads to where we'd gone, and there was no way a horse could get anywhere near it. I didn't have the time or the technical mountain-climbing skills—or the courage—to climb up there, either. It would have been grossly unsporting if the pilot had spooked and driven the herd toward us, but he hadn't. I eventually decided what I'd done wasn't much different from driving a Jeep down a road and spotting a herd of undisturbed antelope, then getting out and moving ahead of them. It made me feel better when I flew out in the same helicopter the next morning and shot a chamois.

This time we landed and walked to the edge of a wide canyon, and I waited until the buck had climbed to the top of the opposite side before I shot it.

Paul had never taken a tahr, so when we spotted another band as we were flying off the mountain, he and the guide got out, and Paul shot one after a short stalk. It went down on a particularly scary place—a steep, shale-covered slope that ended at a fifty-foot drop-off. From the helicopter I watched in horror as the animal suddenly tried to get up when they approached it. When the guide grabbed its horns, they both slid several feet toward the cliff. It was the tahr's last effort, though. The guide and Paul were able to tie the dead animal to the cable with my chamois, and we flew them both to a hunter's shack, where we retrieved them later with a vehicle.

I wasn't scheduled to fly home for another two days, so we took the longer but more scenic route around the island and spent the night in Queenstown before driving on to Christchurch.

My New Zealand visit is something I'll never forget.

Ducks on a Sixth Continent

Natalie Greene, my granddaughter, got her first taste of international travel when she was thirteen and performed with her school's orchestra in Prague. After graduating from high school in three years, she spent the summer backpacking in Europe with two friends. When she was a junior, an Arizona State University program got her to Granada, Spain, for a semester, allowing her to see even more of Europe by Eurail and bus on weekends. When I heard she planned to spend a month traveling alone before a summer-school course in Italy, I met her in Granada, and she and I flew to South Africa, Zimbabwe, Zambia, Botswana, and Swaziland. By the time she was twenty, she had visited twenty countries. [1]

---

[1] My grandson, Logan Greene, showed no interest in traveling to Europe, Africa, or anywhere except Australia while growing up, so we went to Australia after he graduated high school in 2006. We attended an opera in the Sydney Opera House, and he climbed that city's bridge. We saw Ayers Rock from a bus and the Great Barrier Reef from a glass-bottom boat, and fished for barramundi in the Dundee River.

I've told you this so that you'll know that Natalie has inherited my wanderlust. For the past four or five years she has been my "date" at the Saturday evening banquets at Safari Club International's conventions in Reno. We were seated at the Argentina delegation's table at one of those banquets when Natalie told the group I'd hunted on five continents but not in South America and that she intended to travel there with me. Before the dinner was over, she and I were planning a trip to Argentina, with stopovers for sightseeing in Rio de Janeiro, both sides of Iguaçu Falls, and Asunción, the capital of Paraguay. As my translator and nursemaid, Natalie would add three more countries to her curriculum vitae.

Our host in Buenos Aires was José Martinez de Hoz, the SCI Argentina chapter's founding president. He and the chapter's office staff arranged tours in their city and a duck hunt for me at a place called Los Patos (The Ducks) two hours away. With a name like that the shooting should have been great, but it was the last day of the country's waterfowl hunting season, and only a few birds were flying. It didn't matter that the resort's owner and I shot only eight or nine ducks between us. The instant my first South American duck splashed into the pond behind the Los Patos Lodge, I had completed a quest—I had successfully hunted wild game on six continents!

It's Been
a Good Life

Chapter 23

All my working career, I went from one thing to another without a break. For example, I still was the *Tucson Citizen*'s outdoor editor, but the freelance advertising work I'd been doing was slowing down when a woman named Sally Antrobus resigned her post as editor of Safari Club International's *Safari* magazine in early 1983. Before she left, Holt Bodinson (SCI's executive director then) offered me the job. I wasn't interested if I had to report to a committee of volunteers with no journalism or publishing experience and whose faces changed every twelve months. I also enjoyed the local fame that came with writing news stories and twice-weekly opinion columns in a daily newspaper too much to do anything else, or so I thought.

But when Holt said I would report only to him and the club's founder, I went to the newspaper publisher to tell him I was resigning. I was shocked when he asked me to remain his newspaper's outdoor editor while producing SCI's publications. Such an arrangement is almost unheard of in the newspaper business, but I suppose the publisher believed the outdoors portion of his paper was too unimportant to worry about apparent conflicts of interest. His only stipulation was that I use the name William R. Quimby and not Bill Quimby on *Safari*'s masthead. If I wrote bylined articles in the magazine, I had to use a pseudonym.[1]

---

[1] I was "Bill Roberts" for the next four years, before using Quimby again when the *Citizen* got a new publisher. I fooled no one, however. The antihunters on the newspaper's staff (and there were many) somehow found copies of *Safari* magazine and anonymously posted abusive comments on tearsheets of Bill Roberts's articles on the paper's bulletin boards.

Safari Club International claimed it had ten thousand members when I moved into the southwest corner office at its headquarters at 5151 East Broadway in Tucson, but the number was closer to half that. It was printing ten thousand copies of the magazine six times a year, but forty-five hundred copies of each printing were sent directly to a warehouse to be used for advertising manager Eric Hubbell's promotions. When I retired in 1999, membership was on a steep curve, projected to reach fifty thousand within the year.

I had started as a one-man editorial staff, assisted by Hubbell, one full-time secretary, and an intern, publishing a bimonthly seventy-two-page magazine and an annual record book of approximately two hundred and fifty pages. When I retired, the magazine had up to three hundred pages per issue, and the record books were multiple volumes of eight hundred or more pages. My staff included sixteen employees, plus part-timers in Tucson and Johannesburg, and I also published monthly newspapers in North America and Africa and a daily newspaper at SCI's conventions. The club's magazine was losing money when I signed on. When I left, it was the flagship of a prosperous publishing division.

One of the reasons I was able to turn the magazine around was the cooperation I got from Bodinson and the club's founder, C. J. McElroy, who insulated me from the club's petty organizational politics. My marching orders from McElroy were simple: As soon as I could, I was to move the magazine's production and printing away from two men he feared were gaining too much control of the publication. One was the executive director of a state sportsmen's association whose art director also served as *Safari* magazine's production department. The other was a former SCI president who had chaired the magazine committee that was dissolved when I came aboard. He had awarded the contract to print *Safari* magazine to a small printing shop that also did a considerable amount of work for his various companies.

It took only a couple of issues to realize that SCI's deadlines came second to the art director's, who had his own association's magazine to produce. When he fell behind on his magazine's production, it was our magazine that failed to make it to the printer on time, which meant not only that SCI would pay penalties but that Eric Hubbell and I would get angry calls from our advertisers, also complaining that their ads had appeared too late to do their businesses any good.

When I found a pre-press company in Tucson and a printing company in California that specialized in producing short-run magazines economically, I wrote letters to the two men Mac had targeted, thanking them for their past efforts. I also wrote the art director and the printer, telling them their services were no longer needed. I couldn't risk a delay in getting the advertisers' negatives and other printing materials we needed for the next issue, so I had the owner of the pre-press company in Tucson fly to the Midwest and bring the materials back with him. We timed it so he and my letters arrived the same day.

The two men Mac had targeted were not happy with me, of course, but Mac and Bodinson had approved my action, and I was able to show the club's executive committee that my changes had brought an immediate savings of about $8,000 per issue in production and printing costs, which meant the magazine would turn its first profit. Nonetheless, I had made enemies who criticized me at every opportunity at the highest levels of the club, until they both died a few years before I retired.

I did meet some great people during my tenure at SCI, and they opened doors that allowed me to hunt on six continents, but there were others I'd rather forget. Take, for example, a chapter president who stopped by my office when visiting SCI's headquarters to say that although he appreciated what I was doing with *his* magazine, there were a few things he wanted me to do to improve it. I suppose he felt that as a chapter president, he was a member of the club's board of directors and therefore had the authority to tell me what to do. However, there were more than a hundred board members, and most of the club's decisions were made by an executive committee. He obviously didn't know that under my contract I reported only to the president and CEO. I listened politely to his demands and ignored them after he left.

I can't remember how many hunting outfitters called me over the years I directed SCI's publications to ask when their article would run in the magazine, but the number was considerable. When I'd ask them to explain, they'd say something like this: "I had the president of SCI out here hunting, and he promised that he'd run a story about us in the magazine."

When I asked the name of the person who'd promised the caller an article, I'd learn he was president of a local chapter, not the president of the international organization. These were the same chapter presidents who had the words "Safari Club International" printed in large type across the top of their letterhead. Their names, followed by "president," would also be prominent. The chapter names would be in small type, almost hidden in the design of the letterhead.

I was fortunate that I had few problems with Safari Club's executive committee members or officers. One reason none tried to micromanage what I did may be that I was an independent contractor for most of those years. Another had to be the fact that I had taken a magazine that was losing money and built it into an award-winning publication. Every few years, though, a new president or executive committee member would want to know why the club's magazine wasn't sold on newsstands, and I'd have to explain why SCI couldn't afford to put it there. Not only was cost prohibitive, but having to increase advertising rates to pay for printing and distributing many thousands of additional copies would also chase away our present advertisers, outfitters, booking agents, and custom gunmakers. To replace that business, we'd have to try to sell space to big-time advertisers who bought media with much larger circulation than ours. More important, it no longer would be the same quality magazine because it would have to be designed especially for newsstand sales with a dozen glaring headlines across its covers.[2]

I did have a president pull me aside one day, open up a copy of the magazine, and point to advertising he felt should be changed. At first I thought he objected to the content of the ads, but then he said: "Members get tired of seeing the same thing in every issue. You need to tell the advertisers to send you new material."

[2]After I retired, SCI launched a magazine designed for sale on U.S. newsstands. Its emphasis was on North American hunting, and it soon was shut down. *Safari* magazine "owns" the international hunting market, but this attempt to broaden the club's appeal was a predictable failure. There is no shortage of North American hunting magazines on newsstands.

He did not pursue his quest when I explained that we were in the business of selling space to our advertisers, and it was up to them to fill it with whatever message they wanted. As long as it was not libelous, fraudulent, obscene, or detrimental to hunting, we didn't have cause to ask for new material. Besides, I said, few advertisers want to risk changing ads that were still bringing them customers.

A president of a chapter in Europe thought *Safari* magazine should refuse all advertising except ads for high-end products such as top-of-the-line automobiles, English double rifles, expensive leather goods, cameras and optics, fine wines, tailored Italian clothing, and certain hunting outfitters. He didn't like seeing ads for outfitters in South Africa or New Zealand because most of the hunting in those places takes place on fenced estates. I told him I'd work with advertising manager Eric Hubbell on that, and wished him a good flight home.

One of the things I liked most about my position was attending the meetings of SCI's trophy records committee. I enjoyed listening to the panel members talk about their hunts all over the globe, and along the way I got an education about the world's wildlife that I could have found nowhere else.

My teacher was Jack Schwabland, a lumber broker from Seattle. If Jack had been born a hundred years earlier, he would have been called a "naturalist." He was (and is) short-tempered, outspoken, opinionated, and quick to call me whenever I made a mistake, but the work that Jack and his wife, Casey, did while serving on the club's trophy records committee would have been prohibitively expensive if the club had had to pay for it, even if they had charged as little as five dollars per hour. It was a labor of love for them. Casey developed systems for managing members' trophy records, while Jack wrote the natural history text and drew the maps for the record books.

Jack's work made the SCI record books unique and useful for everyone who hunts internationally. Nowhere else under one cover can anyone find as much information about every huntable big-game animal on the planet. Without him, the club's record books certainly would have contained some serious errors in taxonomy. There was great pressure, for example, from outfitters and members who wanted the book to create categories for animals that were not valid species or subspecies. Jack's knowledge and quick temper helped beat down most of them. It wasn't long before at least two well-known wildlife scientists were calling him regularly. Their expertise was limited to certain families of animals, but Jack's large library of natural history material had made him a generalist, with considerable knowledge of the natural history of all big game. A tiny part of that knowledge, I hoped, would rub off on me as I edited the text of Jack's record book.

What surprised me about the club's record books was how some members would do anything to get their names published in them. One member bought a zoo just so he could import certain animals into his country, shoot them, and "make" the book. The committee hadn't yet adopted a policy for "exotics" or "introduced" animals, which is why you'll find Rocky Mountain bighorn and sitatunga shot in Europe listed in the fifth edition of the record book. It was published before the committee realized what was happening. Today, among other things, an introduced animal taken on a hunting estate must be from a breeding population. The rules do not allow it to be released somewhere and shot the next day or even the same year.

There were many blatant attempts by a few members and outfitters to cheat. For example, an outfitter who guided one of the club's presidents to all of the game animals of South Africa gave measurements that placed every animal the president shot while hunting with him among the top ten trophies of all time. Several years later, when the committee voted to have all Top Ten trophies re-measured, nearly all the measurements of the former president's trophies taken with that outfitter were found to have been stretched. Those of us who learned what that outfitter and others had been doing weren't surprised when we heard that several members had refused to have their trophies re-measured, even though they were warned we would remove them from the books if they weren't measured again.

Stretching measurements was not the only way outfitters tried to promote their businesses. More than one told a client he had taken a rare subspecies of something, when the animal actually was a common one. Ultimately, though, it was the members who were to blame for submitting fraudulent entry forms.

Despite the committee's serious efforts to eliminate fraud, SCI's record books do not have a good reputation among the world's hunters. There are reasons for this. For one, the minimum scores needed to enter a trophy are too low. For another, some animals raised in enclosures are listed in the same categories with wild and free-ranging animals. The committee has tried to improve its reputation by writing rules for game-ranched animals and dropping entries of animals suspected of being taken in "canned" hunts, but it has a long way to go. Raising minimums and listing "estate-taken" and introduced animals in a separate book (or eliminating them altogether) would help.

C. J. McElroy could not understand why I wouldn't enter the trophies I took after I was officially named editor of the record books. My chief reason was I felt some might view it as a conflict of interest. I'd also seen too many good people do bad things to get their animals listed.

* * *

As I've shown, Safari Club International gets bad reviews from some hunters because of the problems with its record books and the dumb things a few members do to promote their hunting feats. However, the club deserves recognition and gratitude from hunters all over the world for its role in protecting the hunting tradition. Few realize it, but SCI is the only large, U.S.-based sportsmen's organization whose mission is to both conserve wildlife and protect hunting. Other well-known groups, such as the Foundation for North American Wild Sheep, Ducks Unlimited, and the Rocky Mountain Elk Foundation, do a great job of preserving habitat for their chosen species, but they seldom take a public role in preserving hunters' rights. Part of the reason may be that their nonprofit tax status could be threatened if they became politically involved in hunting issues. Another reason may be that a significant portion of their funding comes from nonhunting sources.

Although the National Rifle Association liked to claim that it alone protected hunters, this was not true. Over the years I directed SCI's publications, the NRA took credit for defending hunters in too many instances, when it was SCI and its local chapters that had rallied the troops and raised the war chest.[3] The NRA's mission is to protect the rights of gun owners, and no other group does this better than the NRA, but it is not alone even in that effort.

* * *

C. J. McElroy's management style was to point his division managers in the direction he wanted them to go and then leave them alone to succeed or fail. I first learned this when I'd been on the job less than a month and knocked at his door with a stack of proofs for the next record book for his approval.

"You handle it. This is all I want to see," he said as he pointed to the pages with his photo and brief text on his life and hunting career. "Just be sure it is in the front of the book, before everybody else."

Although Mac was not involved in the production of record books, he was listed as its editor in each one until the SCI board of directors fired him in 1988. I was given the title after that, and I eventually moved my photo to the back of the books.

I got to know Mac well after he was forced out of his post at SCI, and I like to think we were friends. I respected him for his ability to create and build the world's most influential international sportsmen's organization. He also was responsible for my first hunts in Africa and Europe, and I am proud to have accompanied him on his last African hunting safari. But I cannot deny that Mac was a controversial person.

[3] I was criticized by staunch NRA members on SCI's board of directors when I rejected a two-page ad the NRA submitted for publication in *Safari* magazine. To them, it was as if I had refused a mandate from God. I've forgotten the exact words, but the ad said the NRA was the only organization that protected hunters and hunting. It ignored SCI's considerable efforts and achievements in the local, national, and international political arenas, and I was pleased to see that the SCI executive committee agreed with me that this message had no business being in SCI's magazine.

There were times when, although he should have known better, he did things that guaranteed people would talk about him behind his back. For example, when his first wife died, Mac ran ads in Tucson's newspapers seeking a female companion. Those ads were clipped and sent around the world. Then he married the receptionist at SCI's headquarters, dyed his hair, grew a mustache, and cut a year off his age in the record book's biographical text. Although Arizona is a community property state, it was reported that he did not ask for a prenuptial agreement, and this also fed the gossip mill after his divorce.

His critics charged that Mac used his position to pressure outfitters for free hunts and that he traded the club's prestigious awards for free hunts, but I suspect Mac was deluged with unsolicited invitations from outfitters who wanted to say he had hunted with them. Not all of his hunting was "comped," either. For example, Jan Oelofse, one of Namibia's best-known outfitters, told me Mac booked and paid the full price for a safari with him after Oelofse was named Outstanding Professional Hunter of the Year in 1981.

Mac also gathered critics because he would squash anyone like a bug he saw as a threat to his throne. More than once I saw him give someone an award for past deeds, then remove the man from every committee on which he served.

"He's a taker, not a giver," Mac would say of those he thought might be building a base of political power for themselves.

He was convinced he was the greatest hunter of all time and no one could duplicate his hunting feats. When I named men who already had hunted in more places and taken more types of big-game animals and who had more Top Ten trophies in the SCI record book, he would change the subject. No matter how many times I told him that he would be remembered not as a hunter but for his greatest achievement, the founding of Safari Club International, he would turn the conversation back to his hunting.

The final straw that forced him out of the leadership of the club he'd created came when he and a few of his friends launched a separate foundation and began building a museum to house his personal hunting trophies. He then manipulated things so that SCI would own the facility, and, thus, have to pay its mortgage and future operating costs. This sent the club to the brink of bankruptcy. Even so, the club's leaders were wrong when they treated Mac as if he were a leper after they fired him. Although he attended every SCI convention until he died, it was several years before McElroy was officially recognized from the stage again. Until then, his tables at convention banquets were moved farther and farther from the front of the banquet rooms each year.

Worse, in my opinion, I saw some of the people he had helped in various ways walk past him without saying hello because they didn't want to be seen talking with him. This hurt him deeply. I tried to console Mac by saying this type of treatment was only temporary and that the club eventually would recognize that he was its founder. At the very next convention, then-president Bob Easterbrook presented Mac with an award, and he continued to introduce him at every banquet. I don't know whether Mac thanked Easterbrook, but I know he was moved by his action. After that, people who hadn't wanted to be seen with him were standing in line to have Mac to autograph his books and shake their hands.

After Mac was ousted, SCI hired a succession of executive directors. The problem? As I see it, the club's executive committee has been reluctant to delegate responsibility to the people it hires to run the club's daily operations. Its officers should take a lesson from Mac and point any executive director they hire in the direction they want the club to go, then step aside and allow that person to take it there. Instead, the executive committee appoints committees of volunteers to oversee each of the club's divisions, and, as a result, people who have no experience in education, publishing, conventions, membership sales, and legislative affairs are directing the knowledgeable people hired to direct those activities. They are replaced a year later by another group of volunteers who are equally unqualified, and the club's programs change according to the whims of the new committees.

This has not gone unnoticed within the industry. After a scandal broke involving several prominent SCI members accused of hunting from helicopters in the former Soviet Union,[4] SCI's CEO retired, and at least one well-qualified person was not interested when SCI approached him.

"That's a two-year job," he remarked to me after SCI's offer.

Another of SCI's problems will be tough to solve. When the club was smaller, a member could call headquarters, and the people who answered the phones would know if he was among those who supported the club with money or other donations. Not today. I'm reminded of the turnover of employees every time I visit the club's headquarters. I worked there for many years, but to reach the elevator that takes visitors to the floors with the club's offices, I must talk into a box at a locked door to explain who I am and where I want to go. Fewer than a dozen of the people now at SCI headquarters worked there when I did. Whether or not anyone recognizes me is unimportant, but when someone who has donated hundreds of thousands of dollars or hundreds of hours to the club's programs gets the same treatment, that donor has a right to be unhappy. It's no wonder many of SCI's longtime contributors are taking their time and money to other clubs.

When I retired from my newspaper job in 1994, club officials asked that I change my employment status, and I realized I had no choice. Under the Internal Revenue Service's new rules, I already was a de facto employee, even though I had incorporated myself as a publications company and paid SCI rent for my office and the equipment I used. Fortunately for me, the committees assigned to oversee the publications division in my remaining years at the club were in name only. I continued to report only to the president and CEO.

The stress of working fourteen to fifteen hours daily for more than thirty years in jobs with absolute deadlines eventually affected my health.

---

[4]This was not the only scandal to involve SCI board members and leaders. When I took over *Safari* magazine, I was shocked to see that some of the club's officers at conventions and board meetings considered the women working at SCI headquarters fair game. Unfortunately for the women, this was before federal sexual harassment laws. After such laws were enacted, two women sued the club in separate cases involving alleged harassment by members of the executive committee. One lost her suit; the other accepted an out-of-court settlement.

I probably would have been all right if I'd continued spending only six or seven hours daily at SCI headquarters after leaving the newspaper. Instead, I soon was working ten-hour shifts there. It caught up to me on a Friday night in 1998, when I woke with strong palpitations in my chest. I had suffered from a minor but recurring heart condition for about fifteen years, but I had learned to live with it. This feeling was something different. Jean drove me to a hospital, where my heart rate was recorded at an erratic 195 beats per minute, more than three times its normal rate. Meanwhile, my blood pressure had dropped to a dangerously low level. The emergency room doctors converted me to a normal rhythm several hours later with drugs delivered intravenously. Atrial fibrillation is seldom fatal, a cardiologist told Jean and me in a follow-up interview, but he quickly added that a heart's malfunctioning electrical system often triggers strokes. He prescribed a series of drugs with awful side effects.

No one could explain it, but every Friday night for the next six or seven weeks I would wake up, take my pulse, and ask Jean to take me to the hospital, where I'd spend up to thirty hours in a bed with a tube dripping stuff into my arm. My heart rate approached three hundred beats per minute at least twice. After too many such episodes, I gave SCI notice that I was retiring as soon as I could find and train a replacement.

I was sixty-three years old, just three years from a heart attack, when I turned SCI's publications over to Californian Steve Comus, and Jean and I began dividing our time between our home in Tucson and our cabin in eastern Arizona's White Mountains. A-fib still strikes six or seven times a year, but doctors now use an electric shock treatment to convert me. I no longer rush to an emergency room the instant I feel the palpitations, though. The blood thinner I take lessens the danger of suffering a stroke.

* * *

I was ready to get back into the business when McElroy called a few months after I'd retired to ask me to edit a book he'd written about hunting the world's dangerous game. But I shuddered when he handed me what he called his "manuscript." He had talked into a tape recorder, then had the tapes transcribed word for word by a typist. As with many people in their eighties, Mac couldn't keep his thoughts organized, and he rambled all over the place. One chapter might be titled "Hunting the African Lion," but the narrative would switch from hunting lion to bushbuck to argali to leopard to rhino to Dall sheep in the first few pages. Mac also had his own way of pronouncing certain words. As a result, what I got from the typist for the names of people and places frequently was unintelligible.

After trying to edit what he gave me, I gave up and wrote *McElroy Hunts Dangerous Game* by reorganizing anecdotes and bits and pieces of events taken from the scrambled transcripts and adding things I knew about him, the animals and places he hunted, and the people he hunted with. I used the SCI record books and his earlier *McElroy Hunts Africa* to check the spelling of the names of his outfitters and guides and the dates and places where he had taken his animals. Mac was so happy with the result that he didn't want to stop "writing" and announced plans for at least five more books. I remember him saying that all anyone needed to be an author was a good editor.

"I can't wait to wake up and start writing now," he said each time I visited him at his town home in the foothills above Tucson.

Next came *McElroy Hunts Mountain Game,* the last book that Mac saw released. *McElroy Hunts the Antelope of Africa and Antlered Game* came out after he died of a stroke in 2001. Its bizarre title resulted when publisher Ellen Enzler-Herring of Trophy Room Books had me combine two separate manuscripts I'd written for Mac. She felt her customers were interested only in African topics.

Visiting this once-virile man in his hospital room after he suffered the stroke that kept him from moving and speaking was difficult for me. I could tell from his face that he recognized me whenever I entered the room, but his speech was unintelligible. It was hard to believe that the helpless man in that bed had run away from home as a boy and gone from begging for food and hitching rides on railroad cars to become a self-made millionaire (when a million dollars bought a heck of a lot more than it does today). He had traveled first class around the world;

hobnobbed with politicians, heads of state, royalty, actors, authors, and celebrities of every type; and, more important, had founded the world's largest international sportsmen's organization. I am proud to have known Mac, and to have helped him preserve his stories.

I've kept busy since retiring from my SCI post in 1999. I wrote not only Mac's last three books, but also *Yoshi* with Watson Yoshimoto of Hawaii; *To Heck with It, I'm Going Hunting* with Arnold Alward of New Brunswick; *Wind in My Face* with Hubert Thummler of Mexico; and *Around the World and Then Some* with David Hanlin of Pennsylvania. I also wrote *Royal Quest* (about Prince Abdorreza of Iran), *The History of Safari Club International,* and this book, my autobiography. Last year, I coedited and published a small book about the history of the out-of-the-way village in Arizona's White Mountains where Jean and I have a summer cabin. I also ghost wrote a book for another international hunter.

I enjoyed working on all of these books, and I may write a couple more after that—and maybe I won't—before I see you on the mountain.

Other books by the author

Safari Press, Long Beach, California

To Heck With It, I'm Going Hunting
   by Arnold Alward with Bill Quimby (2003)
Yoshi, The Life and Travels of an International Trophy Hunter
   by Watson Yoshimoto with Bill Quimby (2003)
Royal Quest, The Hunting Saga of H.I.H. Prince Abdorreza of Iran
   by Bill Quimby (2004)
Wind in My Face, The Shikars and Safaris of a Cazador de Mexico. Long Beach: Safari Press,
   by Hubert Thummler with Bill Quimby (2006)
Around the World and Then Some.
   by David Hanlin with Bill Quimby (2009)

SCI Publications, Tucson, Arizona

SCI Record Books of Trophy Animals
   Bill Quimby, editor (1984–1999)
Deer
   Bill Quimby, editor (1984)
Safari Africa
   Bill Quimby, editor (1985)
Safaris Revisited, Best of Safari Magazine of the 1970s.
   Bill Quimby, editor (1991)
Safaris Revisited, Best of Safari Magazine of the 1980s.
   Bill Quimby, editor (1992)
The History of Safari Club International
   by Bill Quimby (2005)

Sincere Press, Tucson, Arizona

McElroy Hunts Asia
   by C. J. McElroy/Bill Quimby, editor (1989)

Trophy Room Books, Agoura, California

McElroy Hunts Dangerous Game.
   by C. J. McElroy/Bill Quimby, editor (2000)
McElroy Hunts Mountain Game
   by C. J. McElroy/Bill Quimby, editor (2001)
McElroy Hunts the Antelope of Africa and Antlered Game
   by C. J. McElroy/Bill Quimby, editor (2002)

Greer Library Friends, Greer, Arizona

Memories from Greer, Tales Told of a Unique Arizona Village
   Bill Quimby and Nadine Stanley, co-editors (2007)